Boundaries of Jewish Identity

Boundaries
of Jewish Identity

Edited by

SUSAN A. GLENN

and

NAOMI B. SOKOLOFF

Jonathan Freedman

A Samuel and Althea Stroum Book

UNIVERSITY OF WASHINGTON PRESS
Seattle & London

This book is published with the assistance of a grant from
the Samuel & Althea Stroum Endowed Book Fund.

Additional support is provided by the Samuel & Althea Stroum Jewish Studies Program,
The Henry M. Jackson School of International Studies, University of Washington.

University of Washington Press
P.O. Box 50096, Seattle, WA 98145 U.S.A.
www.washington.edu/uwpress

Library of Congress Cataloging-in-Publication Data
can be found at the end of the book.

The paper used in this publication is acid-free and recycled from at least 30 percent
post-consumer waste. It meets the minimum requirements of American National
Standard for Information Sciences—Permanence of Paper for Printed Library Materials, ANSI Z39.48-1984.

Chapter 1, by Susan Martha Kahn, originated as the Fifteenth Annual David W. Belin
Endowed Lecture in American Jewish Affairs at the University of Michigan, March
2005. Distributed by the Jean and Samuel Frankel Center for Judaic Studies, University
of Michigan, it is reprinted here with permission of the Center.

An earlier version of chapter 8, by Erica Lehrer, appeared in Imaginary Neighbors: Mediating Polish-Jewish Relations after the Holocaust, edited by Dorota Glowacka and Joanna
Zylinska (University of Nebraska Press, 2007). It is reprinted with permission of the
publisher.

Chapter 9, by Jonathan Freedman, is drawn from his book Klezmer America: Jewishness,
Ethnicity, Modernity (Columbia University Press, 2008), chap. 5. It is reprinted with permission of the publisher.

Contents

Acknowledgments

The essays collected in this volume emerged out of a symposium held in May 2007 at the University of Washington in Seattle. We are grateful to our UW colleagues Michelle Habell-Pallan, Joel Migdal, Janelle Taylor, and Noam Pianko for their valuable contributions as commentators. Their questions and insights catalyzed our thinking as we wrote the introduction and proved to be critical to a number of the authors whose work appears in this volume. The symposium was made possible by the generous support we received from our cosponsors: the Jewish Studies Program, the Samuel and Althea Stroum Endowment, the Walter Chapin Simpson Center for the Humanities, the Arts and Humanities and Social Science divisions of the College of Arts and Sciences, the Department of History, the Department of Near Eastern Languages and Civilization, and UW Hillel.

We would especially like to thank Paul Burstein, former Chair of the Jewish Studies Program, and the current Chair, Gad Barzilai; Kathleen Woodward, Director of the Center for the Humanities; Judith Howard, Dean of Social Sciences; Ellen Kaisse, former Dean of Arts and Humanities; Rabbi Will Berkowitz; John Findlay, former Chair of the History Department; and administrative staff Rochelle Roseman, Jennifer Cohen, and Loryn Paxton for their enthusiastic assistance.

Our appreciation also goes to those who assisted us in the preparation of this volume at the University of Washington Press. We are grateful to the Samuel and Althea Stroum Endowment for a generous subvention in support of publication. We also thank Beth Fuget for her professionalism in guiding this work toward publication and Marilyn Trueblood for expertly shepherding our manuscript through the publication process. Jane Lichty skillfully edited the final version, and Jessica Lee, a doctoral candidate in the Department of History, provided valuable research assistance and much appreciated help at various stages.

On a personal note, Susan Glenn also wishes to thank Jim Gregory,

Ellen Gottheil, and Barbara Boardman for their encouragement and camaraderie. Naomi Sokoloff is grateful to Doug Berry and to absolutely everyone at Seattle Cancer Care Alliance and University of Washington Hospital for their extraordinary support.

Boundaries of Jewish Identity

Who and What Is Jewish?

Controversies and Comparative Perspectives on the Boundaries of Jewish Identity

SUSAN A. GLENN and NAOMI B. SOKOLOFF

The subject of Jewish identity, including the question of who is a Jew and what constitutes "Jewishness," is one of the most vexed and contested issues of modern religious and ethnic group history. This cross-disciplinary volume brings together work by a diverse group of scholars to offer comparative perspectives on what might best be described as the various Jewish "epistemologies" or ways of knowing who and what is "Jewish." Focusing on the twentieth century and the contemporary world, the contributors bring insights from the realms of Jewish law, anthropology, history, sociology, literature, and popular culture to three overlapping areas of debate: definitions of who and what is "Jewish," including controversies surrounding conversion, apostasy, and notions of authenticity; images and self-representation of Jews, including those found in scientific and rabbinical discourse; and boundary issues arising out of the interactions among Jews and non-Jews.

Individually and collectively, these essays raise important questions about how Jews imagine themselves and who defines what it means to be Jewish. While, historically, Jews have often been defined by their enemies or within the discourse of surrounding majorities, Jews themselves have carried on a rich and sometimes rancorous internal dialogue about how Jewishness should be defined. How are those definitions established, enforced, challenged, and transformed? What is considered normative, what is official proclamation, what is imposed and by whom? Studies in many disciplines and Jews from many walks of life have asked, does being a Jew require religious belief, practice, and formal institutional affiliation? One of these? Or all? Do polit-

3

ical behaviors or social associations make someone Jewish? What is the status of the convert to another religion? Is there a biological or physical aspect of Jewish identity? And how do these issues play out in different geographic and historical settings? What is the historical and contemporary relationship between ideal and lived experience?

These are questions that generate multiple answers. What makes this volume distinctive is its attention to ways in which the possible answers reflect the different social, intellectual, and political locations of those who are asking. The essays here highlight the extent to which different ways of knowing and determining what is "Jewish"— genetic, cultural, social, religious, physical, legal, linguistic, literary, and more—produce surprisingly diverse and sometimes contested definitions of identity.

The essays in this volume also emphasize the existence of new kinds of Jews and new issues associated with Jewish identity. The question of who is a Jew has taken on myriad, sometimes startling, new manifestations in the rapidly changing world of the late twentieth and early twenty-first centuries and in the past decade has posed a wide range of unprecedented conundrums. Interest in these issues transcends the realm of academic scholarship. In the past ten years both the national press and Jewish-interest periodicals have drawn attention to the shifting and dynamic aspects of modern Jewish identity and the new face of Jews in North America, Israel, Europe, and elsewhere in the world. Popular exhibits such as "The Jewish Identity Project: New American Photography" at the Jewish Museum in New York City vividly call attention to the varieties of cultural expression and physical appearance among Jews around the world. Much interest concerns the changing demographics of Jewish life, as intermarriage and adoption—along with waves of immigration from the former Soviet Union, Ethiopia, Iran, and elsewhere—have introduced diverse individuals and populations into Jewish communities whose ancestral roots were primarily in Europe. Scholars and the wider public have followed the debates that have arisen over the conflict between Jewish self-identification and established norms of ethnic and religious identity, including the movement of women into positions of religious authority. And these issues have become especially fascinating as Jews who live outside the cultural and social mainstreams of Jewish life (e.g., the Lemba of southern Africa, the Subbotniks of Ukraine, the Bnei Israel in Ethiopia, the Kuki-Chin-Mizo in India, and the Crypto-Jews of the American Southwest) assert their rights to be recognized as Jews. Challenging previous conventional wisdom or assumptions of what is normative, shifts of population have led to awareness that the conundrums posed by the question "who is a Jew?" are ever evolving.

The questions we raise will be of interest not only to readers and scholars of Jewish life and culture but also to those whose primary interest is in the culture and history of other religious, cultural, and ethnic groups, because the case of the Jews provides numerous examples of where novel theories about the nature of group and individual identity might emerge. All the essays in this volume have important insights into the question of how boundaries work, how they are formed, revised, and lived. In shedding light on these issues, the volume provides an excellent opportunity to examine how Jews fit into an increasingly diverse America and an increasingly complicated global society. Recent scholarship points to a heightened awareness of the translingual, transnational, and multicultural aspects of Jewish heritage and with shifting boundaries of belonging.

Contributors to this volume illuminate the varied and contingent meanings of Jewish identity across time and space, suggesting that whatever the formal historical, institutional, or national definitions of "who is a Jew," the experience of identity is layered, shifting, syncretic, and constructed and that Jewish identity can be reforged under new circumstances. Yet, at the same time, the social practices through which individuals and communities of Jews in various parts of the world have challenged conventional understandings of the boundaries of Jewish identity have opened up profound debates on questions of cultural and even biological authenticity.

Our first essay explores some of the fascinating debates concerning authenticity and the genetic boundaries of Jewish identity. In her discussion of the ideological and political implications of new research on population genetics, medical genetics, and assisted reproduction, medical anthropologist Susan Martha Kahn shows how the idea of "Jewish genes" and "the notion of a biological basis for Jewishness" has "gained traction among contemporary Jews." This in turn has brought to the fore important questions about the significance of gender in definitions of Jewish identity. Although, in terms of traditional religious and cultural practices, the term *Jew* has been gendered male, Jewish law, or halakha, defines the term *Jew* as a matter of Jewish maternal descent. Kahn outlines some of the quandaries for religious law that have developed in the wake of new medical technologies. Among rabbis, especially in Orthodox circles that define the term *Jew* as a matter of Jewish maternal descent, questions arise about the legitimacy of assisted reproduction, about whether it is the sperm or the egg that contains the "Jewish" genetic material, and about whether the Jewishness of a mother is determined by who contributes the ovum or by whose womb carries the child. Further disputation concerns whether and when it is appropriate to test for genetically transmitted diseases. As anthropologist Janelle Taylor remarks, Kahn's research has implications well beyond the sphere of Jewish life. It brings a focus on how new biotechnologies are incorporated into specific local systems of meaning and social worlds.* Such issues may prove relevant not only to Jews but to many other contemporary communities facing questions of social self-definition.

Legal scholar Gad Barzilai's essay shifts the focus of debate on boundaries of Jewish identity to the arena of the state. In Israel, shifting populations and the complex relationship between state and religion make for a constant testing of official proclamations on who counts as a Jew for the purpose of citizenship rights. In his work on the "who is a Jew" controversy in Israel, Barzilai considers the question of how communities of Jews who are not officially recognized by the state— including immigrants with no formal ties to the religious community, guest workers and their children, and homosexuals (a group protected in some ways by the secular government but at odds with the Orthodox rabbinate over their civil rights)—have begun to assert their rights to and press their cases for inclusion and the full spectrum of rights afforded by citizenship. As political scientist Joel Migdal has noted, in Israel and elsewhere boundary making is a profoundly social experience, and lived practices have been challenging official categories of Jewishness. Not only do various groups exert pressure

---

*Janelle Taylor and Joel Migdal offered these observations at the May 2007 conference "Boundaries of Jewish Identity" at the University of Washington in Seattle.

on the legal system to adapt to changing realities and newly diverse populations, but different kinds of Jews dress and socialize in ways that mark the boundaries between them. Because these boundaries are also fluid, change can come not only from policy decisions on the part of the state and the courts but from popular behaviors. Thus we find a considerable gap between imposed official discourse (legal and governmental) and social facts on the ground.

Dress and patterns of socializing stand as one kind of observable marker of Jewish identity. A more controversial set of assumptions revolves around the question of whether Jews have distinctive qualities and physical features that visibly distinguish them from the non-Jewish population. What does it mean to act in ways that mark one as "Jewish"? Can you tell who is a Jew just by knowing what to look for? Two essays, one by literary critic Naomi B. Sokoloff and the other by historian Susan A. Glenn, examine the role of stereotypes in the external and internal constructions of Jewish identity.

Sokoloff's reading of two short stories from Israel, one by Jewish writer Aharon Appelfeld and one by Arab writer Sayed Kashua, allows us to think in new ways about the power of stereotypes. She argues that stereotypes have "suffered a bad reputation" because of their association with reductive and racist assumptions. Yet stereotypes can play a far richer role in literature than is often acknowledged. In the fiction she examines, the writers appropriate stereotypes and combine them with other kinds of characterization to create multiple perspectives on the limits of Jewishness. Each story features an abrupt, Kafkaesque metamorphosis that transforms a Jewish protagonist into a non-Jew. Each story also fosters an open-endedness that conveys uncertainty of motive and complexity of character, while at the same time relying on stereotypes that shut down complexity. These contrasting approaches produce the central tensions that animate the texts, and the result, in each case, is to present oscillating possibilities of interpretation. One demarcates and reconfirms schematic, inflexible boundaries of identity; the other critiques those boundaries, circumvents them, disrupts them, or reconfigures them in significant ways.

Stereotypes about the Jewish body have been a centerpiece of anti-semitic ideology in Europe and the United States. But as Glenn argues in her essay, the concept of "Jewish" looks has also played an important part in Jewish self-definition. Looking for Jews is a fundamentally Jewish epistemology—a way of knowing—who is Jewish. Exploring the continuous and shifting public Jewish discourse about whether Jews look "Jewish" reveals the complex and contradictory meanings that Jews in the United States have attached to the notion of their own physical differences. For even as Jewish social scientists attempted to refute scientific racism and to undercut negative stereotypes about the Jewish body, Jewish folk and popular culture perpetuated the idea that Jews themselves "can always tell a Jew" on the basis of looks. This idea became more and not less significant as Jews began to assimilate into the wider American culture, so much so that looks came to be regarded as a significant aspect of modern American Jewish authenticity.

Other essays offer surprising examples of the ways in which social and cultural boundaries are renegotiated as changing circumstances and individual desires dictate. Historian Lila Corwin Berman discusses the attempts of midcentury American Jews to reinforce boundaries by issuing strident warnings about the dangers of intermarriage. This phenomenon turns out to be a typically American one, shaped by a variety of social trends. The tensions surrounding intermarriage were integrally related to debates about women's social roles and obligations within a culture that blamed parents, and especially mothers, for their children's choices even while urging them to let professionals and community institutions take over many parenting roles. These tensions also reflected the rise of parenting experts in North America and a permissive approach to parenting in the postwar era that experts believed would protect children from developing the kinds of personality disorders associated with fascism. We tend to think of warnings against intermarriage as a Jewish story, but Berman explores a moment when the apparatus of boundary drawing reflected as much a sense of American selfhood as it did a commitment to being Jewish. By reframing the issue from a Jewish one to an American Jewish one and then to an American one, she brings new awareness to the question of how social science arrives at its knowledge of Jewish matters.

Sociologist Calvin Goldscheider also reflects on the normative aspects of continuity and discontinuity of Jewish life in North America, and he puts into relief ways in which knowledge is generated as he asks new questions of existing data. In "Boundary Maintenance and Jewish Identity: Comparative and Historical Perspectives," he writes about the effects of mobility on Jewish identity. Goldscheider's analysis of how Jews form and remake community as they move from one locale to the next and operate within a variety of class and professional contexts provides a fresh perspective on long-standing debates about the effects of assimilation. He emphasizes the porous nature of ethnic boundaries among Jews in the United States and Canada. Contrary to popular wisdom about the impact of geographic and occupational mobility, he argues that changes in stratification do more than simply increase the level of interaction between Jews and non-Jews; they also create "new forms of potential interaction among Jews," forms of interaction that can potentially strengthen Jewish identity.

The next three essays deal with groups at the margins of the Jewish establishment, and they put into relief the intensity of the debate about elasticity of categories and claims to inclusion. In our contemporary period, it has often been fashionable to deconstruct identities and question boundaries, but for Jews there are many historical and local circumstances that have made challenges to established boundaries of identity exceptionally fraught. Historian Shulamit S. Magnus demonstrates that the term *Jew* has been highly ambiguous since the beginnings of Jewishness. Context, as historians say, is everything. Magnus's essay on apostasy and the boundaries of Jewish identity in late nineteenth- and early twentieth-century Russia suggests the flexibility of ethnoreligious categories. Magnus shows how under certain circumstances even converts to Christianity might be considered "good" Jews. Her essay uncovers some startling paradoxes that force us to question our assumptions about the boundaries between apostasy and loyalty to the Jewish people. Not every Jew who converted to Christianity did so for personal gain, shows Magnus; ironically, some converted out of "love" for their fellow Jews and used their position as apostates "to uphold the honor of Judaism."

Polish-Jewish boundaries and relationships are the topic of cultural anthropologist Erica Lehrer's essay. Turning to contemporary Poland, Lehrer shows how different stakeholders, including American Jewish tourists and "non-Jewish" Poles who operate the Holocaust tourist industry in Poland, come together with radically different definitions of what "Jewish" means. The issues are delicate, and feelings run high on all sides.

A related set of issues emerges in literary critic Jonathan Freedman's essay on Crypto-Jews in the American Southwest. Freedman illustrates how identity is challenged by and responds to the contexts of multiculturalism. The rediscovery and self-ascription of Jewish roots by Latinos has created both an academic and touristic subindustry devoted to exploring the phenomenon of Crypto-Jewishness and a "vigorous counterresponse" by those who doubt the veracity of those claims. Not only has the "war of words" between claimants and doubters grown increasingly contentious, writes Freedman, but recently a group of "putative Crypto-Jews" has gone so far as to offer genetic evidence to bolster their claims to Jewish authenticity, thereby basing their case on "genetic determinism." Freedman's findings are equally as compelling for Chicano Studies as they are for Jewish Studies. The larger significance of Crypto-Jewish identity claims, remarks Freedman, is that they exemplify the extent to which Jewishness intersects with other cultural formations in ways that are integral to both. Responding to the work of Michelle Habell-Pallan on the cultural borrowings of Latino performers who inject Jewish symbols and folk materials into their songs, Freedman emphasizes the syncretic rather than the foundational aspects of group identity. And like Lehrer, Freedman stresses that groups remaking collective identity out of seemingly disparate materials—including Catholicism, Judaism, Polishness and Jewishness, race and whiteness—are involved in a kind of salvage work that promises to produce a fuller and more elastic concept of identity. Both of their essays show us examples of individuals engaged in the act of weighing the value ascribed to racial and religious determinism against the concept of ethnicity and identity as practice. In that way, their claims mirror the social and political contestation that Barzilai describes for Jews in contemporary Israel.

The concluding essay by anthropologist Laada Bilaniuk provides a useful starting point for thinking about how debates about Jewish identity resonate with identity-related questions among other groups. Although her own scholarship concerns linguistic boundaries among the non-Jewish ethnic majorities in the former Soviet Union, she reflects on how some of the essays in this volume relate to larger themes in the study of boundary making and boundary enforcement. Bilaniuk takes an important step in the direction of comparative studies as she assesses the value of adopting various understandings of identity in Eastern Europe. She asks a question of concern to the other essayists in this volume: what is gained and what is lost by embracing or rejecting dominant nationalist categories of identity? And which version of identity more accurately represents how people actually live their lives?

Bilaniuk's essay indicates how Jews—people whose sense of collective self has a long history of being both nebulous and certain—provide particularly acute examples of the dynamics of self-definition that apply to other groups as well. She argues that those groups and subgroups that define their identity on the margins of what is considered normative can provide particularly illuminating examples of the multivocal conversation through which identities are negotiated and affirmed. In doing so, she points to the "dialogic" nature of identity that connects the multidisciplinary and comparative essays in this volume.

Existing scholarly literature is already rich in its insights into the literary, cultural, and philosophical expressions of identity. The present volume adds significantly to this impressive body of work, however, by emphasizing both the social experience that draws and redraws the boundaries of identity and the differing epistemologies—ways and standards of knowing—that shape our understandings of what is and is not "Jewish." As Sokoloff puts it in her essay on the use of stereotypes in contemporary literature, a key question is not whether the generalization is "true or plausible" but whether it is "endorsed." The authors we include reflect on social experience in all of its varieties: biological reproduction, group claims for public recognition, and the significance of dress, mannerisms, appearance, and spatial interactions in helping define group membership. Our aim is to cast light on the human struggle for ownership of "Jewishness" as different constituencies negotiate with one another over where the border lies between Jews and non-Jews. The overarching question we raise here is, how do they know what they claim to know concerning who is a Jew? Taken together, these essays reveal the complex and shifting social dynamics of boundary making, capturing the relationship of Jews to the social world, past and present.

1

Are Genes Jewish?

Conceptual Ambiguities in the New Genetic Age

SUSAN MARTHA KAHN

Imagining Jewishness as an embodied identity has a long and complicated history. Maimonides posited that Jewishness was not inherently manifest in one's body; rather, it was realized through commitment to Jewish law. Other Jewish philosophers such as Judah Halevi have argued that there is something physiologically different—and superior—about Jews that somehow imbues them with superior qualities and abilities and, by extension, with a unique destiny among humankind.

These philosophical debates take place alongside certain irrefutable Jewish kinship beliefs: anyone born to a Jewish mother is a Jew, suggesting that there is something intrinsically physical about Jewish identity. And yet Jewishness can be acquired via conversion—suggesting that however embodied Jewish identity may be, it is an identity that can be willfully assumed by a non-Jewish body.

In short, opposing concepts of Jewishness, as a product of kinship versus a product of commitment, have always existed in dynamic tension. This tension surfaces periodically in Jewish history, invariably in popular terms that are historically specific. For example, many Jews in the late nineteenth and early twentieth centuries embraced then prevalent notions about eugenics and the concept of racial difference.[1] The inherent ambiguity and disagreement embedded in this question was later evinced in 1958, when David Ben-Gurion, then prime minister of Israel, sought advice from Jewish sages about the nature of Jewishness in order to draft legislation concerning the citizenship status of children born of mixed marriages in Israel. He received dozens of conflicting responses from the most eminent Jewish thinkers of the time.[2]

It is important to note that the question of whether Jewishness is biological is not a debate that has taken place exclusively among Jews. Non-Jews in different times and places have also been obsessed with the question of whether Jews are physically different. Obviously, convictions about Jewish physical difference assumed their most heinous manifestation in Nazi eugenics, in which the biological difference—and inferiority—of Jews was a central tenet.

In this essay, I suggest that we are at an extraordinary historical moment when questions about the biological basis of Jewishness are being reformulated in terms made possible by the advent of new genetic technologies. I seek to illustrate why the notion of a biological basis for Jewishness may be regaining traction among contemporary Jews by parsing the logic and appeal of new genetic technologies in three distinct but intersecting fields: population genetics, medical genetics, and rabbinic discourse on reproductive technologies. It is not surprising that new genetic technologies have proved seductive to a community long preoccupied with its origins, boundaries, and self-definition. For among their many possible applications, these technologies promise to trace descent scientifically, establish a community's geographic origins, identify individual probabilities for disease based on genetic heritage, and isolate reproductive genetic material so that it can be designated as Jewish for purposes of Jewish procreation.

Population Genetics

The goal in population genetics is to trace genetic ancestry among social groups by using methods developed by molecular geneticists to study DNA. In 1997 a team of researchers published an article in the prestigious scientific journal *Nature* in which they claimed to find a so-called Kohen gene.[3] The study identified six polymorphisms (differences in DNA sequences) among 188 contemporary male Jews living in three countries who self-identify as Kohens, or members of the priestly class, a social stratum based on oral tradition that claims a special descent status from father to son. Researchers claim that the identification of these six polymorphisms, known as the Kohen modal haplotype, confirms a distinct paternal genealogy for Jewish priests that differentiates them from the lay Jewish population.[4] Calculations based on variation in the development of mutations among Kohens today suggest a time frame of 106 generations from the ancestral founder of the line. This dates to approximately 3,300 years ago—the approximate time of the exodus from Egypt and the generation of the biblical Aaron. This finding is consistent with oral tradition that there is a priestly class of male Jews who have maintained their lines of descent from Aaron, the first Jewish priest. The authors of the article assert that what makes this finding particularly remarkable is that the difference is observable in both Ashkenazic and Sephardic populations, despite the long geographical separation between the two communities. Thus a Kohen of Russian Jewish descent and a Kohen of Moroccan Jewish descent tend to have more similar Y chromosomes than do a Russian Christian and a Moroccan Muslim. Subsequent studies have expanded on these findings, claiming to confirm that Jewish populations in various parts of the world remained relatively isolated from genetic admixture.[5]

In a related study published in 2002 in the *American Journal of Human Genetics*, researchers examine the mitochondrial DNA of Jewish women from nine distinct Diasporic Jewish communities (from Morocco to the former Soviet republic of Georgia). The authors of the study argue that the striking dissimilarities in the genetic signatures of these women suggest that Diasporic Jewish communities were established when Jewish male traders from the ancient Near East intermarried with local non-Jewish women along their trade routes. Such a hypothesis could also explain why Jews tended to resemble phenotypically their non-Jewish neighbors in various settings.[6]

The problem with these kinds of studies is that mapping Y chromosomes and mitochondrial DNA will "only trace two genetic lines on a family tree in which branches double with each preceding generation," according to bioethicist Carl Elliott and anthropologist Paul Brodwin. They write:

> Y chromosome tracing will connect a man to his father and not his mother, and it will connect him to only one of four grandparents, his paternal grandfather. In the same way, it will connect him to one of his eight great grandparents and one of his 16 great great grandparents. Continue back in this manner for 14 generations and the man will still

be connected to only one ancestor in that generation. The test will not connect him to any of the other 16,383 ancestors in that generation to whom he is related in equal measure.[7]

Connection to one ancestor traced through the male line may be a tenuous reason for constructing a contemporary identity. Yet this kind of genetic evidence is being used increasingly to legitimate diverse claims of Jewish identity. Such claims have been most famously made among the Lemba of southern Africa, whose oral tradition asserts descent from a common Jewish ancestor. The Lemba also maintain a priestly class, with descent status passed from father to son. Remarkably, population geneticists found that about half the men in a priestly Lemba family possess the Kohen modal haplotype, identified among priests in the wider Jewish population.[8] It is important to point out that the Kohen modal haplotype, while widespread among Jews who profess Kohen status, is not unique to Jews. Indeed, this actuality questions the legitimacy of basing an identity solely on this genetic evidence. Moreover, the presence of this haplotype in the DNA of a relatively few members of the community is then used to expand claims of Jewishness for the entire group. Despite these important shortcomings, this research was touted as proof that the Lemba were genetically Jewish.

Such studies must be placed in a larger sociopolitical context where claiming a Jewish identity can have direct impact on a community's access to the rights and resources of world Jewry, whether configured in terms of citizenship rights based on Israel's Law of Return or access to resources, as provided to remote and underserved Jewish communities by organizations such as the American Jewish Joint Distribution Committee.[9] Such claims were hotly contested when made by the Bnei Israel of Ethiopia or, more recently, by the Kuki-Chin-Mizo of northeast India, a small group that asserts descent from the tribe of Menashe.[10] For believers in these kinds of studies, the golden age of Jewish population genetics is at hand, in which geneticists will pursue the origins of the lost Israelite tribes all around the world and allow scientific researchers to "prove" that Jewish populations of the various Diaspora communities have retained their genetic identity throughout exile. Related to these studies that look for genetic evidence to reinforce traditional claims about the historical solidarity of the Jewish community in the Diaspora is an additional category of Jewish population genetics in which genes, ethnicity, and religious belief are conflated with historical theories about the Middle Eastern origins of the Jews. Here genetic studies are used not simply to prove a history of Jewish self-containment and continuity but also to situate Jewish origins conclusively in the Middle East by proving that Ashkenazi Jews have more genetically in common with, depending on the study, Palestinians, Syrians, Lebanese, Kurds, and Anatolian Turks than they do with Northern Europeans, Eastern Europeans, or Russians.

Interestingly, population geneticists generally reject the notion that there is anything called a Jewish gene or that such a categorization would have any merit as a unit of scientific analysis. But because they use social groups, like Jews, as proxies—whether for reproductively isolated groups, ancestral groups, geographically bounded groups, environmental groups, or some combination of these—ample room exists to confuse genetic tests that claim authority for proving group identity with genetic tests that claim authority for proving individual identity. In other words, population geneticists deal with statistical probabilities of genetic relatedness among groups of people, not with genetic tests that prove the religious or ethnic identity of an individual person.

The confusion here is exploited by commercial companies like Family Tree DNA, founded by a Texas Jewish businessman. For $159 and a cheek swab, the company promises to provide you with relevant information about your suggested geographic origins, your possible Jewish or *cohanim* ancestry, and your "deep ancestral ethnic origins." Such tests have as much potential to corroborate identity claims as they do to disrupt them.[11]

Medical Genetics

Perhaps a more familiar domain in which we encounter the purported identification of Jewish genes is in the realm of genetic screening. Here genetic tests are used to identify carriers of mutations for Tay-Sachs and many other genetic diseases that seem to be more prevalent among Ashkenazi Jews. Today routine prenatal screening includes a checklist that asks Ashkenazi Jewish women with Ashkenazi Jewish spouses to self-identify. And once identified, a special prenatal genetic screening panel designed to test for these genetic mutations may be administered at the patient's request and expense. This is to gauge the probability that the developing fetus may be at risk for one of the genetic diseases found to be more common among Ashkenazi Jews.

Such prenatal genetic screening has been put to very specific social uses in the ultra-Orthodox world. The Brooklyn-based organization Dor Yeshorim has created a database of DNA samples taken from young ultra-Orthodox Jews while they were in high school. These samples are then cross-checked before any genetically incompatible "matches" can be made between prospective marriage partners. Through such tests, the community can be sure that prospective spouses are not carriers of the same genetic mutation, which, if combined, could mean that their children are more likely to be born with a devastating genetic disease. In the past twenty years, the organization has met with phenomenal success, and the incidence of genetic diseases in this community has been drastically reduced. Today many young men and women will not even meet on arranged dates unless the other has been screened and checked by Dor Yeshorim. Marital compatibility has been essentialized in genetic terms, and biotechnology dictates marital compatibility.

Ultra-Orthodox Jews are not the only ones to propose innovative uses of prenatal genetic testing. A New York–based philanthropic trust recently launched a project to develop a standard battery of genetic tests that could be offered at low cost to all American Jews. This new Jewish Genetics Project, as it is called, promises to wipe out all of the so-called Jewish genetic diseases in as few as ten years.[12]

While the organized Jewish community in America has largely embraced prenatal genetic screenings for genetic diseases, reactions have been more mixed to medical studies that focus on possible Jewish genetic predispositions toward breast cancer, colon cancer, longevity, schizophrenia, manic depression, and other conditions. For some, these kinds of anticipatory studies have created considerable anxiety, given the possibility that Jews could be perceived as more prone to genetic defects than non-Jews are. For many, targeting Jewish genes in this way resonates with dangerous eugenic overtones. More-over, on an individual level, those who are identified by these tests as carriers of genetic mutations are inevitably faced with ambiguous odds of contracting diseases for which there are often no reliable cures. Nevertheless, many synagogues have organized DNA drives to gather samples to aid researchers. The American Jewish Committee, Hadassah, and other large national Jewish organizations have organized multiday conferences and other events to educate their constituencies about the scientific and practical issues involved in genetic screening, including the risks of insurance discrimination based on test results; these groups have also mobilized their constituents to lobby Congress to work on state and local levels to prevent genetic discrimination. Further, they have organized meetings between top officials from the National Institutes of Health and top rabbis and Jewish community leaders. Widespread public education campaigns have been launched by Jewish organizations on local, state, and national levels aimed at reaching Jewish populations. These communal efforts have effectively galvanized public opinion to recognize the potential dangers inherent in population-specific genetic research and have helped generate public debate about the myriad personal dilemmas presented by this research—including concerns about new experimental treatments for genetic diseases and their implications for individual health.[13]

Certainly, the motivating impulse for this Jewish enthusiasm for genetic screening is understandable. Prenatal genetic screening promises to make reproduction safer and better than ever before. And while genetic screening for adult-onset disease has been recognized as potentially more problematic, its promise has proved to be deeply irresistible. It would seem that Jews in many different contexts have been hopelessly seduced.

Anthropologist Margaret Lock writes that genetic testing "permits us to divine our past and to make that heritage, in the form of genes, into omens for the future."[14] She argues that these tests encourage us to concentrate on the style of reasoning known as biological reductionism or genetic determinism. This kind of thinking allows for other causes of disease, due to social, political, or environmental factors, to be ignored. Instead, disease is understood as the product of inherited, genetic predispositions, thus stigmatizing the individual while eliding the larger, perhaps dangerously unhealthy, environments in which individuals live. Following Lock's reasoning, it would seem that by embracing genetic screening Jews are flirting with the notion that they are the sum of their Jewish genetic parts. This dynamic is reinforced when we juxtapose it with the ways genes are perceived to be Jewish in other domains.

New Reproductive Technologies

An additional field in which genes are expressly identified as Jewish or not Jewish appears in the realm of contemporary rabbinic debates about the appropriate uses of new reproductive technologies. These technologies, including artificial insemination, ovum donation, and in vitro fertilization, depend on the isolation and extraction of reproductive genetic material that is then deliberately manipulated for conception and gestation. Orthodox rabbis have been remarkably lenient in their rulings concerning the permissibility of these treatments and in thinking about their possible applications.

These technologies have forced rabbis to imagine conception in starkly literal terms and to consider basic questions about where Jewishness comes from and, by extension, "who is a Jew." We know Jewishness is transmitted by the mother, but in the age of reproductive technology this transmission becomes less straightforward: is it the mother's egg that transmits Jewishness, or is it the act of gestation and parturition that makes a child Jewish? Contemporary rabbis have debated these questions intensely, and, needless to say, there is much disagreement over proper interpretative strategies in the face of these unprecedented technological developments. Rabbinic rulings on these matters are of direct importance to Jews undergoing infertility treatment, since certain kinds of infertility can only be treated with the use of sperm and/or eggs donated by a third party. Unfortunately for those looking for rabbinic guidance on these matters, there are conflicting rabbinic opinions as to whether it is the egg or the womb that determines Jewishness. Some rabbis argue that the act of gestation and parturition determines Jewishness, and those who wish to conceive a Jewish child may do so using eggs donated by non-Jewish women. Others argue the opposing view, that the egg transmits Jewishness, so to conceive a Jewish child an infertile woman must receive an egg donated by a Jewish woman. By designating the egg as that which confers Jewishness, rabbis holding the latter opinion imbue genetic material with the powerful ability to create Jewish identity.[15] This rabbinic designation has specific repercussions.

For example, a program in New York was recently created to help infertile couples acquire Jewish donor eggs, commodities that for various socioeconomic factors are otherwise very scarce. As part of this program, young, unmarried Israeli Jewish women are flown to New York, their ovaries are hormonally hyperstimulated, and their ova are surgically extracted for donation. All trip expenses are covered, and each young woman receives compensation in the amount of $8,000. Interestingly, not only is the Jewishness of these young women's eggs at a premium here, but the fact that the eggs are being donated while the young women are unmarried also makes their eggs particularly desirable. For eggs donated by unmarried Jewish women are much in demand, especially by infertile Orthodox Jewish couples, who only undergo fertility treatment in strict accordance with rabbinic directives. For these couples, there are additional halakhic complications involved in using donated eggs, since some rabbis have expressed concern about the use of third-party donor material that is introduced into the marital relationship between a husband and wife. Among these concerns is that a child conceived using the husband's sperm and an egg donated by a married Jewish woman who is not his wife could be considered a *mamzer*—a child conceived in an illegitimate act of sexual intercourse—since the child was conceived in a union that if actualized physically, rather than technologically, would be considered adulterous according to Jewish law. In other words, if a married Jewish woman has sex with a Jewish man who is not her husband, a child born of such a relationship would be designated a *mamzer* and subject to a severe stigma in the Orthodox world. By extension, if an egg donated by a married Jewish woman is fertilized by the sperm of a Jewish man who is not her husband, the resulting child could be considered a *mamzer* as well. To circumvent this concern, rabbis make it clear that the egg of an unmarried Jewish woman is preferred for donation, since if a married Jewish man conceives a child with an unmarried Jewish woman, there are no adulterous connotations, and the child is born free from the stigma of *mamzerut*. According to this way of thinking, the egg embodies not only the Jewishness of the woman from whom it is issued but her marital status as well. Clearly, these strains of rabbinic thought seem to indicate that genetic material is capable of embodying different kinds of identity, both religious and temporal.

The rabbinic conceptualization of the egg as the origin of Jewishness is foundational to entrepreneurial efforts like this program that brings unmarried Israeli Jewish women to the United States for ova harvesting. For it is the designation of the egg as the origin of Jewishness that lies at the base of such elaborate effort. This rabbinic strain of thinking about donor eggs is reinforced in a related practice, when infertile Jewish couples seek out Jewish donor eggs directly by advertising for them in college newspapers or on the Internet. These ads often promise up to $50,000 in compensation for Jewish egg donors. Clearly, popular Jewish beliefs about the meaning and power of eggs to transmit Jewishness also shape the market for Jewish donor eggs.

Although they take place under extreme circumstances, high payments and transnational egg flights suggest that the belief in Jewish genes is not an abstract notion. Rather, it is a deeply held conviction, based on explicit rabbinic rulings, worth paying a premium for, and sufficient to justify elaborate networks of transnational exchange and medical intervention.[16]

Conclusions

Jewish genes operate as different units of analysis in each of these three distinct but intersecting fields—population genetics, medical genetics, and rabbinic discourse on reproductive technology. For the population geneticist, Jews are a social category; as descendants of a relatively homogenous ancestral group, Jews embody statistical probabilities that DNA haplotypes will be more prevalent within this group. For purposes of genetic screening, individual genes are nominally designated "Jewish" if they carry genetic mutations statistically more common among Jews. This correlation, between individual Jews and genetic mutations that are more common among Jews, can lead to an easy conceptual slippage, where genes are mistakenly identified as Jewish.

For many contemporary rabbinic decisors, the egg is the essential locus of Jewishness, an identification that has triggered elaborate schemes and high prices for its acquisition. No wonder the boundaries between these discursive domains begin to lose definition as the meanings of genes travel conceptually between them. The basic question here is: if genes seem to be demonstrably Jewish in one domain, how can they not be Jewish in all domains? How can the convincing conjectures generated by population geneticists about the migratory and mating patterns of Jewish communities in the past not suggest that Jewishness has somehow been preserved in DNA? How can the empirical uses of genetic screening to prevent genetic disease among Jews not be evidence of Jewishness as some kind of irreducible genetic category? How can rabbinic designation of, and widespread popular belief in, the human egg as the origin of Jewishness not be reckoned with, particularly since rabbinic authority has determined who is a Jew for centuries? And yet each of these domains constructs the gene in quite different terms.

This confusion creates what anthropologist Victor Turner calls a liminal disorder.[17] Such a state is created when concepts are in transition and turmoil, en route to further elucidation and definition. This ambiguity is amplified when juxtaposed with the profound conceptual tension that has always existed about the biological basis for Jewishness. The question here is whether this contemporary taxonomic chaos is sufficient to create a newly reordered Jewish identity that is explicitly configured in genetic terms. If genetic material is imagined to be a manifestation of some kind of essentialized ethnoreligious self, it would seem to be reminiscent of the racial categorizations developed during an earlier genetic age. But unlike the past, this is not state-sponsored eugenics that seeks to identify Jewish genes in order to control or limit Jewish reproduction. Jews are not coerced to believe in an essentialized genetic self, to endorse Jewish population genetics, to create elaborate infrastructures to study and screen for genetic diseases that use Jewishness as an organizing category, or to launch flights in order to harvest Jewish eggs. On the contrary, Jews themselves have generated these activities.

Indeed, Jews have exhibited a kind of hyper-agency when it comes to embracing new genetic technologies. But how long can this embrace be sustained without reckoning with the conceptual ambiguities and social repercussions it intrinsically engenders?

We already see some evidence of new Jewish social forms emerging from the uses of these technologies. In the case of Dor Yeshorim, marital patterns have shifted to a material base that is configured in terms of genetic compatibility. The routinization of prenatal genetic screening is evidence of a different new social form, where biomedical intervention seems to have become an inevitable part of reproduction for an increasing number of Jews, infertile or not. Certainly, the transnational egg donation program represents another novel social development that has emerged in direct response to these technologies.

Despite the frequent bioethical caution about the social and political dangers of conceptualizing Jewishness in genetically essentialized terms, and the long-standing anthropological argument that identity is socially constructed, contemporary Jews seem to be finding the concept of the Jewish gene irresistible. Indeed, the prominent, Maimonidean strand in Jewish philosophy, which argues against a biological basis for Jewishness, may be undergoing its most profound challenge to date.

The consequences of the Jewish embrace of new genetic technologies are uncertain: will Jews cede the authority to determine Jewishness to technological methods—interpreted through, but ultimately detached from, Jewish tradition? Will traditional practices for reckoning Jewish identity be abandoned? Perhaps the Jewish embrace of these technologies simply amplifies an ambiguity about Jewish identity that has been a constant of Jewish history—for Jewish identity has always been simultaneously fixed and fluid, the product of either kinship or commitment, or both. For some it is a felt identity, for others it is categorical one. Is an identity that is conceptualized as shifting and complex less real than an identity that is reified in genetic terms? These questions become more urgent when one imagines how identity claims can be pitted against one another in various domains, particularly when different kinds of resources are at stake. Needless to say, these questions are relevant for many peoples in the new genetic age, not just for Jews, but they are made particularly urgent for Jews given their rush to embrace these technologies.

Notes

1. Todd Endelman, "Anglo-Jewish Scientists and the Science of Race," *Jewish Social Studies* 11, no.1 (2004): 52–92.

2. Eliezer Ben-Rafael, *Jewish Identities: Fifty Intellectuals Answer Ben Gurion* (Leiden: Brill, 2002).

3. Karl Skorecki et al., "Y Chromosomes of Jewish Priests," *Nature* 385 (January 2, 1997): 32.

4. A haplotype is a set of closely linked DNA polymorphisms inherited as a unit.

5. Almut Nebel et al., "The Y Chromosome Pool of Jews as Part of the Genetic Landscape of the Middle East," *American Journal of Human Genetics* 69, no. 5 (2001): 1095–1112.

6. Mark G. Thomas et al., "Founding Mothers of Jewish Communities: Geographically Separated Jewish Groups Were Independently Founded by Very Few Female Ancestors," *American Journal of Human Genetics* 70, no. 6 (2002): 1411–20.

7. Carl Elliott and Paul Brodwin, "Identity and Genetic Ancestry Tracing," *British Medical Journal* 325 (December 2002): 1470 (reprinted in *BMJ USA* 3 [April 2003]: 225–27).

8. Thomas et al., "Founding Mothers of Jewish Communities."

9. Hillel Halkin, *Across the Sabbath River: In Search of a Lost Tribe of Israel* (New York: Houghton Mifflin, 2002).

10. Interestingly, the Kuki-Chin-Mizo resisted undertaking DNA testing to determine whether there was a genetic connection between them and world Jewry. "Rabbi Shimon Gangte, a Bnei Menashe leader who has lived in Israel for eight years and teaches Torah at a yeshiva (religious school) on the West Bank, argues that the thousands of Ethiopian Jews who emigrated to Israel did not have to undergo DNA tests. He said: 'Over a number of years, Jewish blood has mixed with non-Jewish blood in our community. So would the DNA test show that we are Jewish? Maybe not. So are people then going to say that we are not Jewish and dash the hopes of the rest of the community to move here? Even if it is not proven according to a DNA test, we feel Jewish and we will still be Jewish.'" Inigo Gilmore, "Indian 'Jews' Resist DNA Tests to Prove They Are a Lost Tribe," *Telegraph* (London), November 10, 2002, http://www.telegraph.co.uk/news/worldnews/asia/india/1412777/Indian-Jews-resist-DNA-tests-to-prove-they-are-a-lost-tribe.html (accessed February 11, 2010). Ultimately, genetic tests were conducted on the Kuki-Chin-Mizo with interesting results. "On the one hand, no connection was found on the male side of the genetic chain (the Y chromosome) between the genetic profile of the Kuki and the Jewish profile, or the profile of Middle Eastern peoples in general. However, on the female side of the profile (what scientists call mitochondrial DNA) there is a certain resemblance to the genetic profile

of Middle Eastern peoples and to that of the Jews of Uzbekistan (who also have a tradition of belonging to the 10 tribes)—a closeness that distinguishes the Kuki from the members of other tribes that live nearby." Yair Sheleg, "In Search of Jewish Chromosomes in India," *Ha'aretz*, April 1, 2004.

11. Such tests are appealing not only to Jews. The Family Tree DNA company has found enthusiastic consumers among the African American population, eager to locate their place of origin in Africa. See Amy Harmon, "Blacks Pin Hope on DNA to Fill Slavery's Gaps in Family Trees," *New York Times*, July 25, 2005.

12. *Jewish Daily Forward* (New York), August 17, 2001.

13. See B. P. Fuller et al., "Privacy in Genetics Research," *Science* 285, no. 5432 (1999): 1359–61. The article suggests that Ashkenazi Jews have proved to be a boon for medical genetic researchers for four primary reasons: (1) Ashkenazic Jewish populations exemplify the so-called founder effect, in which a population that is descended from a small handful of ancestors historically shuns intermarriage or is forcibly ghettoized, thereby maintaining genetic lineages (including disease causing mutations). (2) Ashkenazic Jewish history conforms to the theory of genetic drift or bottleneck, which occurs when a genetic mutation becomes common because the population in which it is found dwindles as a result of famine, war, epidemic, or other events, as has happened frequently among Eastern European Jews. (3) Traditionally, Jews have been receptive to science and medicine—making them more willing and prevalent participants in medical studies and research programs. (4) Widespread Tay-Sachs testing in the 1970s among Ashkenazi Jews in the United States resulted in unexpected research payoff; large batches of tissue samples from Eastern European Jews who consented to Tay-Sachs tests have been stored and made selectively available to genetic researchers for further study. Interestingly, these samples were obtained from individuals who had not consented to the use of their tissue for further research, which raises a host of ethical concerns.

14. Margaret Lock, "Breast Cancer: Reading the Omens," *Anthropology Today* 14, no. 4 (1998): 7.

15. This discussion of rabbinic debates on assisted reproduction is drawn from Susan Martha Kahn, *Reproducing Jews: A Cultural Account of Assisted Conception in Israel* (Durham, N.C.: Duke University Press, 2000).

16. Certainly, ascribing identity to reproductive genetic material is not unique to infertile Jews in search of Jewish donor eggs. In the United States, where reproductive genetic material is arbitrated in a market context, donor eggs and sperm are routinely categorized according to the nationality, religion, ethnicity, and physical traits of the donor. Individual consumers expect to be able to choose their sperm and eggs based on presumed phenotypic attributes and other less tangible variables that they deem important. In other words, it is not unusual in this context for people to choose donor material

that they perceive to be "like" themselves, in terms of appearance, ethnicity, national origin, or even shared interests.

17. Victor Turner, *From Ritual to Theatre: The Human Seriousness of Play* (New York: PAJ Publications, 1982).

2

Who Is a Jew?

Categories, Boundaries, Communities, and Citizenship Law in Israel

GAD BARZILAI

Sociopolitical categories construct, shape, and reproduce identities in compound ways. In defining who is in and who is outside a group, different communities may use various categories contingent on specific needs, expectations, interests, and visions of the "good" society and the desirable state. Similarly, any attempt to comprehend citizenship as an exclusively legalistic issue resulting in rights and duties may miss opportunities to look further into state-society relationships and various sociopolitical aspects of citizenship. Citizenship itself, what it grants and what it entails, may be constructed through sociopolitical categories that differently conceptualize the meaning of state-society relations for individuals and communities. The case of Israel represents an example of the gap between official legal entitlements and social arrangements that transgress the boundaries of identity laid out by the state.

In this essay I explore several dimensions of citizenship law that tend to contradict the compound structure of Jewish identities. I examine this conflict in the context of struggles among and between various social groups that are wrestling with the definitions and practices of citizenship while also marking the boundaries with one another, among their own members, and between themselves and the state. Concretely and empirically, I base my analysis here on research I have conducted among Jewish and Palestinian communities in Israel. The main purpose of these studies has been to analyze the convergence and divergence of the lived experience of identities, legal consciousness, social being, and state policies and ideologies. In other words, I am interested in the ways that debates over seemingly legalistic issues are in essence conflicts over sociopolitical boundaries and power. This is a project aimed at unveiling, deconstructing, and in turn theorizing the political interests that propel legal categorizations in identity politics.

Debates about identities, including the contentious question of "who is a Jew" revolve around more than religious and cultural practices; they are constructions that emerge from complex, in-depth realities, especially where communities have tended to impose sociopolitical boundaries. Accordingly, while most studies have related to the issue of "who is a Jew" as a given dilemma, an autonomous ontology with legalistic and political ramifications, my research attempts to move in another direction. It argues that "who is a Jew" is not a static question or a fixed dilemma but rather a dynamic construction of political interests amid struggles of communities over political power. Thus the issue of "who is a Jew" is not an autonomous problem waiting to be politically and legally resolved but rather a social language that serves the political purposes of social engineering. This essay explains how the tendency to assign categories of identity has shaped and reproduced, and also challenged and reformed, sociopolitical boundaries between communities.

My argument is not intended to suggest that Judaism does not have an authentic history. Nor am I implying that Jews are not distinct from other religious peoples. My point is that in Israel, the question of "who is a Jew" is as much about power as it is about religion. The communities in question are *nomos* groups, meaning groups that are in conflict regarding the desirable vision and practices of the "good" society.[1] Accordingly, various communities in Israel have never approached the issue of "who is a Jew" in an attempt to find an intersubjective solution to this dilemma in ways that may engender public consensus. Rather, those communities have sought to monopolize the public debate on who is a Jew to colonize it, even to manipulate it, for purposes of social engineering and political control. In the following section I consider state law in the context of public discourse on "who is a Jew." Then, the essay moves to examine intercommunal interactions before reaching some general conclusions.

The Republican / State Dimension

Zionism, as an aggregate of various Jewish national aspirations, has not clearly differentiated Jewish ethnicity from religion or from nationality. Consequently, public contentions over the issue "who is a Jew" have been paramount for allocations of citizenship rights in Israel since the formal inception of the state in 1948. One of the major national projects was to entrench Jewish domination in the state, preventing the possibility of its territory being settled by an Arab Palestinian majority. Based on the Law of Return (1950) and the Citizenship Law (1952), defining someone as a Jew would automatically grant him or her Israeli citizenship. Conversely, non-Jewish immigrants to Israel would be subjected to separate criteria for being admitted to or denied Israeli citizenship. These two laws were more important in Israel than any other piece of legislation, including the Basic Laws, since they were supposed to entrench Jewishness as the main political force in state ideology, legal ideology, and public policy.

However, various communities have long been in conflict with one another over the "objective" criteria defining who is a Jew. Thus categorization of Jewishness has become a political means to construct formal affiliations with nationality in Israel. Control over decisions regarding the applicability of the category "Jew" has reflected and entailed the shifting dynamics of political power. This explains why partisan conflicts over the political power to categorize Jewish affiliations have even caused severe coalition crises such that Orthodox and ultra-Orthodox political parties have threatened to bring down governments if their demands are not accepted. Commitments to maintain the secular-religious status quo have often been entrenched in coalition agreements between the secular ruling elite and the religious parties. Until the 1990s and under the influence of religious political parties—mainly the National [Zionist] Religious Party (NRP) and the ultra-Orthodox parties Agudath Yisrael and, later, Shas—the Israeli governments had imposed an objective criterion to define who is a Jew. The state required official authorities (namely, the Ministry of the Interior) to check that the Jewishness of any particular individual, both as nationality and as a religion, could be proved through genetic affiliation (namely, a Jewish mother) and appropriate documentation from Orthodox authorities. This issue was debated in two salient court rulings in the 1960s. In the Rufeisen case, the High Court of Justice (HCJ) ruled that one's Jewishness for purposes of nationality and citizenship in the Law of Return should be decided based on objective criteria, in particular, on the ability to provide external evidence to support one's subjective declarations about one's religiosity and nationality. Later, in the Shalit case, the HCJ decided that one's declaration about one's subjective feelings regarding one's religious and national affiliation is sufficient for determining who is a Jew for purposes of the Law of Return and granting Israeli nationality and citizenship.[2] However, that ruling has not been adopted as part of Israeli legislation. That is because in 1970 the Law of Return was amended as a result of severe pressures by the Orthodox and ultra-Orthodox political parties that enabled Orthodox objective criteria to be used to decide Israeli nationality and citizenship. Because of the lack of institutional separation of religion, state, and nationality, this narrow categorization of nationality and religion has monopolized the Israeli political setting.[3]

Thus religious conversions were not recognized unless Orthodox procedures were followed, as proved through formal Orthodox certificates. Conservative and Reform conversions, whether in Israel or overseas, were not recognized by state law as valid for purposes of registration in Israel. The reliance of governmental coalitions on the political power of Orthodox and ultra-Orthodox political parties had made the objective criterion into the practical reality. The "status quo" in state-religious relationships in Israel was embedded in coalition agreements, and it prevented any alterations or reforms. Thus the scope of citizenship was established in the context of struggles over political power, and in turn it affected the meaning of various affiliations to Judaism.

The Orthodox political monopoly on definitions and constructions of citizenship has recently been challenged by non-Orthodox Jews, empowered through a significant wave of Soviet immigrants arriving in Israel in the 1990s. Relatively few among these immigrants had established ties to Jewish institutions. Furthermore, estimates are that about 120,000 among the 800,000 Soviet immigrants to Israel in the early 1990s were not considered "Jewish" by Orthodox and ultra-Orthodox authorities and had no formal ties to the Jewish community.[4]

Nevertheless, Soviet immigrants became active in nongovernmental organizations (NGOs) that have challenged the Israeli establishment, calling for more inclusiveness in the Israeli definitions of citizenship and asking for privatization of religion. In 1995 the Orthodox establishment received another challenge when the Israeli Supreme Court, led by a secular elite of justices, adopted the "subjective" criterion, which obliges the government to recognize non-Orthodox religious conversions, including Reform conversions overseas, and, accordingly, to register anyone who declares himself or herself to be "Jewish" as a Jewish resident. In 2002 the Supreme Court broadened its policy also to include recognition of Reform conversions that were conducted in Israel.[5] The Supreme Court insisted that the objective criterion was no longer considered at this stage to be the only necessary condition for recognizing Jewishness for purposes of registration of residency in Israel. Once the boundaries of the political setting were reformed and enlarged, new and more inclusive categorizations of religion and nationality were adopted.

Consequently, state bureaucracy has had control over who can claim to be a Jew for the purpose of residency in Israel. In this context, affiliation to Judaism is based on the declaration of the immigrant about his or her religion. However, Orthodox and ultra-Orthodox religious communities, and their establishment, have political control over objective criteria that define one's religion for purposes of defining nationality based on the Law of Return. This division of political power between registration for the purpose of residence and construction of nationality has produced a hybrid of practical definitions of who is a Jew, a problem that was not predicted by Zionism. One has to be an "objective" Jew to gain Israeli nationality and a "subjective" Jew to be registered as a resident. Paradoxically, those who feel Jewish may not gain Israeli nationality, if they are lacking objective genetic or Orthodox proofs of being Jewish. Consequently, the Zionist state has excluded some Jews from becoming Israelis (e.g., Jews who were converted to Christianity but want to live in Israel) and excluded some Israelis from being recognized as Jews (e.g., non-Jews who were converted to Judaism in non-Orthodox procedures or those who cannot prove affiliation with Judaism).

In the next section, I analyze struggles between nonruling communities over state law. I designate this dimension of my analysis as the "horizontal dimension," since it enables us to comprehend how debates and conflicts over Jewish identities have marked and molded boundaries between various nonruling communities.

The Horizontal Dimension—Conversions and Who Is Not Jewish

Constructing who is Jewish has been a sociopolitical legal means to mark boundaries between various communities in ways that discipline community members. Hence the debates on the issue have had intracommunal as well as intercommunal significance. Quite obviously, the narrower the definition of "who is a Jew," the more gated the community becomes. Conversely, the more inclusive the definition gets, the larger, and less gated, the community becomes. The example of the Canaanites provides one extreme of the secular spectrum and shows how far some definitions of Israeliness stray from those held by the Orthodox. For the Canaanite movement, the single criterion for granting Israeli citizenship was understood as territorial.[6] Namely, since there is no "Jewish nation," only "a Hebrew / Canaanite nation" based on the histories of ancient Canaan (about 2000 BC), anyone who lives in the "Canaanite" territory is an Israeli, regardless of his or her religion and degree of religiosity. Furthermore, according to the Canaanites any national symbols should be stripped of religious significance, since the distinction between religion and (territorial) nationality is an imperative.[7]

However, the dilemma about what constitutes Jewish identity has not only divided national secularists from religious communities but has also constructed boundaries between religious communities. According to the Reform movement in Israel (known as the Movement for Progressive Judaism in Israel), the dilemma should be solved based on the subjective criterion, while according to the Orthodox, the objective criteria should apply. The former emphasizes the individual's desires to define his or her religion and communal affiliations, while the latter underscores stricter criteria of genetic affiliations and highly demanding criteria of religious conversions. Thus the platform of the Reform movement in Israel states: "Progressive Judaism accepts with greetings those who would like to join the collective of Israel and its religion in a genuine and sincere manner. The conversion that is done by our rabbis is a compound process, with religious, cultural, and educational meanings, which combines the demands of the halakha and the reality of life of the Jewish people nowadays."[8]

Furthermore, ultra-Orthodox communities have demanded communal affiliations of membership as the ultimate guideline for being considered Jewish. Accordingly, various ultra-Orthodox congregations are willing to admit the halakhic validity of conversions only if very strict ultra-Orthodox religious procedures are applied—much stricter procedures than those required by the Orthodox political establishment. These communities are not interested in nationality; rather, they wish to maintain Judaism as a highly gated collectivity, based on a very restrictive set of criteria for who is a Jew. Such restrictive, objective criteria limit access for potential members from other communities, thus reinforcing the homogeneity of Israeli Judaism. Using the problem of identity as a sociopolitical tool of control has resulted in an additional ironic paradox: non-Zionist religious communities have demanded stricter criteria for granting Israeli nationality than have Zionist communities.

Paradoxically, while Zionism has aspired to construct national sovereignty and a unified national citizenship across a defined territory, it has inadvertently generated in practice a multiplicity of citizenships. This multiplicity has constituted seemingly incompatible definitions of rights and obligations in the context of state-society relationships and may be summed up as follows. First, ultra-Orthodox Jews define citizenship based on communally specified criteria for framing what it means to be Jewish. These criteria include blood origins and a very restrictive set of religious procedures. Second, Jewish Orthodox authorities legitimate claims for citizenship that are based on state law, but they define legitimacy under very demanding religious hermeneutics, which do not include personal, subjective, definitions of Judaism. Third, definitions of Jewish non-Orthodox citizenship are based on social resistance to statutory state law, and some Supreme Court judicial rulings advocate for privatization of religion, including Orthodoxy. Accordingly, being a Jew is a matter to be decided by the individual and his or her non-Orthodox community and its non-Orthodox conversion procedures. Fourth, definitions of Jewish territorial citizenship are based on residency and identification with a secular national concept of political membership. Fifth, a source of extreme tension, arguments for non-Jewish citizenship such as those that have prevailed among Israeli Arab Palestinians are based on place of birth. The argument assumes that constructions of Jewish identity have been used to suppress the possibility of Arab Palestinians returning to Palestine/Israel. Quite clearly, once the criteria of affiliations with Judaism became embedded in the definition of nationality and the granting of citizenship, Arab Palestinians in Israel were discriminated against while Arab Palestinians outside Israel were excluded from the possibility of enjoying the right of return to Israel in its pre-1967 borders.[9]

Yet the struggle over definitions has also produced some unlikely coalitions among groups with seemingly irreconcilable perspectives. Because political categorizations of ethnoreligious identities are aimed at engineering boundaries and maintaining control, the most powerful political coalition to support a strict definition of who is a Jew has implicitly been the informal sociopolitical coalition between ultra-Orthodox Jews and the Arab Sharia establishment among Israeli Arab Palestinians. These two groups have infrequently and informally aired support of restricting the definition of who is a Jew, for fear that making it more inclusive would actually erode the status of Jews and Arabs already residing within the geographical boundaries of the state. Both ultra-Orthodox Jews and orthodox Muslims have aspired to monitor Jewish immigration to Israel by generating a broad definition of who is not Jewish.[10] However, in the context of fighting over state resources, ultra-Orthodox Jews have been interested in a narrow category of ethnic Jewish nationality, while Muslims have aspired to enlarge the definition of Israeli territorial citizenship.

Hence the question "who is not Jewish" has been answered through multiple constructions of "who is a Jew." Ultra-Orthodox Jews—the majority of whom have taken part in the Israeli political setting— have aspired to preserve their monopoly in the political establishment through insisting on very formalistic criteria to prove Jewishness, while any more inclusive criteria have been conceived as inviting non-Orthodox forces to be involved in sharing state resources. On the one hand, these strict criteria have formed internal boundaries of communal discipline and authority within the ultra-Orthodox community. On the other hand, those criteria spurred the desire of the ultra-Orthodox groups to enforce the "objective criteria" on the overall Jewish public.[11] Israeli Arab Palestinians have been fearful that any more inclusive state definition of who is a Jew may engender more massive Jewish immigration, even as the return of Palestinians is defined by state law as unlawful. Ironically, while ultra-Orthodox Jews have aspired to incite a more traditional halakhic discourse (based on notions of biological Jewish identity) and Arab Palestinians have encouraged a more secular territorial discourse, their self-interests coincide and result in shared goals of placing limits on who can properly claim to be a Jew in Israel. The politics of identity has also been the politics of nationality.

It is important to note that the objective, stricter criterion of who is a Jew is transnational and not territorial. Thus for ultra-Orthodox Jews, Jewishness as an objective phenomenon based on genetic affiliations does not take into account residency and place of birth. For the adherents of stricter criteria for defining a Jew, Jewish ethnicity becomes a source of domination and it constitutes the essence of Israeli nationality, in both its Zionist and anti-Zionist versions. Conversely, for adherents of broader and more inclusive definitions of who is a Jew, Israeli nationality exceeds Jewish ethnicity and has historically constructed a different vision of Jewish territoriality, which may even completely separate the state from the claims of religion. Paradoxically, the conservative, or objective, criterion for Jewishness is more transnational, while the liberal, or subjective, criterion is more local. From this perspective, the dilemma of how nationality or "Israeliness" should be defined will affect how Jewishness is construed when it comes to the question of who is a Jew.

All these aspects of identity should be conceived and analyzed in the context of dynamic historical trends. Demographic changes in Israel are challenging identity categories and definitions. About three hundred thousand non-Jewish immigrants to Israel since the early 1990s, partly immigrants from the Soviet republics and partly foreign workers, are challenging state authorities and shaping legal categories of citizenship.[12] After the 1970s, the political culture in Israel became more litigious than ever before. Through litigation of NGOs, these immigrants have unsettled the status quo and have demanded more inclusiveness. One of the most important areas of contention has been the degree of Orthodox supervision over religious conversions.

Thus, in the 1990s, the Supreme Court ruled that religious conversions abroad would be recognized in Israel as valid for purposes of registration. Consequently, new modes of religious conversions were adapted with some implicit consent of ultra-Orthodox communities. The result is that the Supreme Court is imposing secular liberal values on established rabbinical authorities. This spirit—of partial privatization of religion and some limited inclusiveness—has radiated to other issues of state and religion as well, in particular, family law (covering marriage, divorce, custody cases, and more). The numbers of civil ceremonies of marriages and contracted civil unions have increased, as have the numbers of non-Orthodox marriages. Furthermore, the Court has ruled that in matters of inheritance and financial benefits, as well as child adoption, a complete equality between homosexuals and heterosexuals should prevail. The Court has evaded the issue of the formal legality of same-sex marriage, due to possible severe opposition from Orthodox religious groups. Yet as a predominately secular elite, the justices have propelled practical privatization of Orthodoxy, using, in this context, inclusive criteria of gender equality.[13] This context—of some pluralization of religious practices and some secularization in culture—has exerted more sociopolitical and cultural pressures on conventional categories of Jewish identity. Human categories do not constitute epistemological islands; rather, they are constituted and reconstituted through the dynamic contexts of social practices.

The social practices of Israelis in daily life have also constituted new identities through which non-Jews, including foreign immigrants from African and Asian countries, may perceive themselves as Israelis and identify with some basic Jewish-Israeli narratives. Indeed, about 40 percent of the Jewish Israeli public has carved out a secular, antitheological definition of a new Israeli nationality in which pluralism of legalities and jurisdictions prevails and in which religious practices are more plural while remaining within the framework of a Jewish state.[14] This means, in practical terms, a significant reduction in the political power of the chief rabbinate, the legality of civil marriage performed abroad and non-Orthodox conversions, and restrictions on the jurisdiction of the rabbinical courts and expansions of the civil jurisdiction of the secular district courts in matters of family law. It has also contributed to the secularization of Jewish holidays in ways that allow them to be redefined as civic festivals. All these issues were debated as a result of controversies over how to define Jewishness, the degree to which the definitions should be restrictive or inclusive, and, more important, which institution and what elite should have the monopoly to impose the criteria for constructing citizenship and membership in the Jewish political body.

Embittered controversies over the scope of military conscription are also part of the dilemma of what it means to be a Jew in Israel. The State of Israel was established based on a system of compulsory military conscription—of about three years of service for all adult men and about two years for all adult women. After the regular military service ends, all citizens are expected to be on reserve military duty for about two weeks every year, with the exception of married women, women with children, and individuals, both male and female, who have special medical or economic reasons to claim exemption. Hence the military has been a very important social-political institution in Israel and the most influential in Israeli culture.[15]

The military has also been the main sociopolitical marker between Israeli Arab Palestinians, who with the exception of the Bedouin and the Druze do not serve in the military, and Jews, the majority of whom do serve. Similarly, it has been a major sociopolitical marker of national patriotism. Zionist Orthodox religious females are exempt from military service but usually substitute "national service" for it. The most meaningful exceptions to the rule of obligatory military conscription have been ultra-Orthodox yeshiva students.[16] For the majority of Orthodox, observant, and secular Jews, military service is the crucial expression of Jewish national identity and patriotism. However, for ultra-Orthodox Jews (with some exceptions), serving in the Zionist military is in severe contradiction to their Jewish faith. Ultra-Orthodoxy considers Jewish nationalism an antinomy to the Jewish fundamental of awaiting the Messiah. The nationalism of the ultra-Orthodox hinges not on the concept of territorial sovereignty but on the religious faith of awaiting an eschatological redemption.

Hence these Jews emphasize more the genetic part of membership in Jewish civilization, while opposing Zionism and its requirements of military service as main criteria for communal affiliation.[17]

In practice, ultra-Orthodox religious political parties have been willing to make political compromises as long as recognition of the Jewish nation-state is only utilitarian—for example, for purposes of taxation—and does not require altering the fundamentals of religious beliefs in eschatological redemption. Yet the issue of mandatory military service has produced a great deal of ferment among contending groups. Secular groups express anger over the issue of exemptions, while the number of ultra-Orthodox Jews asking for those exemptions has been steadily growing. The seeds for this controversy were planted in 1947 when the interim prime minister, David Ben-Gurion, was looking for legitimacy. Early on he agreed to the demands made by ultra-Orthodox political parties and major halakhic figures to exempt yeshiva students from military conscription. Recently, this arrangement has been constitutionally challenged in the Supreme Court. Following several court debates and appeals (by secular groups) that were dismissed, the Court ruled in 1998 to declare the arrangement illegal.[18] Yet fearful of political sanctions against the judiciary, the justices did not declare the arrangement null and void. Rather, they asked the Knesset, the Israeli parliament, to alter the constitutional arrangement. However, because of pressures from the ultra-Orthodox political parties and despite the evident majoritarian opinion of the Court, the exemption arrangement has not been significantly altered as of now.

On the one hand, various segments of Israeli society are negotiating with the state, often challenging its agents and public policy, by articulating and practicing unconventional identities. These groups are a good example of how, despite legal and nationalist frameworks, everyday society constitutes its own informal laws and definitions of group membership. The global economy and technology are part of the picture. In an age when rabbinical yeshiva students are using the Internet to challenge their rabbinical authorities, protesting their sermons, questioning their decisions, and opposing them politically or going to Internet cafés and surfing the Web freely with almost no filtering applied, ramifications for the previously established boundaries of communities and definitions of identities are unavoidable.

Thus the traditional authority of the religious communal leadership has been in some decline.[19] In a very basic sense the communities are becoming more exposed to pressures of various social forces: modernity, secularization, and globalization. In the short run, the ultrareligious authorities are concerned and have been issuing halakhic rulings either prohibiting or warning against private usage of the Internet. But in the long run, Jewish Orthodoxy may acknowledge that a multiplicity of cultural perspectives is part of Judaism. "Who is a Jew" will remain a significant issue, a debatable dilemma, both for internal mobilization purposes and as part of daily national politics in Israel. But with the construction of new practices of identity, new questions may be asked about what constitutes Jewishness.

It is not my intention to predict behavior. The challenge I address is different. My research aims instead to explore and explain some unanticipated consequences of the social, political, and legal categories that have attempted to create a framework for deciding who is a Jew. Rather than see this dilemma, with its historical contingencies, as an independent variable, a cause that requires definite constructions as answers, my essay argues that the politics of categorization has invited public debate around the "who is a Jew" question in ways that reflect and determine political expectations of what the answers should be. However, since identities—inter alia, Jewish identities—are constructed through practices at levels of both elite and grassroots activities, which then are also interacting with the state, predetermined categories are always confronting social criticism. This dynamic paves the way for new types of ambiguities and contestations. The dilemma of defining who is a Jew has not only affected the Jews but has also shaped the broader political, economic, and social landscape of Israel, since communities have used various criteria to maintain their sociopolitical boundaries.

Conclusion

This essay has analyzed various dimensions of legal and practical categories that have constructed the scope and essence of debates on who is a Jew to show how the criteria of constructing and deconstructing Jewish identities have been aimed at framing, coding, and decoding the sociopolitical boundaries among and between various communities in Israel. In the 1950s, state law underscored the Jewishness of the state through legislation that has made Jewish identity the main foundation of legal and state ideology. The question of "who is a Jew" has received a very clear response in state law. Furthermore, the government has relied on the exclusive monopoly of Orthodoxy and ultra-Orthodoxy and its control over definitions of Jewishness for matters of determining nationality. Gradually, however, the ultra-Orthodox categorizations have been subjected to sociopolitical challenges by various nonruling communities of Reform Jews, secular Jews, non-Jews, and Israeli Arab Palestinians. These communities and their assorted NGOs have incrementally altered some of the categorizations that have constructed Jewish identities and citizenship. In this context, my analysis demonstrates that the dilemma of "who is a Jew" has been used to maintain control and mark the boundaries between various communities. Hence what is important is much less the identity dilemma itself than its political usage, which has wide-reaching ramifications for state and society relations.

Notes

1. For the meaning of *nomos* groups, see the following by Robert Cover in *Narrative, Violence, and the Law: The Essays of Robert Cover,* ed. Martha Minow, Michael Ryan, and Austin Sarat (Ann Arbor: University of Michigan Press, 1992): "The Origins of Judicial Activism in the Protection of Minorities," 13–49; "Nomos and Narrative," 95–172; and "Violence and the Word," 203–38.

2. Various court rulings debated this issue. The most prominent and important rulings that also created national political debates were HCJ 72/62 *Rufeisen v. Minister of the Interior* P.D. 16 (4) 2428, and HCJ 58/68 *Shalit v. Minister of the Interior* P.D. 23 (2) 477.

3. Gad Barzilai, *Communities and Law: Politics and Cultures of Legal Identities* (Ann Arbor: University of Michigan Press, 2003), 209–78; Alan Dowty, *The Jewish State: A Century Later* (Berkeley: University of California Press, 1998).

4. For more analysis of the challenges of the migration from the Soviet republics to Israel, see Asher Cohen, *Israeli Assimilation: Changes in the Definition of the Jewish Collective's Identity and Its Boundaries* (Jerusalem: Institute of the World Jewish Congress, 2002).

5. HCJ 1031/93 *Passaro and the Movement for Progressive Judaism v. Minister of the Interior* P.D. 49 (4) 661. The appeal was submitted to the Supreme Court in

1993, and the ruling was granted and published in 1995. HCJ 2901/97, 5070/95 *Naamat v. Minister of the Interior* (February 20, 2002).

6. The original name of the movement that was established in 1939 was the Committee for the Consolidation of the Young Hebrews. After the 1940s it was known mainly as the Canaanites, a name originally given to the movement as an ironic denotation by the poet Abraham Shlonski. Later, it was adopted by the movement as its main title. See a series of interviews with Uzi Ornan, "Anachnu Ha'Knaanim" [We Are the Canaanites], *Svivot* 33 (December 1994), http://www.snunit.k12.il/heb_journals/svivot/33061.html (accessed May 6, 2009).

7. See Yaacov Shavit, *From Hebrew to Canaanite* [in Hebrew] (Tel Aviv: Domino, 1987).

8. See the Web site of the Movement for Progressive Judaism in Israel, in which the platform is published, in Hebrew: http://www.reform.org.il/Heb/IMPJ/Platform.asp#People.

9. Yoav Peled, "Ethnic Democracy and the Legal Construction of Citizenship: Arab Citizens of the Jewish State," *American Political Science Review* 86 (1992): 432–43; Yoav Peled and Gershon Shafir, *Being Israeli: The Dynamics of Multiple Citizenship* (Cambridge: Cambridge University Press, 2002).

10. Kadi Ahmed Natur (chief justice of Supreme Sharia Court of Appeals, Israel), interview with the author, January 31, 1999, Tel Aviv. Yet, obviously, the first preference of the Arab Palestinian minority would be to cancel the Law of Return, if possible.

11. While few ultra-Orthodox groups, like the extreme Satmar, have completely rejected the state, the dominant majority among Israeli ultra-Orthodoxy has taken active part in Israeli politics, has almost routinely participated in governmental coalitions, and has become the leading elite group controlling rabbinical courts and religious councils in Israel. Especially after 1984, while polarization among the non-Orthodox Jewish public has increased, the ultra-Orthodox have gained more power than ever before in Israeli history, including increasing national budgets for their communal purposes. The professional literature testifying to the growing power of the ultra-Orthodox is vast; see, e.g., Joseph Fund, *Pirud o hishtatfut: Agudat Yiśra'el mul ha-Tsiyonut u-Medinat Yiśra'el* [Separation or Participation: Agudat Israel Confronting Zionism and the State of Israel] (Jerusalem: Magnes, 1999); and Menachem Friedman, *Ha-Hevrah ha-Haredit: Mekorot, Megamot ve-Tahalikhim* [Haredi Society: Sources, Trends, and Processes] (Jerusalem: Jerusalem Institute for Policy Studies, 1991); Barzilai, *Communities and Law,* 209–78.

12. According to the Israeli Immigration Police and several NGOs, Israel had about 380,000 foreign workers, of whom 140,000 were defined by state law as "illegal," at the outset of the twenty-first century. See Rebeca Raijman and Adriana Kemp, "The New Immigration to Israel: Becoming a De-Facto Immigration State in the 1990s," in *Immigration Worldwide: Policies, Practices and*

Trends, ed. Uma A. Segal, Doreen Elliott, and Nazneen S. Mayadas (New York: Oxford University Press, 2009), 227–43.

13. See, e.g., HCJ 721/94 El Al v. Danilovich P.D. 48 (5) 749.

14. S. Charles Liebman, Li-heyot be-yahad:Yahase datiyim-hiloniyim ba-hevrah ha-Yiśre'elit [To Live Together: Secular-Religious Relations in Israeli Society] (Jerusalem: Keter, 1990); S. Charles Liebman and Elihu Katz, *The Jewishness of Israelis: Responses to the Guttman Report* (Albany: State University of New York Press, 1997).

15. Gad Barzilai, *Wars, Internal Conflicts, and Political Order: A Jewish Democracy in the Middle East* (Albany: State University of New York Press, 1996); Uri Ben-Eliezer, *The Making of Israeli Militarism* (Bloomington: Indiana University Press, 1998); Yagil Levy, *Israel's Materialist Militarism* (New York: Macmillan, 2007).

16. For more details about Israel's constitutional arrangements of military exemptions, see Menachem Hofnung, *Democracy, Law, and National Security* (London: Aldershot, 1996).

17. Michael Keren and Gad Barzilai, Hishtalvut kevutsot "periferyah" ba-hevrah uva-politikah be-'idan shalom [Inclusion of "Peripheral" Groups in Law and Society in Times of Peace] (Jerusalem: Israel Democracy Institute, 1998).

18. HCJ 448/81 Ressler v. Minister of Defense P.D. 36 (1) 81; FA 2/82 Ressler v. Defense Minister P.D. 36 (1) 708; HCJ 910/86 Ressler v. Minister of Defense P.D. 42 (2) 441; HCJ 3267/97, 715/98 Ressler v. Minister of Defense.

19. Karine Barzilai-Nahon and Gad Barzilai, "Cultured Technology: The Internet and Religious Fundamentalism," *Information Society* 21, no. 1 (2005): 25–40.

3

Jewish Character?

Stereotype and Identity in Fiction from Israel
by Aharon Appelfeld and Sayed Kashua

NAOMI B. SOKOLOFF

In a story called "Transformation" (1968), celebrated Hebrew author and Holocaust survivor Aharon Appelfeld imagines characters at the far edges of Jewish identity.[1] His protagonists, a man and a woman on the run during the Nazi era, undergo a sudden, Kafkaesque metamorphosis. Taking refuge in a forest, they become unrecognizable as Jews, turn into peasants in appearance, and meld into nature. This tale can usefully be read in tandem with another story, from a later era, that similarly features a startling metamorphosis as it explores vexed boundaries between Jews and non-Jews. The story's author, Sayed Kashua, is a Palestinian citizen of Israel who has published widely in the Hebrew press, and in "Herzl Disappears at Midnight" (2005) he imagines a young man who awakes each morning as a Jew and each night becomes an Arab.[2]

These two texts invite comparison, despite their significant thematic and artistic differences, for both carry their protagonists back and forth across ethnic lines to embody non-Jews and Jews and thereby pose the question of what those boundaries demarcate. What are the differences between Jews and others? What constitutes Jewishness, and what are its limits? Does something of it remain after the metamorphoses these characters endure? In both stories, the deployment of stereotype is one of the primary narrative techniques that the authors engage as they wrestle with such questions. Stereotyping depends on and stipulates rigid identity boundaries, yet fiction can use it to richly and creatively address issues of shifting self-definition. Here it serves as a productive tool of representation that contributes to Kashua's and Appelfeld's explorations of Jewish characters and Jewish character.

To be sure, stereotype has suffered a bad reputation. Countless literary and cultural studies have dismissed it as essentialist and reductive or condemned it as downright racist. Some scholars, however, have begun to weary of the stereotyping of stereotype as "always bad, simplistic idiotic, and rigid."[3] The salient question, they say, is how literature has appropriated stereotype and how writers use it. Do authors endorse stereotypes, parody them, flaunt them defiantly, or otherwise transform them when addressing a particular audience?[4] Has the writer struggled with the problem of how to represent groups and how to use markers of identity or simply reinscribed negative clichés? Recognizing that stereotypes are always "already heard"—that is, they are received ideas that have been repeated and rehearsed many times previously—literary investigations have shifted to a model of intertextuality. A variety of studies consider how stereotypes flow and circulate and what their protean instability reveals about those who perpetrate them.[5] Critics advocate asking not if any particular generalization about a collective population is true or plausible but whether such generalizations are endorsed (and by whom) and to what line of previous texts and statements they relate. Furthermore, there has been a call for more literary analysis that is audience-oriented and pragmatic.[6] We might ask, what is the reception accorded to the use of stereotype in literature? Does this material have an impact socially? There is no doubt that the images promoted in literature have played a crucial role over many centuries in shaping cultural identities, fostering ethnic awareness, and even spurring nationalist movements. Therefore, it is important to assess not only how writers deploy stereotype but also how their work functions for and is received by their readership.

In the stories I discuss, Kashua and Appelfeld turn to stereotypes in a way that does not simply reinscribe denigrating images or renounce them but rather forces the reader to confront a conflict—between a world of limitless possibility and one where familiar typologies foreclose a choice about identity. The primary quality the stories share is that each combines two kinds of characterization. Starting with a mode of narration that fosters open-endedness, uncertainty of motive, and complexity of character, each text then switches to a reliance on stereotype that shuts down complexity. Rigid, pejorative imagery, contrasting with the richness of narrative possibility, produces central tensions that animate each story. The result is oscillating interpretations; one demarcates and reconfirms schematic, inflexible boundaries of identity, while the other circumvents, disrupts, or transforms such boundaries in significant ways.

Appelfeld puzzles over perplexities of Jewish identity in an antisemitic Europe, where Jews are both alien others and fully capable of assimilating into the surroundings. He asks readers to ponder whether Jewishness is predetermined and fixed or mutable and as easy to shed as old skin. Is it physically marked or something spiritual, a source of pride or stigma? These are the sorts of conundrums, of course, that Zionism proposed to resolve through a unity of language, people, and territory. Kashua's story, set in Israel decades after the founding of the Jewish state, complicates and challenges any such vision of unity: his writing even puts into question the Jewishness of the Hebrew language, and while the plot delves into the inner world of a Jewish character, it simultaneously asks readers to think about the status of Arabs in contemporary Israel.

Significantly, the two authors invite comparison, precisely because their grappling with the question of "who is a Jew" catapults them into the "who is an Israeli" debates. Both Appelfeld and Kashua represent voices that were once on the margins of Israeli letters, and each moves those voices closer to the center of the canon. Appelfeld has been instrumental since the 1960s in bringing the experiences of Holocaust survivors into Hebrew literature and earning empathy for them. His writing is widely recognized for broadening conceptions of Jewishness in Israeli culture at a time when sabras and Holocaust survivors were often seen as opposites, the former as heroes and the latter as pitiful and even contemptible victims. Kashua, for his part, has been one of the most popular and successful authors to bring Arab voices to a wide Israeli public, through his journalism, novels, short fiction, and television script writing.

Kashua's story treats the margins of Israeli society as an explicit theme, while Appelfeld's does not, but the reception of their fiction shows that both have changed the boundaries of Israeli identity through their literary role as cultural "outsiders" turned "insiders." Part of their outsider status stems from the fact that neither Appelfeld nor Kashua is a native speaker of Hebrew. Adopting that language and writing from the perspective of a Holocaust survivor, Appelfeld reconnects Israeli identity with European Jewish continuity and tradition; in contrast, Kashua's use of Hebrew to convey an Arab voice presents Israel as a site of identity that is anything but cohesive. Both authors turn to stereotype and also to equivocations, as key elements in their art, as they ponder deep divisions between Jews and non-Jews, ill-defined boundaries of Jewish identity, and unsettled, unsettling tensions surrounding perceptions of what constitutes Jewish character.

Aharon Appelfeld's "Transformation"

One of the strengths of imaginative literature is its ability to offer dense, multilayered expression that may attempt to say what could not be said otherwise and what cannot be summarized or paraphrased without losing some of its richness. Poetic prose is known for creating "something unavailable in, and irreducible to, codified language," a description that neatly fits the lyric story "Transformation."[7] Appelfeld's short tale compactly and economically expresses a contradictory vision—of a racist world of rigid exclusions, where boundaries are nonetheless unclear, where Jews cannot be limited to the humiliating views that others have of them, and where Jews are not different from others but still remain Jews.

This tale of Jews in disguise, hiding in a forest, relies heavily on stereotypes. Here, as in much of Appelfeld's fiction, non-Jews are imagined as peasants, associated with physical strength, coarseness, and nature. Inarticulate and narrow-minded, such characters are given to drink and violence. Such a type figure is what the protagonist of "Transformation" becomes. Although Jews in this fictional universe are equated with intellect, weakness, fear, and dishonesty, this Jewish man grows robust and brawny; loses language; learns to fish, hunt, and swim and to make fire and "listen to the wind" (58).

The opening of the narrative makes no explicit mention of Jews or gentiles. Instead, it emphasizes perplexity and abrupt change, presenting puzzling details unmoored in space and time. This beginning will be especially mystifying to an audience unfamiliar with the largely effaced, but pervasive, stereotypes that structure the text. The transformation the characters undergo makes sense only if the reader is aware of the narrative assumption that these are European Jews fleeing Nazi persecution, that Jews and non-Jews are considered polar opposites, and that Jews sometimes escape destruction if they can pass as gentiles. Yet the opening paragraph offers few coordinates setting the locale. The second paragraph includes a brief and cryptic statement, that "for many days the farmers chased after them" (55). However, in order to gather the historical circumstance and external frame of reference necessary to process that information, the reader has to know something about Appelfeld's own childhood during the Holocaust—part of which he spent hiding in forests—or take into consideration the gamut of other stories by him that feature Jews on the run, who camouflage their identities or are unsure where to turn as catastrophe looms.[8]

From the start, "Transformation" is marked by paradox and contradiction, as the plot both establishes stereotypes and undermines them. Jews here are completely different from their neighbors but become indistinguishable from them. In addition, as the tale posits a world of rigid clarities, it creates an air of vagueness and mystery. Precisely because the rigid ideas are so ingrained in the thinking of the characters that inhabit this world, the ability to transform and elude set identities seems amazing, wondrous, paradoxical. The text opens as the principal figure, startled, takes note of sudden changes he is experiencing. The title has already hinted that there will be incongruous qualities to his new circumstances, and, indeed, the original Hebrew title, "Hahishtanut," not only implies "changing" but comes from root letters that also suggest difference and even oddity. This lexical choice points toward the character's estrangement from self. Furthermore, *hahishtanut* is a verbal noun and so indicates that the transformation is a continuing process, not yet complete. All is so new to the man, and newly unfolding, that he finds himself in an uncertain state of mind. The Hebrew prose points to uncertainties and is filled with ambiguity. Here is one possible translation of the opening paragraph:[9]

> "Why, these are not my gestures"—he said to himself and smiled.
> How quick were the changes—like autumn leaf-fall, and also what
> remained wasn't his. An other skin grew on his face, his hands were

hairy. She too changed together with him, in a kind of mutual secret. She lost her face, her gentleness. Her throat reddened from the cold sun. The temperature did with them as it would. There was no escape from this. (55)

What is clear is that the character is glad to see that his gestures and bodily expressions have changed. An assumption that is unspoken but which comes through in a second reading is that peculiarly animated gesticulations have long been associated with negative stereotypes of Jews (this is a motif frequently found in Appelfeld's fiction), and the protagonist here is relieved to be rid of that stigma.[10] More difficult to discern is whether he too looks down on "Jewish" attributes or is just glad to be unrecognizable. Ambiguities of translation include the word *giḥekh*, rendered here as "smiled" but which could instead signify "chuckled" or "smirked." That semantic range would suggest that the character feels a glee mixed with contempt, and "smirked" would bring heightened attention to a dissonance within the man himself. He feels distanced from his usual sense of self, alienated from it, even as an "other skin" grows on his face. He is definitely pleased with his metamorphosis, and he and the woman frequently laugh despite their dire circumstances, but the nuances of their laughter and their motives are open to interpretation.

Ambiguity continues in descriptions of the characters' helplessness. That these two are at the mercy of the elements is evident from the comment, "The temperature did with them as it would." Literally, however, this sentence reads, "The temperature did with them *as with her own* [kivshelah]" (emphasis added). The concept "her own" suggests belonging; the two characters have merged into the landscape and found a home there. At the same time, more ominously, the line might be better formulated in English as "the temperature toyed with them" or perhaps, evoking a sexual overtone, "had its way with them." The forest is both shelter and torment. That "there was no escape from this" reinforces the emphasis on powerlessness. But what is "this"? Is it just the temperature, the elements in general, Jewishness, or something else? Or is it the persecution this pair is experiencing that has not yet been mentioned? The vagueness is deliberate and emphatic. In view of these meanings, the first sentence—"Why, these are not my gestures"—also takes on a new dimension. The word *tenuʿah*, translated as "gestures," more usually signifies "motion" or "movement." The entire story, as it unfolds, will concern the constant wandering, the relentless, forced movement of the protagonists. Does the opening sentence, with its mention of gesture, gesture toward all of that? Perhaps the intention is to express the man's sentiment that the whole circumstance of being on the move, fleeing like a hunted animal, is not of his own doing.

As the personification of the weather demonstrates, an implied narrator is at work here, playing an interpretive role. This narrative voice mediates between the characters and the reader, creating layers of possible meaning through imagery that insists on the ambiguities and oddity of the Jews' situation. Similar use of metaphor throughout the story suggests an assaying of elusive meaning. The implied narrator also turns to simile (e.g., the changes were as quick as "autumn leaf-fall") to create comparisons. Most readers would find Appelfeld's own Holocaust experiences and the characters' plight, hiding in the forest, unimaginable. Similes here suggest approximations; they link an incommunicable reality to a more familiar world that the reader might better understand. In his mediating role, the narrator also turns frequently to the word *ke'ilu* (as if); for example, the man and woman speak little, "as if they were born without words, as if they had no words anymore" (56). This phrase suggests that the narrator is perennially looking for the right words but cannot quite articulate what is happening, even as the characters are living an "as if" situation, an extended impersonation. The conditional conveys the effort it takes to narrate the strangeness and complexity of their experience. Altogether, the narrator is never able to refer to phenomena directly or definitively and so explains them tentatively.

And yet this is the same narrator who later explicitly turns to reductive stereotype. As the plot progresses the characters take on more and more characteristics associated with non-Jews. The man is said to embrace the woman "as drunks do" (59); he begins to beat the woman, and she begs him not to hit her, saying, "after all, you're a Jew not a goy" (60). This kind of crude referential shorthand conjoins jarringly with the elusiveness, vagueness, and emphasis on disorientation at the story's opening. The text that evades well-worn images at first, later embraces them.

How does such stereotyping, disturbing in its crudity, operate in this work? Is Appelfeld simply repeating conventional calumny? In part, the answer is yes, but only in part. His art recreates the prevalence of such thinking within the formative world of his own life; when asked about such images, he responds that he tries to convey the brutal surroundings he knew in his youth and attitudes that were an integral part of that environment.[11] It is crucial to note, though, that it is the characters within the fiction who voice prejudice; they express received commonplaces that the implied author does not necessarily endorse. In "Transformation" it is the woman who says that only a "goy" would beat her. In Appelfeld's novel *Tzili*, similar remarks are made: a gentile prostitute states, "The Jews are weak, but they're gentle too. A Jew would never strike a woman"; a Jew hiding in a bunker insists, "All the Jews are cowards"; a Jewish woman says of her lover that he is "a goy in every sense of the word, drunk and violent."[12] In an Appelfeld story called "The Return," a Jew estranged from his community says of Jews that "their cleverness is used for evil"; in non-Jews, he sees a "kind of primitiveness" and creatures of nature "lacking cunning."[13] Such imagery comes through in many other texts by Appelfeld, including *The Age of Wonders*, *The Conversion*, *Katerina*, *All Whom I Have Loved*, and more.

That this author does not aim primarily for historicity or mimetic documentation should also be kept in mind. He sees stereotypes as a way of conveying primordial fear. He uses them, he says, because at the time of the war, "we came into contact with archaic mythical forces, a kind of dark subconscious the meaning of which we did not know, nor do we know it to this day."[14] Precisely because they are primitive and elemental devices, stereotypes suggest elemental fear and lives reduced by circumstance to primitive measures. The writer, in his fiction, magnifies these images to indicate evil forces of enormous dimension. The stereotypes ask to be taken not as plausible sociological categorizations but as archetypes that resonate collectively. In line with this thinking, some critics have read "Transformation" as a tale of mythic rather than historical orientation, one that reactivates the age-old trope of the eternally Wandering Jew.[15]

Altogether, Appelfeld exaggerates the exaggeratedness of the rude stereotype, the primitiveness of the image of primitive impulses, to create his own distinctive vision of Jewish suffering in a viciously antisemitic world. In "Transformation" two very different techniques working in conjunction with each other make this effort artistically effective. On the one hand, subtle ambivalences, vagueness, and hesitancies point to the puzzling oddity of the characters' world, suggesting the complexity of their personal circumstances; on the other hand, elemental, rude minimalism intensifies the impression of a strange social reality that the author expects will exceed the grasp of the reader. This narrative sketches the imagined realm with highly simplistic, stylized contours as it insists on the base hatred and fear that dominate this environment. Together, the two techniques yield a picture that is eerie and, at once, both elusive and earthy.

Does the story of Jews on the run reach resolution? Do unalterable, impermeable boundaries of identity remain entrenched, or does a vision of adaptable, fluid, complex identity prevail? The issues come to a head at the end, as winter approaches. The woman wants to take shelter with peasants; she feels that she is now unidentifiable as a Jew. The man, though, does not feel safe and wants to hold on to her in the forest. Besides, he cannot move because the frost has frozen and bound his legs. These images of binding, holding, and releasing deepen the thematic emphasis on entrapment and escape. Most pointedly, the man realizes that he must let the woman go, but he determines that, when the frost melts, he will find her and "bind her" (*ya'akod otah*; 62). In his analysis of the story, Alan Mintz notes that these words are inevitably linked in the Hebrew reader's mind with the Akeda, the biblical tale of the binding of Isaac. Mintz interprets the allusion to mean that the character imagines a violent and stereotypically non-Jewish denouement (Jewish tradition focuses on *not* following through with the threat of human sacrifice); yet *ya'akod*, with its echoes of Jewish religious contexts, indicates that the character holds on to vestiges of his Jewishness even when he acts most like the stereotypically brutal "goy."[16]

An alternative interpretation, with a somewhat different emphasis, could be that *ya'akod* is the vocabulary not of the character but of the narrator—someone who crafts the allusive richness of Hebrew in a way that conveys the character's paradoxical, liminal identity. The phrase thereby gestures toward a potential future for the protagonist, calling to mind the life of the author himself—someone who survived the kind of experience his characters suffer, who went on to make a rich narrative art out of his explorations of Jewish cultural tradition, and who feels intimately bound up with his heritage and connected to the past. As Appelfeld puts it, especially in the autobiographical *A Table for One* (2001), such ties to the past are life sustaining and vital to his art. He notes, "When I write, I feel bound [meḥubar] to a time and a place; but when the writing no longer flows, it is as if a cloud descends and my world darkens and narrows."[17]

It is important, then, to keep in mind various kinds of "binding" evoked in Appelfeld's work to understand that final paragraph of "Transformation." For along with the negative reverberations of the word *kevulot* (that is, "bound"—the word used in the text to indicate that the character's feet are roped in by the frost), and *ya'akod* (a verb which is fraught with potential for violence), the implied narrator, like the storyteller Appelfeld, remains bound up with the Jewish past and with tradition (*meḥubar*) in a productive and enriching way. Maybe the Jew in the forest is caught in a world of rigid dichotomies, caught between escaping and embracing his Jewish past, and can never make a full metamorphosis. But maybe Appelfeld crafts a fiction that conveys radical undecidability, such that the character's impasse exposes the entire repertoire of stereotypes that differentiate Jew/non-Jew as constructed and untenable. At the same time, the last words of the story hold out for the value of reclaiming allegiance and identification with Jewish heritage, as the narrator builds his art by reaching out for the emotional and cultural ties that bind.

In his autobiographical essays and memoirs, Appelfeld describes his personal efforts to reach out for such bonds. In the process, he also challenges received notions of Jewish identity by exploring his own lived experience of Jewishness as a variegated and ever-evolving phenomenon. As a child he had very meager Jewish education, religious or otherwise. After the Holocaust, he forged a new life for himself through an extraordinary determination to acquire Jewish literacy. Studying the texts and traditions from the Jewish past gave him the tools for his own art and helped him create characters that run the gamut of Jewish cultural affiliation. All this attests to a more constructivist than essentialist view of identity, as does the fact that his fiction does not limit its representation to a narrow range of Jews. Instead, it portrays a spectrum of types, from religious Jews to assimilated ones, Europeans and Israelis, Communists and faith healers, converts and apostates, Yiddishists and self-hating Jews, and a variety of mute, indecipherable figures. Moving away from rigid stereotypes, his work often includes positive, sympathetic gentile characters as well.

Yet for Appelfeld, Jewishness is not only something chosen or performed, subject to the particular creative adaptations of the individual. In his view it is also inescapable. Because of their history, their family connections, and the prejudices directed against them, Jews cannot deny that they are Jews. What is striking about his artistic techniques is that they hold in balance these multiple, seemingly contradictory definitions. In this conception, Jewishness is multiform, pluralistic, and mutable, yet given at birth, highly determined by society's forces and discourses, but also an inherited sense of self that makes fierce claims to loyalty and commands continuity.[18]

Sayed Kashua's "Herzl Disappears at Midnight"

Kashua's story "Herzl Disappears at Midnight" is another text marked by radical undecidability and contradiction. It features an abrupt metamorphosis that, every night, turns its Jewish protagonist into an Arab and every morning turns him back into a Jew. From the opening sentence the reader knows that there is something contradictory about this character; his name, Herzl Haliwa, indicates his dual existence, for "Herzl" is practically synonymous with Zionism, and "Haliwa" is an Arabic word, meaning "sweet" or "beautiful."[19] In short, this man is named for a culture hero and for ideal qualities, but his duality will turn out to be something much less than ideal.

That this name is intended to invoke stereotype is clear from the outset, because it so closely echoes the name of another fictional character from a story by the popular Israeli writer Etgar Keret. The plot of Keret's "Arkadi Haliwa Takes the Number Five" consists of a gruesome series of non sequiturs and random events that make no claim to plausibility; the narrative aggressively flaunts the lack of psychological complexity in characters representing "disparate ethnic and political factions."[20] Reviled for being part Russian immigrant, part Arab, the protagonist blows up a bus in a surreal and violent satire of contemporary Israeli life. Kashua's "Herzl Disappears at Midnight" begs to be read as response and rejoinder to Keret's narrative. Herzl Haliwa, too, is a patently textual contrivance, and the story indicates quandaries of an individual who, like Keret's protagonist, crosses ethnic lines, but Kashua presents a more humorous, sympathetic, and less violent character. His story is an attempt to defuse stereotype, unsettle rigid boundaries of identity in a deeply divided society, and yet, ultimately, acknowledge an ongoing appeal that stereotypical thinking exerts.

After the opening mention of the name, what is remarkable about Kashua's narrative is precisely the lack of explanatory exposition. The implications of the name "Herzl Haliwa" are not immediately clear. On the contrary, the story offers no explicit summary of the protagonist's situation but, instead, obfuscates reference to place and temporal setting. What the narrative emphasizes is the disorientation of the character as he awakes, startled, unaware of where he is and finding a stranger in bed with him. "Herzl Haliwa let out a cry and jerked his head from the pillow. He recovered very quickly, after all this wasn't the first time, and he stayed silent." This passage underscores a suppression of self, as Herzl stifles his voice and the sound of his movements. The word translated as "stayed silent," *ne'elam*, is a homophone of the word *ne'elam*, "disappeared," which has just appeared in the title. This character is trying to quiet himself and his pounding heart as he hastens to disappear, rushing to get away without waking "Anna von what's-her-name" beside him.

Subsequently, his breathless effort to escape is captured in a string of verbs, all in present tense: for example, he "puts on" his shirt, "picks up" his shoes, "walks on tiptoe," "pulls" slowly on the handle, "looks" one last time at the woman, "leaves" the room, and "walks" quickly through the streets, afraid. In a story that consists of only some four thousand words, one-third of the text is devoted to this account of running away. The style is marked by repetition (the word *maher*, "fast," appears three times), and a run-on sentence intensifies the focus on Herzl's anxiety ("He's almost running, some of the stores are open, he flies by them, doesn't turn his gaze to them"). This technique of characterization, built primarily on a report of actions, focuses the reader's attention on the subjective experience of the protagonist, with a particular emphasis on his uncertainties: the text sums that up clearly, stating, "He has no idea where to go." The reader does not know why Herzl perceives the surroundings to be so threatening. Perhaps he is struggling with guilt about a one-night stand, or panic at having ended up somewhere dangerous, or perhaps he suffers from a psychological disorder, or perhaps some other circumstance obtains altogether. His restlessness and alienation are patent, but his motives are open to various interpretations.

The use of many definite nouns and simple vocabulary suggests a very concrete situation, but the prose is Kafkaesque in its disorienting specificity. Only gradually does the text introduce a few details hinting at the reasons for Herzl's distress. By the end of the second paragraph it is clear that the events take place in the Old City of Jerusalem (thanks to mention of the Jaffa Gate).Though readers receive little information that would ground the action in location and historical period, they learn, a page and a half later, that Herzl is comfortable as soon as he reaches a Jewish neighborhood. Readers can conclude, therefore, that this character is a Jew who feared being alone early in the morning in an Arab area of town. Still, it is notable that the narrative avoids direct definition or classification of Herzl; readers are not told about his appearance, his origins, or his station in life. This technique is very different from standard devices of characterization such as the formal introduction or the thumbnail sketch found in, for example, nineteenth-century realist fiction. The story does not move from the general to the particular or from exposition to scene. It does not typify; rather, it focuses on observable, visible detail that nonetheless leaves the reader without much reference to an external world or set of ideas.

This extended opening is then followed by an abrupt change of emphasis. From a rather lengthy account of actions conveying panicky but ill-defined feelings, the text shifts to a straightforward, even formulaic articulation of Herzl's problem. He has one life by day, another by night. We find this out when the character, searching for a way to justify his nightly absences to his girlfriend, comes up with a pithy, simple explanation that he hopes she will accept.

What will he tell her? Of course, the truth and only the truth, but where exactly to start? Maybe from the end, which is basically that he turns into an Arab after midnight, just like Cinderella, that is, not exactly, but his meaning is clear. It's correct, and Nogah will believe this story immediately, because after all she's completely gullible. And perhaps from the beginning instead.

In other words, he'll start from the fact that his mother, at age forty, hoped for a child and prayed for it "even if he's born half Arab." Apparently, her wish was granted.

So Herzl here invokes fairy tale, referring to a highly familiar folk character to sum up his unstable identity. What is the artistic advantage or effect of this device? First, the reference to a narrow type expeditiously focuses all the earlier anxiety into a clearer picture. The folk figure is a kind of shorthand or abbreviation, something that readers universally will grasp, and so they will get the picture with a punchy jolt of recognition. In addition, the whimsicality of the fairy tale keeps the tone of the story light, while at the same time voicing social protest. The move to typological characterization conveys to the reader that Herzl can be thought of reductively; indeed, in effect he has already been reduced to a stereotype, for the people around him see him not as an individual but as a Jew alone and vulnerable in Arab streets. At the opening, the reader is aware of Herzl as a bundle of emotional energy and unexplained but urgent inner life, perhaps a bit cartoonish in his hyperactivity yet touchingly human in his perplexing distress. Then the anxiety and potential complexity of motive disappear and are replaced by simple summary and definition in terms of others' expectations of him. (Arabs hate him for being a Jew; Jews, it is clear, hate him for the opposite reason—even his own mother has denigrated the idea of being "half Arab.")

In this satirical moment articulating his dilemma, Herzl makes quite a point of noting that his physical being does not change with his nightly metamorphosis. There are no racial differences between a Jew and an Arab, in the sense of distinguishable bodily features that set them apart. And yet everyone can see the difference right away when he undergoes his transformation. Moreover, confirming those differences, Herzl conforms in his behavior to prevalent social stereotypes. When he is an Arab he drinks arrack, and while a Jew he drinks wine. As an Arab he does not know Hebrew. He is a proud Palestinian nationalist and an aggressive activist for his cause. He is hostile to Jews and refuses to go to Jewish neighborhoods so as to avoid the humiliation of being regarded with suspicion. He is dominating and callous toward women. When he is a Jew, in contrast, he does not know Arabic. He is funny, intellectual, vulgar, and timid; he is callous toward women but wracked with guilt over his behavior. While caricature such as this presents absurd simplification, it can be read here not as abandoning verisimilitude so much as aptly expressing the idea that impossible circumstances render the character clownish.[21] The society Herzl lives in suffers a paralyzing simplification, that is, the assumption that Jews and Arabs must live as a dichotomy, and this kind of thinking leaves no room for complex people or for those at the margins of either group. In actuality, Arabs and Jews live in close proximity and make claims to the same space; Kashua suggests that until Jews acknowledge and accept Arabs as occupying both a shared space and a shared history, the prevailing beliefs that leave no room for complexity will always be a source of anxiety, disturbing and disrupting lives even at the most intimate levels.

The use of fairy tale in Kashua's story also suggests that, magically, Herzl's fate could be reversed. Cinderella has a happy ending. Might the same be lurking at the close of "Herzl Disappears at Midnight"? As the conclusion approaches, Kashua makes another shift in characterization, telling the story differently, yet again, and so recasting the reader's grasp of Herzl's identity. Herzl finally takes his girlfriend with him to witness his nightly existence. They visit an Arab bar (where he is ashamed of her being Jewish), but she does not comprehend what is happening. She assumes that the whole episode is a joke, and she calls him "Ahmad," a stereotypical name that she uses in a flip manner to question the seriousness of what she has just seen. They return home, and as he wakes up in the morning, once more a Jew, she disregards the physical evidence she has witnessed. She can only accept his transformation as made up, merely an amusing game.

> "So, what's gonna be with this whole Arab story?" she asked.
> "For my part," he said on the way to the bathroom, "everyone can go to hell."

Nogah's formulation of the situation ("this whole Arab story") posits that Herzl's transformation is a fiction. In this way she raises the possibility that he is creatively telling and acting out his life as a wry and entertaining tale. His response to her, that "everyone can go to hell" (literally, everyone can "burn up"), could be read as confirming that understanding. In other words, now he is writing his own ending; he has acquired a voice of defiance and he has gained agency. He rejects others' views of what is Jewish and what is Arab and relies on his own opinions. Is he thereby forging a redemptive, improvisational self? Can identity become more of an intentionally and individually constructed story, still a difficult and absurd identity, but one over which he has more control because he himself defines it? Perhaps it can. Self-deprecating humor and the development of a self-conscious artistic voice have led to many successes for Kashua, the author, as he writes about painful issues of identity that beset Palestinians living in Israel. It is possible that his fictional character has a similar capacity for bitter, but comic, self-invention.

But the ending of "Herzl Disappears at Midnight" could be read in another manner as well. The way Herzl uses the word *kulam*, his last pronouncement could be translated as "they can all go to hell." However, appearing right after Nogah refers to his "Arab story," the word "they" might refer to Arabs in general. In that case, the last line would therefore mean that the Jew is simply reverting to intolerance and disrespect. This reading would reinstate the dichotomy Jew/Arab and confirm the rigid boundaries between Herzl's contradictory identities. This reading is reinforced by other evidence that indicates Kashua is holding out, at least playfully, for a kind of essentialism. When Herzl states that "basically he turns into an Arab after midnight," the word for "basically" in the original is *be'etsem*—meaning "fundamentally," "essentially," or "at the core"—"basically" in the sense of "at the very base" rather than "more or less." Furthermore, that the last line of the text has Herzl on the way to the bathroom hints that, as a bigoted Jew, he will have his comeuppance; this is because a washroom has been mentioned once before in the story, at a particularly significant juncture. At that moment, Herzl tells his girlfriend that there are no physical differences between his day self and his night self, except that, then again, maybe there are. He remarks, "When I was little I noticed one thing, though; nights when I got up to pee I felt that it had gotten heavier down there, a little bigger than I was used to in those days." The author wryly hints that Arabs really are manlier than Jews. Having appropriated stereotype for sophisticated artistic purposes, having pointed to the limitations of stereotypes and satirized a society for its rigid polarities, Kashua also invokes a stereotype to take a sly jab at Jews. Altogether, this very short text cleverly reaffirms schematic, fixed boundaries of identity, even as it aims to circumvent or get past them. Thus at the very end Herzl Haliwa—as a Jew, as an Arab, as both at once—reverts to preconception and so suggests the tenacious appeal of thinking in stereotypes.

The equivocation at the end of Kashua's story, the undecidable outcome, is put into relief and reinforced by Herzl's earlier, self-conscious statements about storytelling. The character is aware that the structure of a story affects how readers and listeners construe meanings, guiding them toward specific interpretive options. When he muses about whether to tell his story from start to finish or vice versa, he underscores how narratives work, drawing the readers' attention to the importance of endings and beginnings—in general and in the current text in particular. The character explicitly indicates that there is no straightforward way to convey his truth. Thus when he determines to tell his girlfriend the truth, the truth is that he is just like Cinderella, but "not exactly." And he supposes that she will accept his narrative, but perhaps only because she is "gullible." We find an implicit parallel in Kashua's tale, a tale that also expresses a truth that cannot be conveyed unequivocally.

One of the raisons d'être of literature is to attempt to express that which exceeds "familiar norms"—that which could not be said otherwise.[22] Literature as a way of knowing allows for ambivalence and multiple interpretations. Kashua has found a way to say something about boundaries between Jews and Arabs that could not be expressed otherwise with the same richness and ambivalence, irony, humor, and sting. The author's use of stereotype helps him succeed in this task, as one of several modes of (sometimes conflicting) characterization. Furthermore, the prose provides aesthetic pleasure through its combination of approaches. It offers, on the one hand, an economy of style that shuts down complexity and, on the other, a profusion of detail and uncertainties that lead to open-endedness. The reader must take an active role in a game of constructing meaning from the patterns and, in particular, in determining the protagonist's character traits. It is in this sense that, as Roland Barthes famously phrased it, "to read is to struggle to name."[23] In interpreting "Herzl Disappears at Midnight," readers must indeed decide how to assess the dual, symbolic name of the protagonist, Herzl Haliwa, and how to understand the facetious name "Ahmad" that Nogah attributes to him. It is up to readers to assign these names coherence, or to conclude that they signal irreconcilable impasse, or to imagine some kind of resolution that depends on understanding the author's play with identity as humorous performance. Whatever conclusion the reader reaches, the idealized values implied in the protagonist's name at the beginning of the story undergo complication as the story unfolds. Theodor Herzl's novel *Altneuland* (1902) gave rise to the famous slogan about the realization of the Zionist dream: "If you will it, it is not a fairy tale." Kashua's tragicomic spoof on the Cinderella fairy tale presents a highly ironic view of what actually happened when the dream was realized.

Conclusions

Not surprisingly, Kashua's writings, especially his television scripts that reach a mass audience, have met with controversial reception. Jewish journalists welcomed his sitcom *Arab Work* (2007) with great enthusiasm; Arab focus groups decried as misrepresentations of reality the stereotypes that underpin Kashua's humor, and voices in the Arab press assailed him for imagining Palestinian characters who willingly assimilate, integrating themselves into Jewish culture in Israel.[24]

Writing in Hebrew, imagining the inner world of a Jew, and echoing Keret, Kashua situates his story "Herzl Disappears at Midnight" forthrightly in the mainstream of Israeli fiction. In the process, he also transforms Appelfeld into a kind of precursor. Whether there is any direct influence there or not, we can never read Appelfeld exactly the same way again after reading Kashua. Both authors insert themselves into a larger span of Jewish literary tradition, as they recall Franz Kafka's "Metamorphosis"—a narrative that expresses the feelings of a Jewish author alienated by a world that views him with contempt.

Nonetheless, a fundamental and integral aspect of Kashua's art is that it puts a new twist on Hebrew fiction, transforming it through an Arab voice. At a time in Israel when more and more Arab Palestinians are becoming educated in Hebrew, yet growing intensely alienated politically, Kashua's "Herzl Disappears at Midnight" tells a story of Jewish identity from the inside and the outside at the same time.[25] As a result, this story presents its own conundrums and convolutions: the protagonist, like Appelfeld's, is a Jew on the run, but only in part from his enemies; Herzl runs also from himself and cannot quite seem to find a way to coexist with the Arab reality that is also part of him. Appelfeld, too, put a new twist on Hebrew literature when his fiction helped change broadly held attitudes toward the Holocaust. Thanks to his writing, European Jewish characters who had had a minor, even denigrated, role in Israeli literature for several decades met with new empathy and identification on the part of Hebrew readers.

Starting from the position of cultural outsiders in Israeli society, both Appelfeld and Kashua have contributed to major transformations in Hebrew fiction, reflecting and shaping a multicultural Israel. A cacophony of literary voices increasingly has questioned the boundaries that have defined what an Israeli is. Not only have these writers defied and dismantled the once ideal image of the sabra, the new Jew, that prevailed in early Zionist thinking, they have created a pluralistic vision that encompasses the perspectives of Mizrahi and Sephardi Jews as well as Ashkenazi Jews, religious as well as secular individuals, women as well as men, European-born Holocaust survivors as well as sabras, and Arabs as well as Jews.

Notes

1. The story "Transformation" appeared in the collection *Bekomat hakark'a* [On the Ground Floor], by Aharon Appelfeld (Tel Aviv: Daga, 1968), 55–62. Further citations to this story are given in the text. All of the translations are my own.

2. Sayed Kashua, "Herzl ne'elam beḥatsot," *Ha'arets*, October 3, 2005, http://www.haaretz.co.il (accessed December 8, 2007). All translations are my own. An English version from 2006 by Vivian Eden appeared under the title "Cinderella" in *Words without Borders: The Online Magazine for International Literature* http://www.wordswithoutborders.org/article.php?lab=Cinderella

(accessed February 5, 2010). However, I use my own translations in this essay in order to capture more of the nuances I think are crucial to interpretation of the story.

3. Mireille Roelle, quoted in Carrie Tirado Bramen, "Speaking in Typeface: Characterizing Stereotypes in Gayl Jones' *Mosquito*," *Modern Fiction Studies* 49, no. 1 (2003): 133.

4. For a helpful summary of how the field of literary study has shifted toward these questions, see Ruth Amossy and Anne Herschberg Pierrot, *Stéréotypes et clichés: Langue, discourse, société* [Stereotypes and Clichés: Language, Speech, Society] (Paris: Nathan, 1997); Joep Leerssen, "The Rhetoric of National Character: A Programmatic Survey," *Poetics Today* 21, no. 2 (2000): 267–92; Leerssen, "Types, Tropes, and the Poetics of Conventionality," *Poetics Today* 22, no. 3 (2001): 691–96; and Leerssen, "The Downward Pull of Cultural Essentialism," in *Image into Identity: Constructing and Assigning Identity in a Culture of Modernity*, ed. Michael Wintle (Amsterdam: Rodopi, 2006), 31–52. On the study of stereotype from the field of social psychology, see Marco Cinnirella, "Ethnic and National Stereotypes: A Social Identity Perspective," in *Beyond Pug's Tour: National and Ethnic Stereotyping in Theory and Literary Practice*, ed. C. C. Barfoot (Amsterdam: Rodopi, 1997), 37–52. I have also found helpful a discussion of stereotype and self-writing in Juan Velasco, "Automitografías: The Border Paradigm and Chicana/o Autobiography," *Biography* 27, no. 2 (2004): 13–38.

5. See, e.g., Bryan Cheyette, *Constructions of "the Jew" in English Literature and Society: Racial Representations, 1875–1945* (Cambridge: Cambridge University Press, 1993); and Cheyette, ed., *Between "Race" and Culture: Representations of "the Jew" in English and American Literature* (Stanford, Calif.: Stanford University Press, 1996). Sander L. Gilman has written many studies on stereotypes of Jews and the history of those images. See, e.g., Gilman, *The Jew's Body* (New York: Routledge, 1991); and Gilman, *Smart Jews: The Construction of the Image of Jewish Superior Intelligence* (Lincoln: University of Nebraska Press, 1996).

6. Leerssen, "Rhetoric of National Character."

7. Benjamin Harshav, *Explorations in Poetics* (Stanford, Calif.: Stanford University Press, 2007), 45.

8. For an overview of Appelfeld's life and writing, see, e.g., Yigal Schwartz, *Aharon Appelfeld: From Individual Lament to Tribal Eternity* (Waltham, Mass.: Brandeis University Press, 2001); and Naomi B. Sokoloff, "Aharon Appelfeld," in *The Dictionary of Literary Biography*, vol. 299, *Holocaust Novelists*, ed. Efraim Sicher (Detroit: Gale Research, 2004).

9. My thanks to Or Rogovin for discussing this translation with me.

10. For an illuminating discussion of public discourse on the topic of "Jewish" gestures, see Susan A. Glenn, "'Funny, You Don't Look Jewish': Visual Stereotypes and the Making of Modern Jewish Identity," in this volume.

11. Aharon Appelfeld, *Beyond Despair*, trans. Jeffrey M. Green (New York: Fromm International, 1994), 74–76.

12. Aharon Appelfeld, *Tzili: The Story of a Life*, trans. Dalya Bilu (New York: Dutton, 1983), 77, 51, 184.

13. Aharon Appelfeld, "Hashivah," in *Bekomat hakark'a*, 80, 75 (my translation).

14. Appelfeld, *Beyond Despair*, 66.

15. See, e.g., Gershon Shaked, "Appelfeld and His Times: Transformations of Ahashveros, the Eternal Wandering Jew," *Hebrew Studies* 36 (1995): 87–100; and Alan Mintz, *Ḥurban: Responses to Catastrophe in Hebrew Literature* (New York: Columbia University Press, 1984).

16. Mintz, *Ḥurban*, 220–23.

17. Aharon Appelfeld, *'Od hayom gadol* (Jerusalem: Keter and Ben Zvi, 2001), 116 (my translation). The passage is found in a different form in Appelfeld, *A Table for One: Under the Light of Jerusalem*, trans. Aloma Halter (New Milford, Conn.: Toby Press, 2006), 100. For discussion of Appelfeld's life and writing and his entrance into Hebrew literary tradition, see Naomi B. Sokoloff, "Life/Writing: Appelfeld's Autobiographical Work and the Modern Jewish Canon," in *Arguing the Modern Jewish Canon: Essays on Literature and Culture in Honor of Ruth R. Wisse*, ed. Justin Cammy, Dara Horn, Alyssa Quint, and Rachael Rubinstein (Cambridge, Mass.: Center for Jewish Studies, Harvard University, 2008), 371–85.

18. This take on Appelfeld differs significantly from interpretations of his work by critics who emphasize his imagery of Jews and non-Jews as polar opposites. See, e.g., Gershon Shaked, *Sifrut az, kan, ve'akshav* [Literature Then, Here, and Now] (Tel Aviv: Zmora-Bitan, 1993), 143–51.

19. My thanks to Amal Eqeiq for her input on the meaning of this name.

20. Yaron Peleg, *Israeli Culture between the Two Intifadas: A Brief Romance* (Austin: University of Texas Press, 2008), 80. Keret's story appeared in the collection Etgar Keret, *Tsinorot* [Pipelines] (Tel Aviv: Am Oved, 1992).

21. Robert Alter notes that stereotypes may be "approximations rather than misrepresentations" of reality. He has in mind Dickens's comic grotesque figures that are walking embodiments of a metaphor and not "an abandonment of verisimilitude but bold stylizations that catch the terrible, absurd simplicity with which some people can reduce their lives." Robert Alter, *The Pleasures of Reading in an Ideological Age* (New York: Simon and Schuster, 1989), 57, 64.

22. Alter, *Pleasures of Reading*, 183–84.

23. Roland Barthes, *S/Z*, trans. Richard Miller (New York: Hill and Wang, 1974), 92, quoted in and discussed by Shlomith Rimmon-Kenan, *Narrative Fiction: Contemporary Poetics* (London: Methuen, 1983), 36.

24. See, e.g., Ruta Kupper, "Kol yisrael 'aravim zeh lezeh" [All Israelis Are Responsible for One Another], *Ha'aretz*, November 13, 2007.

25. Arabs now make up the majority of students in many Hebrew language and literature classes in Israeli universities.

4

"Funny, You Don't Look Jewish"

Visual Stereotypes and the Making of Modern Jewish Identity

SUSAN A. GLENN

"If you want to compliment a Jew . . . tell him that he does not look like one. What a depth of degradation for a people to have reached," observed the Anglo-Jewish writer Israel Zangwill in 1904.[1] Fifty years later, a popular joke among American Jews reveals the persistent pre-occupation with the question of Jewish looks. In the joke, an older woman approaches a "dignified" looking gentleman on the subway and proceeds to unmask what she suspects are his ethnic origins. "Pardon me for asking," she inquires, "but are you Jewish?" He coldly replies, "No," he is not Jewish. A few minutes later she asks again. "Are you sure you're not Jewish?" And he repeats that he is definitely sure. But the woman is not convinced, and she approaches him a third time. "Are you *absolutely* sure you're not Jewish?" Finally, he breaks down and confesses, "All right, all right, I am Jewish." "That's funny," remarks the woman. "You don't look Jewish."[2]

When sociologists Bernard Rosenberg and Gilbert Shapiro discussed this joke in their 1958 article on ethnic "marginality" and Jewish humor, they used it as an example of the "psychological ambiguity" that was characteristic of modern Jewish self-consciousness. To the sociologists, the joke suggests that although Jews are "quite literally everywhere," they are often "in disguise" and can be detected "only if one knows the proper signs."[3] But what were "the proper signs," and why did some Jews feel that it was imperative to know them? One answer of course was virulent antisemitism. Historian Sander L. Gilman suggests that turn-of-the-century European Jews were so fully "fixated" on the idea of their physical visibility that even after they began to "pass" in gentile society, they remained rightly skeptical about their capacity for "invisibility." Since Jews in Europe were perceived to be a distinctive and inferior "race," Gilman argues, neither genteel manners nor the alterations of plastic surgery that became available to Jews at the turn of the century could erase the taint of inferiority. The paradoxical effect was that each attempt at Jewish invisibility only created a new "sign of difference."[4] Nevertheless, as I argue, risk and fear are not the only reasons that Jews have been historically fixated on the issue of bodily difference. Physical self-classification has also played an important part in the assertion of Jewish collective identity. Jews have historically defined the question of *who* is a Jew on the basis of "blood logic." The child of a Jewish mother was and still is "counted" as a Jew, yet the notion of physical difference has also played a part in how Jews have defined "*what* is to be counted as Jewish."[5] For American Jews, and perhaps for Jews throughout the Diaspora, the idea of "Jewish looks" has been one of many sources of collective self-definition. Over the course of the twentieth century, notions of Jewish physical difference constituted a major source of anxiety for Jews who wished to normalize their status as Americans *and also* a central element of modern American Jewish ethnicity. The idea that Jews know what a Jew looks like became more and not less important as Jews gained entry into mainstream American society. Concepts of physical difference—in the case of Jews' facial features and "bodily practices" such as gesture— have not only shaped the history of racial and ethnic persecution, but have also helped Jews define what is "Jewish" and what is not.[6]

To study Jewish engagements with the question of Jewish physical differences is also to reconsider the question of Jews and racial identity in the United States. Historians and anthropologists have documented the process by which Jews—once considered racial others—came to be accepted as "Caucasian" and took their place on the white side of the American color line. But far less attention has been paid to the articulation of Jewish racial self-description, which has less to do with skin color than with the idea of difference itself—seen and unseen. As historian Eric Goldstein has shown, many Jews in the United States were not prepared to accept the "price" of whiteness if it meant the erosion of Jewish group solidarity. So they adopted the vague but emotionally powerful language of "race" to set themselves off from others who were also classified as "Caucasians."[7] The Jewish discourses on "race" and "looks," while conceptually related, were not one and the same. While few, if any, twentieth-century American Jewish commentators openly challenged the "blood logic" by which Jews historically defined group membership, the question of whether all or most Jews looked "Jewish" was much harder to resolve. And the very confusion and consternation that this effort produced were themselves important aspects of the way Jews publicly shaped a sense of Jewish group identity.

In this essay, I explore the continuous and shifting conversation about Jewish looks in the United States as it moved among formal social scientific theorizing, popular culture, and kitchen-table gossip. This conversation about looks, this very public effort to puzzle through the issue, is, I argue, one of the formative discourses of American Jewish identity. I am concerned with two related historical patterns and the paradox they produced. The first is the effort of Jews to dispel stereotypes about Jewish looks—not only physiognomy (facial features) but also the claim that "Jewish" postures and gestures were fixed at the level of genetics. The second is the way that Jewish understandings about the quality of looking Jewish and the gestural patterns associated with Jews came to be understood as an aspect of ethnic "authenticity" among Jews.

What interests me is the unresolved tension in secular Jewish public discourse—a tension produced by attempts to erase and the compulsion to acknowledge Jewish physical difference. The tension appears in several locations: folk discourse, popular media, and social science. In what follows, I examine three key periods of public discourse on the idea of Jewish looks. In the first period, from the 1910s through the end of World War II, Jews in the field of anthropology—most notably Franz Boas and his students—attempted to replace biological and moral concepts of Jewish physical difference with cultural and environmental explanations. They argued that there was no uniform Jewish physical "type" since Jews varied from locale to locale as a result of environmental influences. In the second period, roughly from the end of the 1940s through the 1960s, when psychological experts—many of whom were Jews—took over the field of anti-race science, Jewish and non-Jewish psychologists would make even bolder claims, insisting not only that Jews were virtually indistinguishable from non-Jews but that anyone who believed otherwise was probably racist at best and, at worst, a proto-fascist. Fittingly, this was also a time when Jews were engaging in ever more deliberate attempts to conceal or minimize externally visible signs of ethnic difference, as both name changing and plastic surgery became common practices. During this same period, psychologists also began to consider the possibility that for Jews, the idea of "Jewish looks" had positive social value because it served as a physical common denominator that symbolized their distinctive group identity. In the third period, roughly from the 1970s to the present, when Jews found greater social acceptance and when groups promoting racial and ethnic pride began to dominate American cultural politics, the idea of "Jewish looks" reemerged in Jewish public discourse as a key signifier of ethnic authenticity. With a few exceptions, the tensions and transitions in social scientific and popular discourse remain largely unanalyzed by scholars; this essay is an occasion to revisit those issues.

Jewish Looks as an Anthropological Paradox

In the late nineteenth century Jewish anthropologists and physicians challenged antisemitic ideology about the diseased body and mind of the Jew. Yet as historian Mitchell B. Hart has shown, rather than abandon the idea of Jewish physical difference, the Jewish nationalists among them emphasized the positive value of an identifiable Jewish face as a symbol of ethnic unity and racial purity.[8] Contrary to what the enemies of the Jews suggested, the appearance of "Jewish" features even in the children of mixed marriages signified "the superior tenacity" of the Jewish "racial type."[9]

In the first two decades of the twentieth century, however, Jewish social scientists increasingly insisted on the changeability of Jewish features. Cosmopolitan Jewish scientists, most famously, Franz Boas, a Columbia University anthropologist, and pioneering environmentalist Maurice Fishberg promoted Jewish assimilation by stressing the physical variety and plasticity of Jews. Both argued that the more Jews mixed in culturally, socially, and biologically with the surrounding non-Jewish population, the less "Jewish" they looked. To refute the most popular antisemitic stereotype—the idea of the "hooked" Jewish nose, which externalized the supposedly evil nature of the Jewish character—Fishberg conducted his own visual ethnographies among Jews living in New York City, Western Europe, and North Africa. The most prevalent type of nose among Jews is not hooked but "straight, or Greek," according to Fishberg, and, more important, he claimed that "it is not the body which marks the Jew; it is his soul."[10] Centuries of confinement in the ghetto, social ostracism, and persecution helped produce a characteristic psychic quality that manifests in the Jew's "melancholy, thoughtful, piercing eyes."[11] The cure, argued Fishberg, was assimilation, since "the peculiar Jewish expression disappears in Jews who have been out of the Ghetto for a few generations."[12] In simultaneously verifying the idea that Jews looked Jewish and challenging the notion that Jewish looks were immutable, Fishberg produced a paradox that would continue to haunt liberal anthropology for the next forty years.

Although Boas, an immigrant from Germany, eschewed psychological explanations for differences among groups and races, he was equally committed to proving what he called the "instability of human types."[13] Boas was a physical anthropologist who cultivated a stance of cosmopolitanism and scientific detachment and insisted on being known as a German rather than a Jew, but he also worked hard to combat the biological determinism that undergirded anti-semitism, arguing that Jewish physical difference was a product of culture and environment, not genetic destiny. In 1912, in the context of growing calls for immigration restriction by eugenicists and others who believed that Jews could not assimilate, Boas published a study designed to prove that the physical traits associated with various groups and races were not fixed at the level of biology but responded to new environmental conditions.[14]

The triumph of eugenic thinking and the ominous implications of Nazi racial ideology in the late 1920s and early 1930s deeply disturbed Boas, and he used "every resource he could muster" to combat racialist thought.[15] Yet that project, especially as it pertained to the issue of Jewish looks, was fraught with paradox. Like Boas, most of his Jewish graduate students were secular modernists who wrote about other "others" (such as Native Americans and Africans).[16] However, some of these scholars also took an interest in the issue of Jewish race and the question of Jewish looks. In doing so, they both encountered and produced contradictions. One such scholar was Alexander Goldenweiser, a Russian Jewish immigrant, who begins his 1927 article "The Jewish Face" with the observation that one thing Jews and antisemites had in common was their certainty that "you can always tell a Jew." Although his purpose was to argue that Jewish looks and mannerisms "are not in-born but acquired, not biological but cultural," he clings to the notion that the Jew possesses a distinctive "physiognomy" characterized by his "hunched nose, the mobility of his face, his hair . . . the fact that he uses his hands . . . as a major means of conversation."[17] Two decades later, when social scientific attacks on biological determinism and race science had reached their peak in the aftermath of the Holocaust, another former Boas student, the famous physical anthropologist M. F. Ashley Montagu, used almost identical language. In the 1946 volume of *The Jewish People: Past and Present*, Montagu insists that it is impossible to describe a universal "Jewish type." But then he concedes that "there undoubtedly exists a certain quality of looking Jewish," due to "certain culturally acquired habits of expression: facial, vocal, muscular, and mental," traits that may gradually disappear over generations in individuals who abandon Jewish culture.[18]

The work of the Jewish Boasians was clearly a refutation of the Nazis and other racist ideologues, who held that both looks and gestures were fixed at the level of the genes. Rabid nationalists and xenophobes on both sides of the Atlantic posited that Jewish behavior was governed entirely by genetics; hence Jews were incapable of becoming anything other than "Jews" and thus posed a threat to the cohesiveness of national culture. Yet even those Jewish social scientists who attempted to repudiate genetic explanations for the gestural repertoire of Eastern European Jews vividly described the ability to pick out Jews on the basis of their peculiar and easily identified bodily movements. The most famous was Boas's student, the Argentine-born Jewish anthropologist David Efron. In the mid-1930s Efron began a study that he and Boas hoped would provide the empirical evidence to refute the Nazi scientists who insisted that the peculiar gestural habits of the Jews were an inherited and immutable aspect of their "psycho-racial traits." Working in partnership with New York illustrator and muralist Stuyvesant Van Veen, Efron analyzed sketches and moving pictures of the body language of some twenty-eight hundred Eastern

The distinctive physical gestures of "ghetto" Jews in New York were illustrated by Stuyvesant Van Veen for David Efron's study, *Gesture and Environment* (New York: King's Crown Press, 1941). These are examples of what Efron described as the "gestural promiscuity" of Eastern European Jews, who touched, grabbed, and poked their conversational partners.

European Jewish and southern Italian subjects. His intention was to show that assimilated Jews and Italians resembled one another to a far greater extent than they resembled the members of their "traditional" group.[19]

Published in 1941 under the title *Gesture and Environment*, Efron's book documented the differing gestural and postural repertoires of "traditional," "semi-assimilated," and "assimilated" individuals.[20] This project, which began as an attempt to refute the Nazi racialist claims, eventually took on a life of its own. In studying gesture from a cultural rather than a biological standpoint, Efron ended up amplifying rather than downplaying the issue of whether Jews looked Jewish. The pages of Efron's book are filled with passages describing the characteristic postural "slump" and "turtle-like" head movements of the typical ghetto Jew.[21] He provides elaborate detail on the "comic character" and "frequent puppetlike" movements of gesticulating ghetto Jews and attributes these to the "almost spasmodic" changes in speed within a single "gesture-pattern."[22] And he writes at length of the "gestural promiscuity" of Eastern European Jewish men who could not converse without touching, grabbing, and poking their conversational partners.[23] Sometimes this took the form of "gestural fencing," whereby two Jewish men "clamped" on to each other's hands or coat lapels and fought out the battle "by means of head motions only."[24] The most extreme display involved a conversation in which "the two interlocutors were enthusiastically talking and gesturing at the same time" and one of the speakers "not only grasped the arm of his impatient opponent, but *actually gestured with it!*"[25]

Jews don't look Jewish, but yes they do. The contradictions in the self-representations of Jews in anthropology in part reflected the ambivalent position of second-generation American Jews who were steeped in but struggling to distance themselves from traditional Jewish life. Immigrants and children of immigrants, they had learned to distinguish and perhaps to appreciate the sights and sounds of Jewish difference and to decipher the faces and gestures that separated the unassimilated Jewish "them" from the assimilated, cosmopolitan "us."[26] More emphatic in rejecting notions of Jewish physical and gestural difference was anthropologist Melville J. Herskovits. In his 1949 essay "Who Are the Jews?" he emphasized both the physical heterogeneity and the diverse historical experiences of Jews, concluding that although "stereotypes die hard," there were no typical "Jewish" characteristics.[27]

This conclusion emerged in part out of experiments Herskovits and Boas had conducted a decade earlier, experiments designed to demonstrate that "Jewish" looks were largely in the eye of the beholder. In the mid-1930s, against the backdrop of the intensifying Nazi threat, Boas had designed a bold classroom experiment "intended," in his words, "to show how far it is possible, for an *inexperienced* observer, to determine the race of an individual from a general impression."[28] During the first week of class, each student, identified only by a number, stood before his fellow students, who wrote down "what they thought his origin to be, their degree of certainty in drawing this judgment, and why they classified him as they did." In one of Boas's experiments 40 percent of students tested at a New York college mistook Italians for Jews, and equal numbers thought Jews were Italians.[29] Herskovits duplicated this experiment at Northwestern University, where the majority of the student body came from Northern European backgrounds and had little familiarity with people of "Mediterranean stock." There the non-Jewish students mistook dark-haired gentiles for Jews and lumped the blond Jews in with the Northern European groups.[30] Moreover, their "Midwestern judgment," led these students to classify one another simply as "American."[31]

Although the social scientists used their authority as scholars to challenge racist stereotypes of Jews as biologically immutable and inferior, Jewish social scientific writings on Jewish looks were never fully consistent with their public agendas to deracinate and thus to "normalize" the Jewish image. The same could be said of literary and cinematic texts of the wartime and postwar eras that attempted, not always successfully, to challenge the idea that Jews bore a distinctive physical cast. Arthur Miller's 1945 novel *Focus* showed how easily a gentile could be mistaken for a Jew. Laura Z. Hobson's best-selling 1946 novel, *Gentleman's Agreement*, which was made into an Academy Award–winning film the following year, explored the phenomenon of passing and attempted to invalidate the idea of "Jewish" looks. The plot of Hobson's novel and the film revolves around a handsome gentile journalist called Phil Green who decides to pass as a Jew in order to write about how Jews experience antisemitism. Because he is new in town and nobody knows his actual background, Phil reasons that all he has to do to convey that he is "Jewish" is to just "say" that he his. In a critical scene, Phil calculates his chances of passing as a Jew by measuring his own physical characteristics against the stereotypes associated with Jewish looks. Phil was tall and lanky, his "nose was straight," and therefore he "didn't look Jewish," but neither did "a hell of a lot of guys who were Jewish," including his best friend, Dave. Phil "had no accent or mannerisms that were Jewish," and therefore he did not "sound Jewish," but "neither did a lot of Jews." Further scrutinizing his own features, Phil excitedly concludes that, with his "dark eyes, dark hair," and "a kind of sensitive look," pretending to "be Jewish" for six weeks ought to be "a cinch."[32]

The intended message here is that gentiles can pass themselves off as Jews because not all Jews look "Jewish." However, it does not hurt his chances that Phil has dark features and brooding looks (as opposed to blond hair and blue eyes). Conversely, Hobson's novel suggested that Jews with certain stereotypically gentile features and a willingness to change their Jewish-sounding names could easily pass as Wasps (white Anglo-Saxon Protestants). Phil's secretary at a New York publishing house successfully passes as gentile because she is blond, and "Scandinavian" looking, and because she has changed her name from Walovsky to Wales.[33] Waspish good looks and a name change also enable journalist Rick Dohen (formerly Richard Cohen) to pass as a gentile, allowing him to join "the best clubs, *The Social Register*, the whole routine."[34] Here Hobson comments negatively on what had become a widespread practice of attempting to conceal ethnoreligious origins behind a more neutral sounding moniker. Just a few years after the publication of Hobson's book, one researcher, who analyzed the patterns of name changing in the 1940s and 1950s, estimated that of the approximately fifty thousand people who applied to state courts to change their names, around 80 percent were Jews, more than half of whom were trying to adopt more "gentile"-sounding names.[35]

To blend in, Jewish men changed their names; Jewish women changed their noses. As Gilman observed, it was no accident that the most significant increase in nasal plastic surgery began in the 1940s, a time when it became increasingly dangerous to be seen as a Jew.[36] In the 1940s and 1950s, more than half of those seeking rhinoplasties in the United States were Jews, most of them female adolescents hoping to attain a more "normal" American appearance without abandoning their Jewish identity. Non-Jewish women also had rhinoplasties to avoid being categorized as Jewish. And the trend continued over the next several decades.[37] By changing "the contour of their noses," observed anthropologist Frances M. Cooke Macgregor in a 1953 study of motivations for plastic surgery, they hoped to escape the stigma of minority group membership and to become "indistinguishable from other [white] Americans."[38]

In *Gentleman's Agreement*, Hobson insisted that with or without name changes and plastic surgery, most Jews could not be easily distinguished from gentiles. However, like the writings of liberal anthropologists, Hobson's novel both advocated and undercut its own liberal universalism. It said, in effect, that there is no universal Jewish type. It maintained that because Jews and gentiles can and do share many of the same physical traits, they can physically pass, undetected, into each other's social milieu. At the same time, it verified that there was indeed some "quality of looking Jewish." For example, in an unguarded moment in the novel (but not in the film), Phil begins to study Dave's face, asking himself, "Does Dave *look* Jewish?" Phil confesses, "Yes, he supposed he did, now that he asked it." He could find nothing obviously Jewish about Dave, "no hint of hook or curve" in Dave's "short," even "stubby," nose. "Yet if you thought, you'd know this man was Jewish. It was there somewhere," perhaps, he speculated, "in the indented arcs of the nostrils," the "turn of the lips," or "the quiet eyes." No matter, Phil abruptly reminds himself: "It was such a damn strong good face."[39]

However, not every Jewish face in the novel qualified as "damn strong good." The phrasing itself suggests as much. The figure of Professor Joe Lieberman, a world-famous physicist, possesses "the face of a Jew in a Nazi cartoon, the beaked nose, the blue jowls, and the curling black hair."[40] Yet it is this "Jewish"-looking Jew who adamantly adopts the stance of scientific universalism. "I have no religion, so I am not Jewish by religion," he announces to Phil. As a scientist, he knows that "there's no such thing as a distinct Jewish race" and "not even such a thing, anthropologically, as the Jewish type." Joking about his new "crusade" to prove the point, the professor tells Phil, "I will go forth and state flatly, 'I am not a Jew.'" "With this face," he concedes, "that becomes not an evasion but a new principle. A scientific principle."[41] As cultural historian Matthew Frye Jacobson points out, the "new principle" proposed by Professor Lieberman is not the same as the new principle proposed by the author of *Gentleman's Agreement*. In Hobson's story as in Miller's novel *Focus*, characters can "look Jewish" without being Jewish and "be Jewish" without looking Jewish. Yet both arguments are premised on the idea that "there *is* in fact such a thing as 'looking Jewish,'" an idea that Hobson validates in Professor Lieberman's unmistakably "Jewish" face.[42]

Seeing Jews: "Bigotry" or Cultural "Survival"?

In the decade after World War II popular understandings about Jewish racial difference persisted in spite of or, as one Jewish sociologist suggested, perhaps even because of the anti-race scientists' "incessant concentration" on the question of group differences. That was the view of Melvin J. Tumin, who wrote in a 1949 essay that while science "emphatically denies the popular notion of race," the public was still more inclined to trust the "clear-cut evidence" of their own "senses," which told them that "it is often possible to tell a Jew from a Gentile, just by looking at him."[43]

Such attitudes prevailed despite changes in the bodies, gestures, and outward appearance of Jews in the United States that would differentiate them from their European ancestors. Some of this was the result of changes in diet, dress, and cultural conditioning. Some of it was accomplished through plastic surgery. If Jews looked more "American" in 1949 and 1950 than they had in earlier decades, what then did it mean for American society, and for Jews, that many people continued to believe that one could "sense" who was a Jew, on the basis of looks? Was this necessarily a negative or a dangerous sensibility? Could it have some practical or valid purpose? These were questions that engaged the social psychologists who took over the field of anti-race science in the late 1940s and early 1950s. Their debates are especially fascinating not only because they reveal the shifting paradigms within the sciences about the social meanings of physical difference, but also because popular Jewish attitudes about what makes Jews "Jewish" were also in turmoil. Ironically, even as the Boasians proved to be correct in their predictions that Jews would eventually become less easy to identify on the basis of looks, the postwar psychologists began to analyze why "Jewish" looks mattered both to Jews and to non-Jews. Rather than dismiss the notion that Jews looked Jewish, they began to take seriously the emotional underpinnings of racial and ethnic self-perception.

Initially, psychologists were determined to prove that seeing Jews was a figment of the bigot's imagination. Postwar psychological experts such as Gordon W. Allport designed "racial awareness" experiments that would demonstrate once and for all that physical differences between Jews and non-Jews were so minor and undetectable that the average well-adjusted individual would fail to detect them. Their experiments are revealing, not for what they prove or disprove about the psychological dispositions of the participants who saw or failed to see Jewish physical difference, but, rather, because they perpetuated both the question and the confusion about Jewish looks.

In keeping with postwar challenges to fascist and authoritarian ideological systems, psychologists incorporated new theoretical work on the so-called authoritarian personality into their examinations of the relationship between extreme bigotry and racial perception. Unlike the "tolerant" and "unprejudiced" personality, psychologist Else Frenkel-Brunswik suggested, the "totalitarian personality" displayed "overly rigid" defense mechanisms—which manifested in a tendency to see the world in terms of absolute categories of good and evil and the need to make "conformity" an "all or nothing affair."[44] Beginning in the late 1940s psychologists adopted Theodor W. Adorno's "F[ascist]-scale" (a diagnostic instrument used to measure what Adorno called "the authoritarian syndrome") to experiments testing the "racial awareness" of prejudiced and unprejudiced individuals. In 1946, for example, Allport and Bernard M. Kramer tested the ability of Harvard and Radcliffe students to identify Jewish faces in photographs. They found that students who scored high on the F-scale because of their strong prejudices against Jews, blacks, and Catholics also tended to judge more faces as "Jewish" than did less prejudiced students. They also found that the students with the highest degree of antisemitic prejudice also tended to be the most accurate in their selection of Jewish faces. The authors hypothesized that "the bigot apparently learns to observe and interpret both facial features and expressive behavior so that he can more swiftly spot his 'enemy.'"[45] Although the test was designed to demonstrate that Jewish looks were a cultural myth, it actually verified the notion of Jewish physical difference. While the relatively unprejudiced individuals had failed to learn or detect the outward signs of Jewish difference, the bigots had become connoisseurs.[46]

The behavior of Jews who participated as "judges" in these racial awareness experiments created the greatest interpretive challenge for psychologists trying to gauge the relationship between perception and racial bigotry. In some experiments, Jewish judges proved to be what one study called "unexpectedly incompetent" in identifying Jewish faces; however, in others they demonstrated extreme tendency to see Jewish faces. A good deal of hand-wringing ensued about the significance of these contradictory findings. Psychologist Hans H. Toch and his colleagues speculated that the allegedly "incompetent" Jews had strong egalitarian feelings and may have considered it an "affront" to be asked to distinguish "physiognomic differences" among Jews and non-Jews.[47] Others suggested that assimilation had eroded their ability to detect their coreligionists by sight. One psychologist noted that when asked to judge photographs, young American-born Jews "hesitated at length, often made mistakes, and not infrequently insisted that the very division between Jewish and non-Jewish faces was a figment of the imagination."[48]

Equally controversial, but for different reasons, was the behavior of Jews who proved especially competent in picking out Jewish faces. For example, in 1957, in an experiment using photographs, social psychologists Alvin Scodel and Harvey Austrin found that Jews taking the test judged more faces to be "Jewish" than all of the non-Jewish judges did.[49] The authors concluded that all Jews (and not just those who scored high on the F-scale) had picked out more Jewish faces because they had accepted the majority group's negative stereotypes of Jewish facial traits. As a consequence, Jews who may have felt anxious about being seen as Jewish had developed a "disposition" toward visual hypervigilance because they felt their own "security" as Americans would be "enhanced by this type of projective assimilation."[50]

Other psychologists came to the opposite conclusion about Jewish accuracy. They argued that Jews had learned to tell the difference between the faces of Jews and non-Jews not only because of their greater level of social experience with Jews, but also because of the ethnic "survival value" of knowing how to make such distinctions. This was a position argued by Toch and endorsed by Polish-born psychologist Leibush Lehrer, who insisted that the "easy recognizability of the Jew" on the basis of physical traits, facial expressions, and gestures "fulfilled a major function in internal Jewish life" because it provided the Jew with "a sense of kinship and strengthened his sense of security."[51] Lehrer's experiments, conducted in the late 1940s and early 1950s, led him to conclude that Eastern European–born Jewish participants more readily identified Jewish faces and seemed perfectly comfortable in being asked to make such distinctions because they had a stronger sense of "Jewish belongingness" than their American-born counterparts.[52] In Lehrer's view, loss of Jewish knowledge about Jewish physical difference posed a threat to ethnic continuity.

Lehrer's perspective represented an important shift in Jewish public discourse about the question of Jewish looks. He and some of his

contemporaries provided the first attempts to theorize the larger significance of the Jewish folk practice of visually distinguishing Jews
and non-Jews on the basis of presumed physical differences. Unlike
the Boasian anthropologists who had tried to universalize Jews, the
psychologists examined the question of looks from the point of view
of Jewish emotions and emphasized the Jewish need to see Jews as an
aspect of ethnic identity. In the late 1940s, Los Angeles psychoana-
lyst Anton Lourie argued that the "uncontrolled loud voices and . . .
vehement gesticulations" of traditional Jews were important aspects
of what Jews considered authentic Jewishness. He believed that "deep
in their hearts, traditional Jews are proud of their emotionalism; they
identify it with warmth and naturalness and consider it a necessary
attribute of the genuine Jew."[53] Terms such as "genuine Jew" and
"authentic Jew" were themselves highly polemical categories among
Jews in postwar America. Frequently deployed in intra-Jewish debates
about promoting group "survival" and the proper and legitimate way
of being Jewish in America, these terms pitted community leaders
who demanded group loyalty against self-styled "free thinking" intellectuals who insisted upon individual rather than collective definitions
of Jewishness.[54]

Modern Rituals of Jewish Visual Connoisseurship

Despite their theoretical and ideological differences, social scientists in
the 1950s and 1960s agreed upon one thing: whether or not gentiles
viewed Jews as marked by physical differences, Jews themselves not
only believed in the concept of "Jewish looks" but attached significant
positive and negative social meaning to the notion. The social scientists
who analyzed jokes such as "Funny, You Don't Look Jewish" viewed
this humor as reflecting the anxieties of assimilation. "The mannered
punchline" of Jewish identity jokes, Rosenberg and Shapiro suggested
in their 1958 article on humor and ethnic marginality, "demonstrates
that the leopard's spots remain unchanged." They argued that jokes
such as this one helped mediate the conflict between assimilation and
"traditional loyalty" by conveying the idea that "Jewish identification
is permanent" even for converts, because for Jews "the real unalterable self remains intact."[55] To the antisemite, the "secret Jew" posed a

threat, observed Rosenberg and Shapiro. To assimilating Jews, he was a potential ally, who held out the possibility of "mutual support" in the Jewish "fight for survival" as a distinctive group.[56]

For Jews in the postwar decades, the various versions of "Funny, You Don't Look Jewish" worked both as a cautionary tale about the taboos of passing for gentile and as a meditation on the growing importance of Jewish visual connoisseurship to the development and maintenance of an ethnic Jewish identity. In each of the midcentury versions of the joke, a "persistent" woman variously described as an "old lady," a "lady," or a woman with a Jewish-sounding name such as "Mrs. Moskowitz" or "Sarah Finkel" represents the authentic or more traditional Jew. The younger well-dressed male she encounters on a train, a bus, or a subway symbolizes the assimilated Jew whose hidden ethnic identity she seeks to unmask. He is variously described as "distinguished looking," "handsome looking," "cultured," or "blond, blue-eyed"—all synonyms meant to suggest that he is a successful individual who could physically pass for a gentile. Her task in each case is to use her Jewish powers of visual discernment to properly guess his true ethnicity and then to force him to confess it in front of a social audience.[57] Although the joke suggests that *looking* Jewish and *being* Jewish may or may not be one and the same, it simultaneously reinforces the Jewish folk belief that "you can always tell a Jew" just by looking at him.[58] For Jews, in other words, Jewishness can be read on the body.

Jewish rituals of visual connoisseurship were not new in the postwar era, but they took on new meaning as Jews began to assimilate culturally and geographically.[59] As American Jews continued to move out of their immigrant ghetto communities into the wider American society, often by relocating to the suburbs, and as intermarriage was increasingly perceived as a threat to a stable Jewish community, developing a "visual epistemology" that allowed them to divide the world into "genuine" Jewish looks, surgically altered "Jewish" looks, and non-Jewish looks gained a new urgency. In the early twentieth century, Jews may have taken for granted their ability to sort out the members of their own so-called tribe, but by the late 1950s and 1960s, as looks and social locations had changed, the practice took on a new urgency.[60]

These visual games were accompanied by what anthropologists in the 1970s called the rituals of Jewish "ethnic signaling"—whereby Jews peppered conversations with Jewish colloquialisms and incorporated Jewish gestures into social interactions to determine if a stranger, perhaps with a Waspish-sounding name or "Nordic" looks, would positively respond to the ritual cues of a fellow Jew.[61] "How to Tell a Jew," an article published in the 1986 newsletter of the Union of American Hebrew Congregations, summed up the pattern by concluding that the best way to tell who is a Jew "is if he is looking for other Jews."[62] "Jews are excellent cryptographers," remarks another writer, a young Jewish woman who was interviewing subjects for a story on the same theme almost fifteen years later. She wondered about why "we spend our days proffering and receiving a vast melange of shibboleths as a way of announcing our existence to one another, but not to the rest of the world," and interviewed a man who told her confidently: "If I meet a woman with Jewish looks. . . . If she's got the nose, her name is Rachel, and she's from Long Island, you've got a 90% chance [that she is Jewish]."[63] Thus looking and seeing "Jewish" was itself a form of Jewish identity.

By the 1970s, when the ethnic pride and feminist movements made physical "difference" a symbol of identity politics, "Jewish looks," became a highly politicized issue as women were urged to "take back their noses and their names" in a rebellion against the Wasp standards of physical attractiveness.[64] In the late 1970s, for example, Berkeley psychotherapist Judith Weinstein Klein tried to "heal the wounds" of "Jewish self-hatred" by conducting "ethnotherapy" workshops where women and men were encouraged to value rather than to disdain physical qualities associated with Jewish looks.[65] For some, flaunting Jewishness—whether culturally or physically—became a badge of ethnic pride. It also became a source of intra-ethnic connection. "I liked being marked that way," writer Lisa Jervis says of her "Jewish" nose; it made her "instantly recognizable to anyone who knew how to look."[66]

Postmodern Jewish artists, many of them influenced by feminist and gay subcultures, have been especially confrontational in their presentation of images associated with stereotypical Jewish faces, often by "exaggerat[ing] the exaggeratedness of the rude stereotype."[67] In the catalogue for the deliberately controversial 1996 art installation "Too

Jewish?" at the Jewish Museum in New York City, curator Norman Kleeblatt explained that the work of several artists who played with stereotypes of "the Jewish nose" confronted the social pressure "to negate or eradicate" images of Jewish difference.[68] No stereotype received as much attention from Jewish artists in this show as the "Jewish nose" did. Creating a parody of the classificatory systems of racial science, artist Dennis Kardon made and painted forty-nine sculptures of the noses of Jewish artists, curators, and collectors and labeled them with the names of his models. Adam Rolston produced a series of highly technical drawings depicting the surgical procedures of rhinoplasty.[69] An attempt to explore how Jews have been represented in American popular culture and how they represent themselves, the "Too Jewish?" exhibit used parody and humor to reiterate and then to critique physical stereotypes of Jews. In doing so, argues art historian Carol Ockman, the artists in this show were "calling bigotry's bluff in order to expose it as reductive." Equally important, the "Too Jewish?" show demonstrated what Ockman labeled as "the mired relationship between identity and stereotype."[70] Yet to dismiss Jewish engagements with stereotypes of Jewish physical difference as "mired" or to equate them, as some have, with "Jewish self-hatred" is to ignore a more complex and contradictory set of meanings that American Jews have attached to the idea of "looking Jewish."[71]

Take the example of *Heeb*—a contemporary magazine that encourages ethnic pride among young readers, in part by claiming as "Jewish" unconventional images and individuals on the margins of Jewish (and gentile) society, from punk rockers to pimps, from queers to tattoo artists.[72] *Heeb* traffics in Jewish insider-knowledge, playing with well-worn stereotypes not only to debunk them but for their nostalgic effect. In "The Goy Issue" (one of a series of themed issues), an advertisement for the magazine used "before" and "after" photographs of a silhouetted young woman that completely reversed normative expectations about the desirability of Jewish versus gentile looks. The "before" photograph had a somber-looking young woman with a small, upturned nose (presumably the result of rhinoplasty), while the "after" photograph showed the same woman with a large (presumably "Jewish") nose and a happy smile on her face. The caption read: "Be the way you want to be. Heebmagazine.com."[73]

The recent coinage of the term "Jewdar" (a variant of the term *gaydar*) suggests that "Jewish looks" remain a salient aspect of Jewish self-definition.[74] According to one "urban dictionary," this word implies that Jews have a visual radar that enables them to pick out other Jews in a crowd, even those who do not conform in any obvious way to stereotypes of the Jew.[75] Illustrating this idea in a piece of autobiographical self-confession, Jewish writer Baz Dreisinger discusses Jewdaring as a "favorite mall sport." She and her sister, a recent graduate from a yeshiva high school, have devised a list of "unofficial rules and regulations" for the game they call "Spot the Jew": "A sampling: Jewish = frizz; Goyish = the glossy stuff of Pantene commercials. Jewish = long skirt with sneakers; Goyish = Juicy sweat suit. Jewish = breast reduction; Goyish = breast implants. Jewish = bumpy nose; Goyish = button nose. Jewish = five-foot-seven for men; Goyish = five-foot-seven for women." Dreisinger, who insists that the "essence of my Jewish identity . . . lies in my [ample] breasts," which were "handed down to me from my maternal grandmother," speculates that the "insuppressible nature" of "Jewishness" is having something that is "out-of-proportion": "something that maybe sticks out a bit too much, is too dark, hairy, bulbous, or bulging—something you long ago pinpointed which marks you as a Jew . . . or some highly inconvenient feature you're vastly relieved you *don't* have."[76]

Yet as the controversy surrounding a now-famous comedy sketch on the long-running television show *Saturday Night Live* attests, these rituals of Jewish life have different implications when played out on a larger American public stage. Brandon Tartikoff, the former head of NBC entertainment, recalled that no comedy sketch caused him as much "grief" as the "Jew / Not-a-Jew" game show, written by Al Franken and aired in 1988.[77] In the sketch, emcee Bob Tomkins (played by Tom Hanks) shows the two pairs of contestants—the Knutsons and the Johnsons—photographs of famous people and asks them to guess if the person is Jewish. Before the game begins, Hanks interrogates the couples about their own ethnic and religious lineage. When the dark-haired Greg Knutson says that he is Swedish and Lutheran, Hanks replies, "Gee, I thought all Swedes were blond." His wife, Deborah, announces that she is "hard-core Protestant." The Johnsons proclaim, "We're both Wasps." When the first photograph on the screen shows the blond actress Penny Marshall, the Knutsons debate for a few seconds and then decide to go for "Jew." Wrong, corrects Hanks, she's really Italian Catholic. The last photograph belongs to the former mayor of New York City, Ed Koch. And with no debate, the Johnsons immediately identify him as a Jew. Ironically, even those Jews who complained that the sketch was antisemitic acknowledged that privately they also played the game. Tartikoff's mother reportedly expressed her distress over the airing of the sketch on national television, but then added: "Besides . . . I always thought Penny Marshall *was* Jewish."[78] Likewise, a representative from the Anti-Defamation League who contacted Franken in response to complaints about the sketch explained that he personally understood the humor because "he did the same thing in his house. . . . tried to figure out which of the performers on TV was Jewish."[79]

Rather than deny the idea that Jews look "Jewish," social critics in the contemporary period have come to terms with how real and imagined physical differences both mark Jews as stereotypically other and serve as symbols in a shared ethnic identity. Jews have been deeply invested in the idea of their own physical difference, but the terms of that engagement have shifted over time in response to both external and internal pressures. Whether trying to prove to racists and xenophobes that Jews would eventually cease to look stereotypically "Jewish," or seeking plastic surgery to normalize their appearance, or playing the game of visual connoisseurship, American Jews have acknowledged and even embraced physical difference as an aspect of what makes Jews "Jewish." In a society that now mainly classifies Jews as "white" and "Euro-American" and in an era where many people who call themselves "Jews" have no tangible connection to religious institutions or organized ethnic community life, games like "Spot the Jew" and the centuries-old practice of "Jewhooing"—the naming and claiming of Jews by other Jews on the basis of biological descent—are part of the secular rituals that help maintain a sense of uniqueness and historical connectedness among Jews.[80]

Jewdaring, like Jewhooing, has a continuous but changing history, a history that has been shaped and mediated by secular institutions, at least some of which have been devoted to disproving the idea of Jewish physical difference. This essay suggests that the more than century-long Jewish fixation on the idea of Jewish looks was not simply a result of internalized stereotyping. The continuous but shifting discourse on the question of whether Jews look "Jewish" was both a product of social scientific inquiry and a manifestation of the struggle over Jewish ethnic self-definition in an era when Jews began to enter "white" society on an equal footing for the first time. A central irony of Jewish self-definition has been the tribalistic perspective of a group that has also been committed to the idea of liberal universalism. Jews have defined themselves tribalistically, relying upon the concepts of ancestry, descent, physical difference, and historical memory as the basis of belonging and obligation. But Jews have also played a pivotal role in the development of institutions and ideas that have championed the value of universalism and cosmopolitanism: social sciences such as anthropology and psychology, the publishing industry, the arts, literature, and Hollywood. These secular institutions promoted the idea of universal commonality among human beings of different backgrounds and races. Paradoxically, they also helped legitimate the social practices through which Jews would attempt to maintain primordial concepts of Jewish identity. "Funny, you don't look Jewish" plays on both sides of the divide, invoking both universalism and tribalism in an anxious ritual of Jewish connoisseurship.

Notes

1. Quoted in Maurice Fishberg, *The Jews: A Study in Race and Environment* (New York: Charles Scribner's Sons, 1911), 178. See also John Efron, *Defenders of the Race: Jewish Doctors and Race Science in Fin-de-Siècle Europe* (New Haven, Conn.: Yale University Press, 1994), 97–98.

2. This version of the joke appears in Bernard Rosenberg and Gilbert Shapiro, "Marginality and Jewish Humor," *Midstream* 4, no. 2 (1958): 70.

3. Ibid., 77–78.

4. Sander L. Gilman, *The Jew's Body* (New York: Routledge, 1991), 192, 193, 236. For other perspectives on the "problem of the body" in Jewish history, see Howard Eilberg-Schwartz, ed., *People of the Body: Jews and Judaism from an Embodied Perspective* (Albany: State University of New York Press, 1992).

5. I borrow the who/what framework from Virginia Dominguez. Although she does not address the issue of looks or phenotype, she offers a compelling analysis of the practice and significance of ethnic group self-classification. See Dominguez, *People as Subject, People as Object: Selfhood and Peoplehood in*

Contemporary Israel (Madison: University of Wisconsin Press, 1989), 3–20, 128, 190–91. On Jews and blood logic, see Susan A. Glenn, "In the Blood? Consent, Descent, and the Ironies of Jewish Identity," *Jewish Social Studies* 8, nos. 2–3 (2002): 139–52.

6. Siniša Malešević, *The Sociology of Ethnicity* (New York: Sage, 2004), 135. Paul Connerton discusses the importance of "bodily practices" to the shaping of cultural memory and group identity in *How Societies Remember* (Cambridge: Cambridge University Press, 1989), 1–4, 72–75, 79–82, 104; quotation on 104. Anthropologist Barbara Kirshenblatt-Gimblett remarks that studies of embodied notions of Jewishness have provoked considerable anxiety in the Jewish Studies field, where the traditional emphasis has been the study of texts and ideas. Kirshenblatt-Gimblett, "The Corporeal Turn," *Jewish Quarterly Review* 95, no. 3 (2005): 447–61.

7. On the process by which Jews attained white racial status, see Matthew Frye Jacobson, *Whiteness of a Different Color: European Immigrants and the Alchemy of Race* (Cambridge, Mass.: Harvard University Press, 1998). On Jewish racial self-description, see Eric Goldstein, *The Price of Whiteness: Jews, Race, and American Identity* (Princeton, N.J.: Princeton University Press, 2006); and Karen Brodkin, *How Jews Became White Folks and What That Says about Race in America* (New Brunswick, N.J.: Rutgers University Press, 1998).

8. Mitchell B. Hart, *Social Science and the Politics of Modern Jewish Identity* (Stanford, Calif.: Stanford University Press, 2000), 176–79, 181–91; Hart, "Racial Science, Social Science, and the Politics of Assimilation," in *Science, Race, and Ethnicity: Readings from Isis and Osiris*, ed. John P. Jackson (Chicago: University of Chicago Press, 2002), 99–128; Efron, *Defenders of the Race*, 7–8, 63–65, 81–90.

9. Fishberg, *The Jews*, 102, 220. For further discussion of nationalist uses of photography, see Hart, *Social Science and the Politics of Modern Jewish Identity*, 181–91. In the 1917 study *The Jewish Child*, W. M. Feldman presented a photographic genealogy to show that the mating of racially pure Jews with Jewish "hybrids" (children of Jewish and gentile parents) produced offspring who were just as likely to be "Jewish-looking" as "non-Jewish looking." W. M. Feldman, *The Jewish Child: Its History, Folklore, Biology, and Sociology* (London: Baillière, Tindall and Cox, 1917).

10. Fishberg, *The Jews*, 79, 165.

11. Ibid., 169.

12. Ibid., 171.

13. See Leonard B. Glick, "Types Distinct from Our Own: Franz Boas on Jewish Identity and Assimilation," *American Anthropologist* 84, no. 3 (1982): 545–65.

14. See Melville J. Herskovits, "Franz Boas as Physical Anthropologist," in *Franz Boas, 1858–1942*, ed. A. L. Kroeber et al., *American Anthropologist*, n.s., 45, no. 3 (1943): 43–49; and Gelya Frank, "Melville J. Herskovits on the African and Jewish Diasporas," *Identities* 8, no. 2 (2001): 177–79.

15. Herskovits, "Franz Boas as Physical Anthropologist," 45.

16. The most comprehensive study of the Jewish Boasian anthropologists is Karen Ann Russell King, "Surviving Modernity: Jewishness, Fieldwork, and the Roots of American Anthropology in the Twentieth Century" (Ph.D. diss., University of Texas at Austin, 2000).

17. Alexander Goldenweiser, "The Jewish Face," *Reflex*, October 1927, 10.

18. M. F. Ashley Montagu, "Race Theory in the Light of Modern Science," in *The Jewish People: Past and Present* (New York: Jewish Encyclopedic Handbooks, Central Yiddish Culture Organization, 1946), 1:8.

19. David Efron, *Gesture and Environment: A Tentative Study of Some of the Spatio-temporal and "Linguistic" Aspects of the Gestural Behavior of Eastern Jews and Southern Italians in New York City, Living under Similar as Well as Different Environmental Conditions* (New York: King's Crown Press, 1941), 1–4, 40–42. On the origins of the study, see the collection background description in the David Efron Gesture Research Collection, Stuyvesant Van Veen Illustrations (1930–40), National Anthropological Archives, Smithsonian Institution. See also "Interview with Stuyvesant Van Veen" by Emily Nathan, May 5, 1981, in the Archives of American Art, Smithsonian Institution. Kirshenblatt-Gimblett ("Corporeal Turn," 456) describes Efron's book as "the richest account ever of the gesture system of East European Jews."

20. Efron, *Gesture and Environment*, 40–42, 130–31.

21. Ibid., 56. The Jewish "slump" when sitting and the "stooped posture" of standing Jews are described in David Efron, "Some Observations on the Conversational Bodily Postures of 'Traditional' and 'Assimilated' Jews and Southern Italians in New York City," typed manuscript, in David Efron Gesture Research Collection. Along with this original manuscript, the collection contains extensive study notes and numerous illustrations.

22. Efron, *Gesture and Environment*, 61.

23. Ibid., 64–65, 123, fig. 21. See also Anton Lourie, "The Jew as Psychological Type," *American Imago* 6 (June 1949): 123–25, 144–45.

24. Efron, *Gesture and Environment*, 65.

25. Ibid. (italics in original); see also 143, fig. 19.

26. This was not unique to Jews and in fact may be characteristic of all minority groups and all multicultural societies.

27. Melville J. Herskovits, "Who Are the Jews?" in *The Jews: Their History, Culture, and Religion*, ed. Louis Finkelstein (New York: Harper and Brothers, 1949), 2:1166–67.

28. Franz Boas to Melville J. Herskovits, September 12, 1934 (italics added), Professional Correspondence of Franz Boas, microfilm reel 37, University of Washington Library, Seattle (hereafter cited as Boas Correspondence). Originals are located in the library of the American Philosophical Society, Philadelphia.

29. Herskovits, "Who Are the Jews," 2:1167–68.

30. Ibid., 2:1168.

31. On the "American" look, see Herskovits to Boas, October 24, 1934, Boas Correspondence, microfilm reel 34. On mistaking Jews and non-Jews at Northwestern, see Herskovits, "Who Are the Jews," 2:1168. None of these experimental studies was ever published, and Herskovits makes only brief references to them in "Who Are the Jews." Herskovits's lecture notes from Boas's 1922 course on Anthropological Methods contain detailed discussion on the question of "what makes for change" in the physical characteristics of humans. See especially the notes from November 22, 1922, box 164, folder 1, Herskovits Papers, Northwestern University. I am grateful to anthropologist Kevin Yelvington for sharing copies of Herskovits's methods notes with me.

32. Laura Z. Hobson, *Gentleman's Agreement* (New York: Simon and Schuster, 1946; New York: Dell, 1962), 63–64. Citations are to the 1962 edition.

33. Ibid., 96–97.

34. Ibid., 196–97.

35. J. Alvin Kugelmass, "Name-Changing—and What It Gets You: Twenty-five Who Did It," *Commentary* 14 (August, 1952): 145–50; Werner Cohn, "The Name Changers," *Jewish Digest* 30 (September 1984): 16–22.

36. Sander L. Gilman, *Making the Body Beautiful: A Cultural History of Aesthetic Surgery* (Princeton, N.J.: Princeton University Press, 1999), 193.

37. Ibid.; Elizabeth Haiken, *Venus Envy: A History of Cosmetic Surgery* (Baltimore: Johns Hopkins University Press, 1997), 184–89, 192–93; Richard B. Aronsohn and Richard A. Epstein, *The Miracle of Cosmetic Plastic Surgery* (Los Angeles: Sherbourne Press, 1970), 37.

38. Frances M. Cooke Macgregor, *Facial Deformities and Plastic Surgery: A Psychosocial Study* (Springfield, Ill.: Charles C. Thomas, 1953), 66.

39. Hobson, *Gentleman's Agreement*, 125 (italics in original).

40. Ibid., 117.

41. Ibid., 199. See also Jacobson, *Whiteness of a Different Color*, 130–31.

42. Jacobson, *Whiteness of a Different Color*, 196.

43. Melvin J. Tumin, "The Idea of 'Race' Dies Hard," *Commentary* 8 (July 1949): 81.

44. Else Frenkel-Brunswik, "Summary of Interview Results," in *The Authoritarian Personality*, by Theodor W. Adorno, Else Frenkel-Brunswik, Daniel J. Levinson, and R. Nevitt Sanford (New York: Harper, 1950), 281–86.

45. Gordon W. Allport and Bernard M. Kramer, "Some Roots of Prejudice," *Journal of Psychology* 22 (July 1946): 17. See also Gardner Lindzey and Saul Rogolsky, "Prejudice and Identification of Minority Group Membership," *Journal of Abnormal and Social Psychology* 45, no. 1 (1950): 37–53. Several other studies found little or no relationship between antisemitic attitudes and ability to identify Jews in photographs. See, e.g., Donald N. Elliott and Bernard H. Wittenberg, "Accuracy of Identification of Jewish and Non-

Jewish Photographs," *Journal of Abnormal and Social Psychology* 51, no. 2 (1955): 339–41; Launor F. Carter, "The Identification of 'Racial' Membership," *Journal of Abnormal and Social Psychology* 43, no. 3 (1948): 279–86.

46. Gordon W. Allport, *The Nature of Prejudice* (Boston: Beacon Press, 1954), 119–20.

47. Hans H. Toch, Albert I. Rabin, and Donald M. Wilkins, "Factors Entering into Ethnic Identifications: An Experimental Study," *Sociometry* 25 (September 1962): 298, 299.

48. Leibush Lehrer, "Jewish Belongingness of Jewish Youth," *YIVO Annual of Jewish Social Science* 9 (1954): 137, 139; quotation on 139.

49. Alvin Scodel and Harvey Austrin, "The Perception of Jewish Photographs by Non-Jews and Jews," *Journal of Abnormal and Social Psychology* 54, no. 2 (1957): 279.

50. Ibid.

51. Toch, Rabin, and Wilkins, "Ethnic Identifications," 298; Lehrer, "Jewish Belongingness," 161–62.

52. Lehrer, "Jewish Belongingness," 137, 139–40. See also Lehrer, "The Dynamic Role of Jewish Symbols in the Psychology of the Jewish Child in America," *YIVO Annual of Jewish Social Science* 6 (1951): 72. On Lehrer's background and career, see Milton R. Konvitz, "YIVO Comes to Morningside," *Commentary* 3 (January 1947): 53–54.

53. Lourie, "The Jew as Psychological Type," 125, 144.

54. See Susan A. Glenn, "The Vogue of Jewish Self-Hatred in Post–World War II America," *Jewish Social Studies* 12, no. 3 (2006): 95–136.

55. Rosenberg and Shapiro, "Marginality and Jewish Humor," 72.

56. Ibid., 78.

57. The various collected versions can be found in Richard Raskin, *Life Is Like a Glass of Tea: Studies of Classic Jewish Jokes* (Philadelphia: Jewish Publication Society, 1992), 213–15. See also William Novak and Moshe Waldocks, eds., *The Big Book of Jewish Humor* (New York: HarperCollins, 1981), 7.

58. Novak and Waldocks, *Big Book of Jewish Humor*, 7.

59. Historian Aviva Ben-Ur describes how Ashkenazim in early twentieth-century New York City often misrecognized Sephardic Jews, mistaking them for non-Jewish immigrants from the Mediterranean and Middle East. See Ben-Ur, "Funny, You Don't Look Jewish! 'Passing' and the Elasticity of Ethnic Identity among Levantine Sephardic Immigrants in Early Twentieth Century America," *Kolor* (Brussels), no. 2 (November 2002): 9–18.

60. Martin S. Jaffee, "Jewish Radar: A Superannuated Technology" (unpublished manuscript, in the author's possession, 2007). Jaffee uses the term "visual epistemology" to discuss the radar he developed to tell Jews apart from Italians and other non-Jewish ethnics in his Long Island suburb in the 1950s. See also Jaffee, *The End of Jewish Radar: Snapshots of a Post-ethnic American Judaism* (2009), http://www.iuniverse.com (accessed August 28, 2009).

Nancy K. Miller comments on how the "Funny, You Don't Look Jewish" joke played out in her family's anxieties over the issue of intermarriage with gentiles. See Miller, "Hadassah Arms," in *People of the Book: Thirty Jewish Scholars Reflect on Their Jewish Identity*, ed. Jeffrey Rubin-Dorsky and Sheller Fisher Fishkin (Madison: University of Wisconsin Press, 1996), 154–56.

61. Leon Plotnicov and Myrna Silverman, "Jewish Ethnic Signalling: Social Bonding in Contemporary American Society," *Ethnology* 17, no. 4 (1978): 414. See also Erving Goffman, *Stigma: Notes on the Management of Spoiled Identity* (Englewood Cliffs, N.J.: Prentice-Hall, 1963; New York: Simon and Schuster, 1986), 101, 114. Citations are to the 1986 edition.

62. Robert Sloan, "How to Tell a Jew," *Keeping Posted* 31, no. 5 (1986): 13–15.

63. Tilia Klebenov, "*Chai* There: Subtle Ways Jews Tell Other Jews They're Jewish," *Jewish Magazine* 29 (February 2000), http://www.jewishmag. com/29mag/chai/chai.htm (accessed June 17, 2005). Others reported the anxiety of being misrecognized by Jews because they lacked the stereotypic traits associated with Jews. See Laurel Richardson, "Looking Jewish," *Qualitative Inquiry* 9, no. 5 (2003): 815–21; Daria Vaisman, "My Life as a Shiksa Jew," *Jewish Student Press Service*, June 9, 2005, http://www.shmoozenet.com/jsps/stories/0998Daria.shtml (accessed June 17, 2005); Susan Schnur, "As an Adopted Child, All I Wanted Was Real Jewish Hair," *Lilith* 20, no. 1 (1995): 15.

64. Miller, "Hadassah Arms," 161, 166.

65. Judith Weinstein Klein, *Jewish Identity and Self-Esteem: Healing Wounds through Ethnotherapy* (New York: Institute on Pluralism and Group Identity, American Jewish Committee, 1980), 18–19; quotation on 24.

66. Lisa Jervis, "My Jewish Nose," in *Adiós Barbie: Young Women Write about Body Image and Identity*, ed. Ophira Edut (Seattle: Seal Press, 1998), 66.

67. The phrase in quotation marks is one I borrow from Naomi B. Sokoloff, "Jewish Character? Stereotype and Identity in Fiction from Israel by Aharon Appelfeld and Sayed Kashua," in this volume.

68. Norman Kleeblatt, "'Passing' into Multiculturalism," in *Too Jewish? Challenging Traditional Identities*, ed. Norman Kleeblatt (New York: Jewish Museum; New Brunswick, N.J.: Rutgers University Press, 1996), 8. Contemporary Jewish cartoonists have also flaunted the "too Jewish" body. See Andrea Most, "Re-imagining the Jew's Body: From *Self-Loathing* to 'Grepts,'" in *You Should See Yourself: Jewish Identity in Postmodern American Culture*, ed. Vincent Brook (New Brunswick, N.J.: Rutgers University Press, 2006).

69. Kleeblatt, "'Passing' into Multiculturalism," 10–11, 13.

70. Carol Ockman, "'Too Jewish? Challenging Traditional Identities': Jewish Museum," *ArtForum* 35, no. 1 (1996): 106.

71. Following the lead of Gilman, Elliott Horowitz suggested that the exhibit was meant to explore "an internal category of Jewish self-hatred." See Horowitz, "Too Jewish? And Other Jewish Questions: A Review Essay," *Modern Judaism* 19, no. 2 (1999): 195–206.

72. My thanks to Sarah Lindsley for sharing her astute observations on *Heeb*'s engagement with the outrageous and unconventional.

73. Rebecca Weiner, "In the Beginning," in "The Goy Issue," *Heeb* 15 (Winter 2007): 6. The before/after images follow on 74.

74. Joseph Epstein, "Funny, but I Do Look Jewish: The Photos of Frédéric Brenner's 'Diaspora,'" *Weekly Standard* 9, no. 14 (2003), http://www.weekleystandard.com (accessed June 17, 2005).

75. *Urban Dictionary*, s.v. "Jewdar," http://www.urbandictionary.com/define.php?-term=jewdar (accessed June 17, 2005).

76. Baz Dreisinger, "Spot the Jew," in *The Modern Jewish Girl's Guide to Guilt*, ed. Ruth Andrew Ellison (New York: Dutton, 2005), 173–75 (italics in original).

77. Quoted in David Zurawik, *The Jews of Prime Time* (Hanover, N.H.: University Press of New England/Brandeis University Press, 2003), 2. *Saturday Night Live*, season 14, episode no. 247, first broadcast October 8, 1988, by NBC; the sketch is also available on *Saturday Night Live: The Best of Tom Hanks*, DVD (Santa Monica, Calif.: Lions Gate Entertainment, NBC Universal, 2005).

78. Quoted in Zurawik, *The Jews of Prime Time*, 3.

79. Ibid.

80. On "Jewhooing," see Glenn, "In the Blood."

5

Blame, Boundaries, and Birthrights

Jewish Intermarriage in Midcentury America

LILA CORWIN BERMAN

To study the debates about Jewish intermarriage over the past half century is to be confronted with a politics of blame. In both scholarly and popular discussions, the desire to assign blame has remained a constant theme. For example, Steven M. Cohen, a sociologist well known for his statistical studies, lambasted American Jews in 2007 for not doing enough to stem the tide of intermarriages. Either address the problem, he exhorted, "or you can watch the Jewish population start to contract as my generation of baby-boomers begins leaving this world for the next, to be replaced—or not—by a numerically much smaller cohort of Jewish descendants."[1] And one would be hard-pressed to find many rabbis in the past half century who have not delivered reproachful sermons on this same topic.

In their public pronouncements, twentieth-century American Jewish leaders blamed no one more than parents for intermarriage woes. Other targets presented themselves: social, cultural, and educational forces that affected Jewish patterns of socialization or weakened religious authority; or children themselves who staged rebellions. Parents, however, bore the brunt of this criticism when communal leaders sought to explain why Jewish boundaries were shifting and, in some cases, dissolving. In accusing parents of not properly patrolling boundaries, and, eventually, creating a child-oriented apparatus intended to serve in loco parentis, Jewish leaders and scholars have often failed to confront deeper questions about the nature of Jewish boundaries and the meaning of Jewish community in modernity.

As Jews gained acceptance into American society, particularly from the 1950s on, markers between Jews and non-Jews that had once seemed nearly immutable grew far less stable. While much of Jewish

law is concerned with methods for maintaining communal boundaries, explaining and enacting them in a putatively liberal, pluralistic
society was no easy task.[2] A simultaneous and related crisis in Jewish
authority further complicated the project. Who or what could compel
Jewish behavior in the modern world: law, divinity, tradition, social
custom, popular culture, education, clergy, family?

Even as the boundary lines between Jews and non-Jews blurred
and sources of Jewish authority vied for power, most American Jews
throughout the twentieth century married other Jews. The instances
when they did not, however, served as some of the most emotionally
percussive subjects for Jewish leaders to craft modern-day jeremiads.
On one level, by drawing persistent public attention to Jewish intermarriage, they affirmed that Jews could love, and be loved by and
legally committed to, a non-Jew. Yet these leaders spoke through the
one vocabulary they hoped might salvage their authority to reconsti-
tute Jewish boundaries: that of condemnation.[3]

Often Jewish leaders tried to balance the weight of American
belonging and Jewish survival on the shoulders of the American family.
They encouraged Jews to follow American trends and to use their
family life as a pathway for Americanization, while they chastised
them for dissolving the boundaries between the Jewish family and the
American, or non-Jewish, family. In declaiming communal behavior
and identifying a source for it—who or what had failed to act properly—Jewish leaders suggested a remedy, respinning reproach into
repair. This was the best case; sometimes, however, the blame was crip-
pling, causing those casting the blame to feel removed from responsibility and those being blamed to feel alienated.

Jews were not alone in analogizing family stability and social stability. Indeed, a long-standing component of American political
thought maintained that families were small versions of the state, thus
drawing family order into a larger national purpose.[4] The social sciences, which held great sway by the early decades of the twentieth
century, operated under a similar premise: that small units, whether
individuals, families, or minority groups, stood for the whole.[5]

By the mid-twentieth century, regnant American thought endowed
parenting with incredible cultural and national power, so great that
experts worried that most parents were not up to the task. Just as

American leaders attempted to create institutions and social services that could stand in for parents unable to fulfill the lofty ideals of American parenthood, Jewish leaders as well began to establish an entire infrastructure of Jewish life to serve as surrogate—or better—parents. Idealizing the family, especially parents, only to scold it for falling short, American and Jewish authorities disempowered the very institution that they had built up, causing widespread alarm about the fate of the American nation and the Jewish people.

Children and Visions of the Self at Midcentury

In an era marked by reverence for experts, surveys, and the social sciences, parenting drew new scrutiny.[6] According to exponents of the "child sciences," which emerged in the 1920s and flourished in the interwar and postwar eras, children were products of empirically observable forces, and thus who a child grew up to be was no great mystery.[7] Child-rearing guides tended to agree that parents, through the environment they created, controlled their children's destiny. With the possibility of control came new obligations for parents and, in many cases, new blame. A child's pathway to delinquency or rebellion clearly started at his or her parents' feet. Mothers, assumed to be core agents of their children's socialization, drew particular ire even when they were not named. The term *parent* itself was gendered female, evidenced by the kinds of magazines in which experts on parenthood published their studies and by the broader context of postwar family life. At the same time, experts agreed that children needed mothers and fathers in order to develop properly.

At the root of cultural authorities' rising focus on parenting were warring American ideals about selfhood. How was the self formed and by whom? Religion had once been the purveyor of this kind of existential knowledge, but scientific discourse increasingly intervened. Far from univocal, twentieth-century scientific frameworks depicted the self as both entirely malleable and precisely prefigured. By the early decades of the century, cultural anthropologists were dismantling race science and biblical narratives, replacing both with a radical vision of human adaptability. Accordingly, they envisioned the self as environmentally determined and therefore mutable.[8] Yet in the same years, Freudian and developmental psychology drew attention to childhood, especially early childhood, as the most critical period of personality formation. Once beyond those years, an individual carried a deeply lodged unconscious and multiple layers of repression alterable only, if at all, through therapy.[9] The implication of these two reigning discourses of personhood was to celebrate human adaptability while putting serious limitations on it once a person passed through childhood.

Children's behavior—and especially their behavior as adults—had not always been understood as a reflection of their parents' child-rearing decisions. America's early Calvinists, for example, believed that babies entered the world marked by sin; sin was organic, not a result of something one did, but a precondition of sentience.[10] Yet new modes of scientific knowledge drew attention to human activity and the lived environment as the causal factors in shaping individuals and communities. These were empirically observable variables. Parents— not God—and home—not heaven—shaped children. Certainly, before the twentieth century, many people would have thought of parents as exercising special authority over their children. Nevertheless, the scientific apparatus for quantifying and reifying that authority emerged only in the twentieth century. Most important, through psychology and its popularization in advice literature, parents were saddled with the task of forming not just the present but also the future of children's lives. What parents did—how they disciplined or even when they toilet trained—had consequences far beyond the individual family. Whole communities and nations depended on proper parenting.

A National Purpose for the Jewish Family

For American Jews, the high stakes of parenthood were only heightened by their new postwar communal obsession: intermarriage. Much as their attitudes toward parenting reflected a larger American discourse, so did their understanding of marriage. Of course, Jewish endogamy had a history quite independent of its American career. Since at least the codification of rabbinic law in the early centuries of the millennium, Jews have been instructed to marry within the Jewish group. While the biblical basis of the injunction against marrying non-Jews is less than obvious, certain prophets and then the rabbis who worked to recreate Judaism after the destruction of the Second Temple enshrined endogamy with the power of normativity.[11] Among myriad laws mandating Jewish communal separation, it often reigned supreme.

In the modern era, marrying in posed a real and symbolic obstacle to Jewish integration into liberal nation-states. American Jews were granted citizenship without the existential struggles that ensued in Europe, but they still felt a similar disjuncture between citizenship ideals and religious or ethnic ideals. The metaphor that would hold the greatest sway over American life throughout the twentieth century— the melting pot—was animated by the dramatic possibility of inter-marriage.[12] In the Progressive decades of the early twentieth century, intermarriage indeed presented a way to resolve the tension between America's ever-growing diversity and its leaders' investment in uni-fying and strengthening the nation.

American Jews were well aware that their endogamy chafed against Progressive visions. In 1909 a group of Reform rabbis, members of the liberal wing of Judaism, debated whether it still made sense to adhere to the traditional interdiction against intermarriage. Back and forth they argued, seeking to arrive at the perfect balance between a religious ideal that stood at the core of Jewish group identity and a political ideal that stood at the core of American Progressive thought. Although most Reform rabbis could hardly imagine breaking with the practice of endogamy, their Progressive loyalties and Enlighten-ment origins bred a painful self-consciousness about endogamy. Amid high-minded statements endorsing universalism and Americanism, endogamy stuck out as clannish and atavistic. In the end, the rabbis resolved only that intermarriage should be "discouraged," offering very little explanation of why.[13]

While the rabbis argued, most Jews remained steadfastly endog-amous, less because of stated religious conviction than because of the conditions of early twentieth-century America. The channels for contact between Jews and non-Jews were limited, given the socio-logical circumstances of the time. Moreover, few Americans, Jewish or not, were interested in bridging the divide, especially through sexual intimacy. Most mainstream American religious groups mandated endogamy among their adherents.[14] More important, despite its paeans to American assimilation, the Progressive Era was awash with fear that new immigrants were contaminating and weakening the nation. Such fears fed an obsession with maintaining American purity by guarding presumed scientific and biological boundaries. A pervasive cultural belief that marriage between blacks and whites—so-called miscegenation—was unnatural came to inform scientists' and policy makers' valuation of marital homogeneity.[15]

By the 1930s, social scientists and marriage experts characterized endogamy as an essential component of marital success.[16] Most prominent among them was the University of Chicago sociologist Ernest Burgess, who concluded in a comprehensive study of marriage co-authored by Leonard Cottrell of Cornell University that "similarity of cultural background is favorable and . . . dissimilarity . . . is unfavorable to adjustment in marriage."[17] With the exception of racial difference, which most assumed was an obvious marital hazard, marriage experts tended to highlight religious difference as a crucial source of marital incompatibility.

Jewish leaders found great utility in experts' testimony on behalf of endogamy. Instead of being marked as unassimilable because of their marital behavior, endogamous American Jews could position themselves as guardians of social stability.[18] After all, interwar studies had determined that the more homogenous a couple, the more likely their marriage was to succeed and stand as a foundation for a stable society. A series of reports that divorce rates were higher in interfaith marriages than in other marriages offered seemingly irrefutable proof that religious endogamy served the interests of stability.[19]

Children as Victims

Less quantifiable than divorce rates but more emotionally stirring were the wounds that sociologists and clergy believed interfaith marriages inflicted upon children. Children's proper social adjustment and identity formation, according to experts, depended on the sort of stability a religiously consistent home ensured. Those parents who were unable to raise their children in a singular religion could expect to encounter problems corrosive to family life and children's development. Their decision to marry across faith lines, which initially may have represented the triumph of romance over convention, or individual happiness over communal pressure, all too quickly revealed a deeper, more disturbing, and far less individualistic dimension. When it came to intermarriage, "the child is the loser," concluded a midcentury sociologist in the pages of the *Christian Century*.[20]

According to experts of the day, the offspring of interfaith couples stood as testimony that a single intermarriage was capable of creating a web of dysfunction, imperiling children, families, and, ultimately, a nation. Politicians, clergy, and family experts increasingly described religion as a child's right and a parent's obligation. In 1949 Rabbi Bernard J. Bamberger, a Reform rabbi in New York City, wrote in the *Reconstructionist*: "Above all, every child is entitled to a religious upbringing—to *one* religious upbringing which will be a source of security and not an occasion of inner conflict."[21] Similarly, James Pike, an Episcopal priest, informed readers of his book *If You Marry Outside Your Faith* that children raised in mixed-faith homes were by definition deprived of a crucial building block of identity essential to their psychological well-being.[22]

One family expert, mincing no words, wrote in *Redbook* that interfaith marriage precipitated a "cold war" at home, potentially as dangerous as the one abroad.[23] As many historians have noted, religion carried rising cultural and political currency during World War II and the postwar era. What mattered about religion when it came to nationalistic goals was not its doctrinal complexity but rather its assurance of stability and goodness. Social critics and some clergy might have bemoaned this state of affairs, but none could dismiss the power of religious rhetoric in American self-definition.[24] In the name of stability—familial and national—experts instructed Americans to avoid crossing boundaries in their marital behavior.

According to American cultural mores, the most dangerous marital crossings were racial ones, yet so certain were most Americans of the ill consequences of these unions that experts and the popular media fixed far less attention on them than they did on interfaith marriages, especially those entered into by Jews and non-Jews.[25] Though most Americans by this time assumed Jews and non-Jews were members of the same race, they also continued to perceive the two populations as gravely different from one another.[26] Thus these marriages threatened social divisions beyond denominational affiliation. Children born in households with one Jewish and one non-Jewish parent were imagined as clear illustrations of the identity crises wrought by intermarriage.

A series of personal essays published in *Commentary* in the 1950s charted the child-centered anxiety stoked by marriages between Jews and non-Jews and revealed how deeply experts' statements about faith and marriage struck. For example, Eleanor Felder, a Presbyterian woman married to a Jewish man, averred that while she and her husband were not religiously minded people, she was certain that "children have a right to be exposed to religion."[27] With a sentimentality that did not match her own beliefs, she continued, "The concept of a God who watches over each sparrow may give the child a deep sense of warmth and protection."[28] Yet because she and her husband did not share a faith (and were, in any case, cool to religion), they had never offered their son the chance to feel the comfort of religion or the sense of belonging it conferred. "Can conscientious parents," she continued, "arbitrarily deprive their children of this possibility?"[29] A few months later, as if in answer to Felder's question, *Commentary* printed an article penned by the troubled son of a Jewish father and non-Jewish mother. Children surely suffered their parents' marital misdeeds, according to the author, and if they found ways of constituting a stable identity, they did so only out of creativity borne from necessity.[30]

The fact that non-Jewish mothers appeared in both of these articles was not a coincidence. In those years, Jewish men married non-Jews far more frequently than Jewish women did.[31] It may have seemed logical, then, that if Jewish leaders were to blame anyone for rising rates of intermarriage and the ill consequences that ensued, it would have been Jewish men. Yet because by Jewish law mothers passed down religious identity to their children, and by social convention mothers socialized their children, women, as mothers—and not men, as husbands—received reprobation. Negligent Jewish mothers produced sons who intermarried and daughters who did not know how to make themselves attractive to Jewish men. Ironically, just as parents, especially mothers, learned from Dr. Benjamin Spock to trust themselves, experts and religious leaders worried precisely that parents were not to be trusted with raising children. Indeed, even Spock's best-selling *Common Sense Book of Baby and Child Care* implied that parenting was so far from a commonsense activity that one needed to be trained how to do it.

The Problem with Jewish Parents

By midcentury, Jewish leaders increasingly directed their attention not to mixed-faith couples themselves but rather to Jewish parents, who, they feared, were raising a generation destined for intermarriage. The fact of the matter was that mixed-faith couples were rare enough that it made little sense for Jewish institutions to invest sustained energy in dealing with them. Jewish parents, however, posed a new kind of threat to normative Jewish family ideals. They had chosen to marry other Jews, so the problem was not anything they had done. Rather, the problem was what they were not doing: raising properly Jewish children. In the very terms that rabbis and other Jewish leaders employed to talk about intermarriage, they simultaneously empowered parents and defined them as incompetent. According to child-rearing wisdom of the day, these parents controlled their children's future. According to menacing statistics, their children were increasingly headed into the arms of non-Jews. As early as 1941, a rabbi recounted a meeting with a distraught mother. Her son, she told him, was planning on marrying a non-Jew. "She made it clear that she was not fanatical about religion, nor did she have any personal objections to her son's 'intended.'"[32] In the rabbi's view, this was the heart of the problem. Here was a parent who had not communicated proper Jewish family ideals to her child. At one time, she had the power to convince him to marry a Jew—when he was young and impressionable—but now her cries were meaningless. As a parent, she had failed to raise a Jewish child.

Some rabbis suggested that the political climate as much as bad parenting was endogamy's foe. Rabbi Bamberger, for example, admitted that liberal rabbis like himself were "busily engaged in creating conditions that favor intermarriage." In fervently fighting segregation and attempting to break down barriers among groups, the rabbi explained, increased social contact between Jews and non-Jews was inescapable and would "sometimes lead to love and marriage."[33] A commitment to integration meant that categorical difference, whether defined by law, race, religion, or an individual's attitudes, was an embattled concept. Many rabbis and Jewish leaders were so ardent in their support for integration because they saw their own survival and protection as dependent on it.[34] Yet Jewish survival—or the perpetuation of a distinctive Jewish identity—would come unhinged unless leaders and parents could convince children that, at least when it came to marriage, a categorical difference existed between Jews and non-Jews.

An outspoken sociologist and open defender of Jewish endogamy, Marshall Sklare asserted that if the political climate had made endogamy more difficult to maintain, parents' toothlessness had sealed its sorry fate. In 1964 he wrote, "The liberalism of the Jewish parent—his commitment to the idea of equality and his belief in the transitory character of the differences which distinguish people from one another—serves to subvert his sense of moral rectitude in opposing intermarriage."[35]

Very few Jewish leaders, however, were comfortable disavowing liberalism or the parenting style—what experts termed permissive parenting—that accompanied it.[36] Praised as a modern method, permissive parenting offered children a sense of independence and encouraged them to challenge authority. As a theory, it had taken on a moral and Jewishly inflected status in the postwar era. Searching for ways to regain a sense of order and meaning after the Holocaust, important Jewish intellectuals portrayed evil in pathological terms and suggested that bad moral behavior could be altered much as an illness could be cured or, better, prevented. Bruno Bettelheim and Morris Janowitz, both employed by the American Jewish Committee, argued that children raised with more laxity, free to explore the world as they saw fit, would be less likely to harbor intense hatred for others than would children raised in so-called authoritarian households. As a product of their environment, children could develop immunity to the allures of totalitarianism and bigotry so long as they were properly raised. Democracy at home, in other words, bred democracy outside the home.[37]

While some social researchers implied that Adolf Hitler might have been stopped had more parents been permissive in raising their children, Jewish leaders worried that American Jewish parents were choosing permissiveness at the expense of Jewish survival. Often themselves adherents and advocates of permissive parenting, very few rabbis or Jewish leaders were in the position to advise parents simply to prohibit their children from intermarrying. In 1964, even as Albert Gordon, a Conservative rabbi, instructed parents to try to "the very best of their ability . . . [to] dissuade their children from intermarrying," he nonetheless emphasized that they must do so "lovingly . . . always realizing that their most important 'possession' is their child."[38]

By many measures, midcentury Jewish parents were confused about how their actions and attitudes might mold their children's future behavior. A 1953 poll found that 42 percent of Jewish parents surveyed would approve if their child wanted to marry a non-Jew, seemingly an indication of their child-centered permissiveness.[39] Yet another survey taken later in the 1950s found that fully one-half of Jewish parents were affiliated with a synagogue primarily for the sake of their children's identity formation, evidence of their attempts to control their children's development.[40] Herbert Gans, a sociologist who studied suburban Jewish life in the fifties and sixties, contended that just this kind of ambivalence was at the heart of a new style of American-Jewish life: "symbolic Judaism." Instead of living Judaism as part of daily life, American Jews were choosing the few activities, objects, and places that enabled them to "feel and express their Jewishness" without being bound by it.[41] As parents, they gave their children token Jewish experiences, but according to many Jewish leaders, they did not give their children the tools to live a fully Jewish life. A rabbi in 1969 explained pointedly: "Parents will have to learn that just because they feel Jewish does not mean that their children think they are Jewish."[42]

On many fronts, Jewish leaders in the 1960s were becoming convinced that parents, indeed, needed to be educated about what it meant to raise a Jewish child. Likely aware of their own diminished authority, rabbis worried that parents had no recourse when their children behaved in Jewishly impermissible ways. Monford Harris, a rabbi and professor of religion, writing in a Conservative publication in 1966, described what he believed was becoming a common situation: "The young Jew at the brink of marrying a gentile is challenged by his parents. Their argument against intermarriage is usually a religious one. But the young man (or woman, as the case may be) is quick to point out that he has seen no evidence of a deep commitment to Jewish piety and practice in his parents' life." At that point, according to the rabbi, the parents had to concede. Most Jewish parents, he believed, were more liberal and permissive than they were "authentically religious."[43] Their discomfort with intermarriage paled in comparison with their habituated permissiveness and their liberal belief that a person should be able to marry whomever he or she loves.

If Jewish parents' powers of persuasion were so limited, how then could they convince their children not to intermarry? For Rabbi Harris, the solution had little to do with children; rather, it had to do with how parents understood their own Jewishness. The reason that parents' religious arguments against intermarriage floundered was because the vocabulary of religion could not capture why most Jewish parents, who were otherwise unmoved by Jewish laws, still wanted their children to marry Jews. He explained: "Tenuous as their conscious religious affirmations and actions may be, [parents] are often deeply if unconsciously committed to covenantal Jewish existence."[44] Rabbi Harris's point was that if parents could first appreciate their own Jewishness, then they would know how to raise children who intuitively eschewed intermarriage. Influenced by Jewish thinker Mordecai Kaplan, the rabbi suggested that even secular Jews sensed that they were part of a covenant—or peoplehood—but most Jews did not know how to articulate or enact this connection. Kaplan, in his early to mid-twentieth-century writing, had proposed that the only way Judaism would survive modernity was for it to become a "way of experience," so real and basic that no one would question whether or not to be Jewish.[45] Entire communities, not just children, had to feel an intense intimacy between their existence and Judaism. As rich as this vision of Judaism seemed, it also suffered from its impractical pragmatism.

In Loco Parentis

Reeducating an entire community, whether in Kaplan's vision of peoplehood or in the fundamentals of Jewish law, seemed a hopeless endeavor to many Jewish leaders by the mid-1960s. In 1963 the *American Jewish Year Book* published the results from several intermarriage studies, all of which appeared to document a rising rate of intermarriage.[46] The next year, the widely read magazine *Look* featured an article titled "The Vanishing American Jew."[47] Panicked, William Abrams, a Conservative lay leader, concluded that parents were, in effect, a lost cause. In a 1973 article, he dismissed parents, explaining they could no longer be relied on to "transmit Jewish values . . . in the way they personally conduct themselves."[48] Jewish children needed parenting that their parents simply could not give them. Abram's solution was to replace parents with institutions better suited to doing the work of Jewish child rearing. Day schools, extracurricular Jewish programs, especially for high school students, and accredited Jewish Studies programs at universities all struck him as ripe for expansion. In his vision, the new function of Jewish institutional life was readily apparent.

Blundering parents were pushed to the sidelines as Jewish leaders and institutions positioned themselves in loco parentis. Frequent statistical studies of intermarriage, sometimes performed or financed by these same leaders and institutions, legitimated their claim over Jewish children. Armed with empirical data, many Jewish leaders concluded that they were offering a necessary renaissance—rebirth—for Jewish children. A massive philanthropic apparatus supported these new parenting initiatives. Told that their dollars could insure Jewish survival and reminded of studies documenting rising rates of intermarriage, Jews funded new instruments of child rearing alienated from homes and parents. In many cases, parents with financial resources were also convinced to pay for surrogates to do the work of Jewish parenting; sometimes doing what was best for one's child meant admitting that one did not know what was best.

Summers became the most crucial months for Jewish leaders to reparent children, as family vacations gave way to camp. For a month or more, children lived apart from their parents in a new kind of Jewish home. According to one scholar who has studied youth culture and Jewish summer camps, camp leaders "yearn[ed] to socialize Jewish children in a manner that they believed was often lacking at home."[49] She reports that often campers would return home with a sense of authority over their parents' Jewishness, correcting how they observed the Sabbath or insisting that the family abide by certain dietary laws.[50] Better than a youth group, summer camp transported children to a distant, often bucolic, setting that became a young person's "total institution" for a month or two, with parents' presence restricted to letters and perhaps a brief visiting day.[51]

Teen trips to Israel, which started in the 1950s and flourished by the mid-1960s, placed even more distance—literally thousands of miles—between parents and their children.[52] Often run by institutions with very specific agendas, such as Zionist groups, these trips explicitly aimed to resocialize Jewish youth. Not coincidentally, the most popular program by the early twenty-first century was called "Birthright," a birthright bestowed on children not by parents but by a philanthropic Jewish institution. Started in 1999, Birthright funded ten-day trips to Israel for Jews primarily between the ages of eighteen and twenty. In reports evaluating its effectiveness (and presumably shown to potential donors), researchers highlighted that participants "report a greater commitment to marrying Jews and to raising children that they may have in the future as Jews" than Jews who do not participate in the program.[53] According to the authors of a recent study of the Birthright experience, "The trips, both covertly and overtly, create links between the major threats to Jewish existence in recent decades—the Holocaust, the Arab-Israeli conflict, assimilation, and intermarriage—and Israel as a response to these threats."[54] Targeting young adults, putting them in close quarters, and, often, orchestrating emotionally heightened situations, Birthright, like other organized tours to Israel, may also function as a *shadchan*, or matchmaker, taking on a role most Jewish parents forsook at least a century ago.

Day schools, university-level Jewish Studies programs, and Hillel, all of which grew astronomically in the last three decades of the twentieth century, similarly stemmed and benefited from deep communal anxiety about intermarriage and inadequate Jewish parenting. Certainly, other forces fueled the creation of these institutions, but their logic was embedded in the community leaders' mission to step in and take responsibility for Jewish children, even at the expense of marginalizing Jewish parents. In reaction to this, some Jewish leaders started to suggest family education plans, intended to embrace entire families and not leave parents waiting at airport gates or driving away from rustic bunks.[55]

Throughout the twentieth century, child-rearing experts all seemed to agree that children needed better parenting than most parents could give. Convinced, on the one hand, that parents should be able to control the development of their children—the effect of a radically nurture-based turn in how Americans thought about child rearing— and certain, on the other hand, that professional experts would be far better up to the task than untrained parents would, American parents and Jews among them learned to doubt themselves. Thinking about child rearing as a communal activity had incredible potential to realign wealth and power toward a more systematic commitment to child welfare (the old "it takes a village" idea). In the case of American Jews, however, it seemed to draw children into communal politics of blame and often to treat them as statistic-making entities and fund-raising objects. Sometimes it seemed as if children and parents simply got lost in the mix.

In the process of trying to reassert the importance of Jewish boundaries, Jewish leaders drew those lines in some unexpected places— even between parents and their children. Communities, of course, need ways of distinguishing themselves. Throughout history, marriage rules have aptly done just that. The problem of alienation that follows boundary making may be inevitable; someone must always be excluded for others to feel included. Yet tragedy came in those instances when the Jewish community became fixated on boundary maintenance, exclusion, and blame at the expense of creating meaningful community.

Notes

1. Steven M. Cohen, "The Many Dangers of Looking at Intermarriage through a Pair of Rose-Colored Glasses," *Jewish Exponent* 221, no. 23 (2007): 29.

2. On Jewish efforts to explain their Jewishness in the United States, see Lila Corwin Berman, *Speaking of Jews: Rabbis, Intellectuals, and the Creation of an American Public Identity* (Berkeley: University of California Press, 2009).

3. My reference to jeremiads and the function they play in community transformation draws on Sacvan Bercovitch, *The American Jeremiad* (Madison: University of Wisconsin Press, 1978).

4. On the early history of the political understanding of American family life, see Mary Beth Norton, *Founding Mothers and Fathers: Gendered Power and the Forming of American Society* (New York: Knopf, 1996).

5. Dorothy Ross, *The Origins of American Social Science* (New York: Cambridge University Press, 1991).

6. On American expert culture and the power of the social sciences, see Sarah Igo, *The Averaged American: Surveys, Citizens, and the Making of a Mass Public* (Cambridge, Mass.: Harvard University Press, 2007).

7. See the introduction to Barbara Beatty, Emily Cahan, and Julia Grant, eds., *When Science Encounters the Child: Education, Parenting, and Child Welfare in Twentieth-Century America* (New York: Teachers College Press, 2006).

8. See Elazar Barkan, *The Retreat of Scientific Racism: Changing Concepts in Britain and the United States between the World Wars* (New York: Cambridge University Press, 1992); Carl Degler, *In Search of Human Nature: The Decline and Revival of Darwinism in American Social Thought* (New York: Oxford University Press, 1991); and George W. Stocking, *Race, Culture, and Evolution: Essays in the History of Anthropology* (Chicago: University of Chicago Press, 1982).

9. See Andrew Heinze, *Jews and the American Soul: Human Nature in the Twentieth Century* (Princeton, N.J.: Princeton University Press, 2004); Eva Moskowitz, *In Therapy We Trust: America's Obsession with Self-Fulfillment* (Baltimore: Johns Hopkins University Press, 2001); and Anne C. Rose, "The Discovery of Southern Childhoods: Psychology and the Transformation of Schooling in the Jim Crow South," *History of Psychology* 10, no. 2 (2007): 249–78.

10. Steven Mintz, *Huck's Raft: A History of American Childhood* (Cambridge, Mass.: Belknap Press, 2004), chap. 1.

11. See Shaye J. D. Cohen, *The Beginnings of Jewishness: Boundaries, Varieties, Uncertainties* (Berkeley: University of California Press, 1999); and Christine Hayes, *Gentile Impurities and Jewish Identities: Intermarriage and Conversion from the Bible to the Talmud* (New York: Oxford University Press, 2002).

12. Israel Zangwill's 1908 play, "The Melting Pot," staged this metaphor for American life through a romance that culminated in marriage between a Jewish man and a non-Jewish woman. Edna Nahshon has written an informative introduction to and commentary on Zangwill's "Jewish" plays. See Edna Nahshon, ed., *From the Ghetto to the Melting Pot: Israel Zangwill's Jewish Plays* (Detroit: Wayne State University Press, 2006). Also, on the symbolism of the term, see Philip Gleason, "The Melting Pot: Symbol of Fusion or Confusion?" *American Quarterly* 16, no. 1 (1964): 20–46.

13. See *Central Conference of American Rabbis Yearbook* 19 (1909): 115. On the effects of the Enlightenment on Jewish thought, see Shmuel Feiner, *The Jewish Enlightenment*, trans. Chaya Naor (Philadelphia: University of Pennsylvania Press, 2004).

14. Anne C. Rose, *Beloved Strangers: Interfaith Families in Nineteenth-Century America* (Cambridge, Mass.: Harvard University Press, 2001).

15. See Martha Hodes, *White Women, Black Men: Illicit Sex in the Nineteenth-Century South* (New Haven, Conn.: Yale University Press, 1993); Peggy Pascoe, "Miscegenation Law, Court Cases, and Ideologies of 'Race' in Twentieth-

Century America," *Journal of American History* 83, no. 1 (1996): 44–69; and Peter Wallenstein, *Tell the Court I Love My Wife: Race, Marriage, and Law—an American History* (New York: Palgrave Macmillan, 2002).

16. On the rise of marriage experts, see Beth Bailey, "Scientific Truth . . . and Love: The Marriage Education Movement in the United States," *Journal of Social History* 20, no. 4 (1987): 711–32; and Rebecca Davis, "'The Wife Your Husband Needs': Marriage Counseling, Religion, and Sexual Politics in the United States, 1930–1980" (Ph.D. diss., Yale University, 2006); and Moskowitz, *In Therapy We Trust*, chap. 3.

17. Ernest Burgess and Leonard Cottrell, *Predicting Success or Failure in Marriage* (New York: Prentice-Hall, 1939), 12.

18. See Lila Corwin Berman, "Sociology, Jews, and Intermarriage in Twentieth-Century America," *Jewish Social Studies* 14, no. 3 (2008): 32–60.

19. The three most important studies that correlated interfaith marriage with increased divorce rates were Howard Bell, *Youth Tell Their Story* (Washington, D.C.: American Council on Education, 1938); Judson Landis, "Marriages of Mixed and Non-mixed Religious Faith," *American Sociological Review* 14, no. 3 (1949): 401–7; and H. Ashley Weeks, "Differential Divorce Rates by Occupations," *Social Forces* 21, no. 3 (1943): 334–37.

20. Murray Leiffer, "Mixed Marriages and the Children," *Christian Century* 66, no. 4 (1949): 106. His research findings were also summarized in *Time*. See "Interfaith Marriages," *Time*, January 31, 1949, 63.

21. Bernard J. Bamberger, "Plain Talk about Intermarriage," *Reconstructionist* 15, no. 16 (1949): 12.

22. James Pike, *If You Marry Outside Your Faith* (New York: Harper and Brothers, 1954).

23. Ardis Whitman, "Children of Interfaith Marriage," *Redbook*, June 1963, 112.

24. On religion in the cold war context, see Patrick Henry, "'And I Don't Care What It Is': The Tradition-History of a Civil Religion Proof-Text," *Journal of the American Academy of Religion* 49, no. 1 (1981): 35–49; Mark Silk, *Spiritual Politics: Religion and America since World War II* (New York: Simon and Schuster, 1988); and Stephen Whitfield, *The Culture of the Cold War* (Baltimore: Johns Hopkins University Press, 1991).

25. In the post–World War II era, social scientific studies of interracial marriage tended to focus on the psychological deficiencies of those people who married across the color line. See Renee Romano, *Race Mixing: Black-White Marriage in Postwar America* (Cambridge, Mass.: Harvard University Press, 2003), 53–58.

26. On Jews and whiteness, see, e.g., Karen Brodkin, *How Jews Became White Folks and What That Says about Race in America* (New Brunswick, N.J.: Rutgers University Press, 1998); and Matthew Frye Jacobson, *Whiteness of a Different Color: European Immigrants and the Alchemy of Race* (Cambridge, Mass.: Harvard Uni-

versity Press, 1998), chap. 5. For a recent study that draws on "whiteness" scholarship but offers a subtle reading of how Jews thought about race and whiteness, see Eric Goldstein, *The Price of Whiteness: Jews, Race, and American Identity* (Princeton, N.J.: Princeton University Press, 2006).

27. Eleanor Felder, "My Child: Jew or Christian?" *Commentary* 14, no. 3 (1952): 232.

28. Ibid.

29. Ibid.

30. Richard Goldhurst, "Growing Up between Two Worlds," *Commentary* 16, no. 1 (1953): 30–35.

31. On the gender imbalance in intermarriage, see Todd Endelman, ed., introduction to *Jewish Apostasy in the Modern World* (New York: Holmes and Meier, 1987), 1–19; and Susan Weidman Schneider, *Intermarriage: The Challenge of Living with Difference between Christians and Jews* (New York: Free Press, 1989), 6.

32. Jacob J. Weinstein, "The Jew and Mixed Marriage," *Reconstructionist* 7, no. 10 (1941): 5.

33. Bamberger, "Plain Talk about Intermarriage," 11.

34. See Marc Dollinger, *Quest for Inclusion: Jews and Liberalism in Modern America* (Princeton, N.J.: Princeton University Press, 2000).

35. Marshall Sklare, "Intermarriage and the Jewish Future," *Commentary* 37, no. 4 (1964): 52. For biographical information about Sklare, see Marshall Sklare, *Observing America's Jews* (Hanover, N.H.: University Press of New England / Brandeis University Press, 1993), chap. 1; and Jonathan D. Sarna, "Marshall Sklare (1921–1992)," *Proceedings of the American Academy of Jewish Research* 58 (1992): 33–35.

36. Peter Stearns, *Anxious Parents: A History of Modern Childrearing in America* (New York: New York University Press, 2003), chap. 3.

37. See Ann Hulbert, *Raising America: Experts, Parents, and a Century of Advice* (New York: Knopf, 2003), 202–3; and Stuart Svonkin, *Jews against Prejudice: American Jews and the Fight for Civil Liberties* (New York: Columbia University Press, 1997), 39–40. For a broader discussion about postwar interest in authoritarianism, see Glenn, "The Vogue of Jewish Self-Hatred."

38. Albert Gordon, "Intermarriage: A Personal View," *Jewish Spectator* 29, no. 9 (1964): 10.

39. Morton Sontheimer, "Would You Approve Your Child's Marrying a Protestant? A Catholic? A Jew?" *Woman's Home Companion*, March 1953, 31.

40. Albert Gordon, *Jews in Suburbia* (Boston: Beacon Press, 1959), 119.

41. Herbert Gans, "American Jewry: Present and Future," *Commentary* 21, no. 5 (1956): 427.

42. Allen Stephen Maller, "New Facts about Mixed Marriage," *Reconstructionist* 35 (March 1969): 29.

43. Monford Harris, "On Marrying Outside One's Existence," *Conservative Judaism* 20, no. 2 (Winter 1966): 61.

44. Ibid., 62–63.

45. Mordecai Kaplan, *Judaism as a Civilization: Toward a Reconstruction of American-Jewish Life* (New York: Schocken, 1934; Philadelphia: Jewish Publication Society, 1994), 182.

46. Erich Rosenthal, "Studies of Jewish Intermarriage in the United States," in *American Jewish Year Book* (Philadelphia: Jewish Publication Society of America, 1963), 3–53.

47. Thomas Morgan, "The Vanishing American Jew," *Look*, May 5, 1964, 42–43, 45–46.

48. William Abrams, "Intermarriage: Catastrophe or Challenge," *United Synagogue Review*, Spring 1973, 13.

49. Riv-Ellen Prell, "Summer Camp, Postwar American Jewish Youth, and the Redemption of Judaism," in *The Jewish Role in American Life: An Annual Review*, ed. Bruce Zuckerman and Jeremy Schoenberg (Los Angeles: University of Southern California Casden Institute, 2006), 79.

50. Prell mentioned these examples at a workshop in the summer of 2001.

51. Sociologist Erving Goffman theorized the idea of a "total institution." See his *Asylums: Essays on the Social Situation of Mental Patients and Other Inmates* (New York: Doubleday, 1961), chap. 1.

52. For an analysis of American Jews' travel to Israel, see Saul Kelner, "Almost Pilgrims: Authenticity, Identity, and the Extra-ordinary on a Jewish Tour of Israel" (Ph.D. diss., City University of New York, 2002).

53. Leonard Saxe, Ted Sasson, and Shahar Hecht, "Taglit-Birthright Israel: Impact on Jewish Identity, Peoplehood, and Connection to Israel" (report issued by the Maurice and Marilyn Cohen Center for Modern Jewish Studies, Brandeis University, Waltham, Mass., 2006), 8. The nonparticipants polled had all applied to the program but not taken the trip.

54. Barry Chazan and Leonard Saxe, *Ten Days of Birthright Israel: A Journey in Young Adult Identity* (Hanover, N.H.: University Press of New England / Brandeis University Press, 2008), 49.

55. For example, the Jewish Education Service of North America (JESNA) published a report in the summer of 2003 titled "Jewish Family Education" that outlined the various Jewish institutions that were starting to use this educational approach. For access to the report, see http://www.jesna.org/sosland/resources/Complementary-Education/Spotlight-Paper-3A-Jewish-Family-Education/details (accessed January 29, 2010).

6

Boundary Maintenance and Jewish Identity

Comparative and Historical Perspectives

CALVIN GOLDSCHEIDER

Who and what is "Jewish," and how do we know? The sociological way of knowing that I examine relies on two key social science concepts: community and stratification. Community can be defined by the connections among persons who share history and experience and the spatial boundaries within which people live, work, and interact. Stratification refers to the specific economic, educational, and status location of individuals within that geographically located community. In the twenty-first century the boundaries that make Jewish identity distinctive and mark Jewish communities off from others are porous. Since they are not fixed or rigid, individuals move in and out of the Jewish community. Moreover, the contemporary communal boundaries are more porous than they were in the late nineteenth and early twentieth centuries, when movement in and out was exceptional. The boundaries of contemporary Jewish communities are also diverse, and no universal set of characteristics can be found in all Jewish communities. Therefore the following interrelated questions about boundary maintenance cross-nationally and historically need to be addressed. First, what factors maintain the boundaries between Jews and others? Second, how have the boundaries changed over time, and how have the factors that sustain the boundaries shifted? And, third, what does the comparative and historical evidence show about the maintenance of these boundaries and the factors that sustain or maintain them?

Some of these questions can be answered by comparative-historical data about Jews and others available for a variety of countries around the world. Some of the answers may be derived from incomplete evidence and remain hypotheses to be tested. I submit that there is now considerable and reasonably reliable evidence to allow several relatively firm conclusions and to allow for generalization and theory construction. I focus on some of the critical themes that have emerged in the sociological study of Jewish communities. Most of what I present focuses on stratification as a key form of boundary maintenance and distinctiveness in the contemporary period. I also briefly touch on other forms of distinctiveness.

What is meant by the *boundaries* that are associated with the maintenance of Jewish communities and that shape Jewish identity? This should be made clear from the beginning. We are accustomed in social science to think of the reverse processes of "boundary dissolution"—the diminishing of the maintenance of boundaries, that is, assimilation into the larger community where religious or ethnic identity is no longer salient and where communities are no longer distinctive. But it is no less significant sociologically to explore those factors that *sustain* communities than to study those that result in their disintegration. Indeed, by asking the maintenance question, we are able to revisit and revise some past theoretical and empirical generalizations about ethnic and religious group changes.

I focus here primarily on stratification, and I refer to the standard indicators used to study the stratification of groups: education, occupation, income, and, by inference, social class (lifestyle and life chances). When examined over time and between groups, the focus becomes social mobility, inequality, and social class diversification. Associated with these indicators are the networks and institutions that characterize ethnic/religious groups (in this illustrative case, the Jews) and their communities. Hence the core question becomes, what is the relationship between these complex forms of stratification and the maintenance of community and the reinforcement of Jewish identity? While there is a considerable amount of information on many of the indicators of stratification, there are no systematic data on the quality of the educational experience, the relative importance of economic-kinship networks, or the interaction among religio-ethnic groups within schools or on the job or in neighborhoods and nothing on extended family networks. Data on income are generally weak and rarely extend beyond current income to measure wealth.[1]

It is certainly accepted wisdom in the social sciences that we need to make systematic comparisons in order to address analytic issues. It would be untenable to address these comparisons fully and systematically in one short presentation. I review findings on the largest Jewish community in the world (comparing Jews and non-Jews) over time in the United States and include some significant comparisons to immigrant Jewish communities of Canada. I have selected these communities because they are instructive about the diversity of relationships between stratification and boundary maintenance among Jews. They also point to some common processes of boundary maintenance that are shared cross-nationally.

Transformation

In the late nineteenth and early twentieth centuries, when Jewish immigrant communities in North America were relatively cohesive, religious/ethnic identity and stratification were closely connected. There was little social class diversity within Jewish communities (with a small proportion of wealthy Jews and a very large group of poor Jews) and very little ethnic/religious diversity among Jews, if one could separate the two at all (i.e., peoplehood, Jewishness, and religion were closely connected). There were of course some cultural differences between German and Eastern European Jewish immigrants, but most of these were a product of social class and length of exposure to American society. Over time national origin differences among American Jews diminished considerably. Between the late 1920s and the 1950s, the Jewish middle class expanded and social class diversity increased. With increased educational and occupational opportunities Jews in the United States worried that upward social mobility would erode the religious/ethnic cohesion in these communities. Societal openness meant that religious and ethnic identity became increasingly voluntary and separable. Empirically, the data available suggest that from the 1920s to the 1960s there was a clear connection: the higher the social class, the greater the probability of diminished commitment to Judaism and to Jewishness (and the reverse—the lower the social class, the greater the commitment to Judaism).[2] All of this applied in a context of options and opportunities. With some opportunity and choice (as in the modern democratic state) higher social class tended to result in disaffection from the ethnic and religious (i.e., the Jewish) community.

But this is not the end of the story. Money, education, and occupational opportunities over time resulted in the formation of new types of Judaic expressions and Jewish cultural options. These new forms of Jewishness, and of Jewish identity, increasingly have been disentangled from social class and from the indicators of social class. Thus it is no longer the case in twenty-first-century America that Jewish Orthodox religious practice is associated with the lower social classes or that Jewish cultural expressions are primarily religious. Identifying Jewishly in diverse ways has become the norm, as the entire stratification picture among American Jews has been transformed. In short, there are many factors that sustain or diminish Jewish identity and the boundaries of the Jewish community, but social class is no longer the culprit. Social class has become more a context than a determinant of boundary shifts.

Stratification and the Cohesion of the American Jewish Community

What happens to the community boundaries and to ethnic and religious identity among Jews in the United States as social mobility, high educational attainment, and professional occupational achievement have become master characteristics of the American Jewish population? Stratification has become one of the conspicuous forms of communal cohesion even as the boundaries of the Jewish community have become more porous. A review of the educational and occupational characteristics using evidence accumulated over the past century (national data sources—U.S. censuses and sample surveys on Jewish men and women and in comparison to other white, non-Hispanics) reveals that Jews in the United States have become the most educated group of all American ethnic and religious groups, of all Jewish communities around the world, and of all Jewish communities ever in recorded Jewish history.[3] This accomplishment is quite a feat, given the low level of education of the American Jewish community three to four generations ago. It reflects both the value that Jews place on education *and* access to the educational opportunities available in the

United States (through their own financial resources and through the availability of these opportunities). More than 90 percent of contemporary American Jewish young men and young women go on to college, and they are the children of mothers and fathers who also have studied in college—two generations of men and women who are college educated. Many also have grandparents who have some exposure to college education. Increases in the educational level of the American Jewish population have been documented in every study carried out over the past several decades, and the level attained is a distinguishing feature of American Jewish communities. It may be a core value of contemporary American Jewish culture.

These educational patterns have been translated into occupational changes in the United States. In the two generations to 1970, the Jewish occupational pyramid was upended: shifting from a majority of Jewish males in worker or service positions in 1910 to a majority (seven out of ten) in professional and manager positions by 1970; from almost three-fourths of Jewish females with jobs classified as worker or service categories in 1910 to half of the females in professional and managerial jobs by 1970. Between 1970 and 2000 there was a further increase in professional occupations among Jewish men and women along with a rather sharp decline (more than 50 percent) in managerial positions among Jewish men.[4]

These radical shifts over time in the occupational structure and in job classification have resulted in new forms of the Jewish occupational distinctiveness in the United States when compared to white, non-Hispanics in metropolitan areas. Particularly conspicuous is the greater concentration of Jews in professional jobs, paralleling their educational attainments, reinforced by residential and regional concentrations of Jews in the United States. While there was a strong residential concentration at the beginning of the twentieth century, there remains a reconcentration of Jews residentially through group migration. An inference from the occupational, educational, and residential concentration of Jews is the development of new and powerful networks of interaction among Jews. Just as stratification changes open up the opportunities for interaction between Jews and non-Jews, so it creates new forms of potential interaction among Jews. Hence, in part, social class network shifts are occurring that reinforce and sustain ethnic/

religious boundaries. Social class transformations parallel transformations in ethnic and religious identities.[5]

Therefore, there are two responses to the question of whether social class transformation is linked to "boundary maintenance" or assimilation among Jews in the United States. On the one hand, increases in educational attainment and the diversification of occupational types result in greater interaction with "others" who are not Jewish. These new contexts of interaction between Jews and non-Jews challenge the earlier segregation of Jews and in turn the cohesion of Jewish communities. On the other hand, the institutional contexts of schooling and the workplace may also expose Jewish Americans to new networks and alternative values that are not ethnically or religiously Jewish. In the present context that means an increase in porous boundaries, with many more leaving than entering, at least during some periods of the life course, particularly in young adulthood, before marriage and the presence of children in families.[6] The combination of interaction and exposure may erode the distinctiveness of the community over time through family changes and generational discontinuity. In this view, stratification is associated with new options for intergroup interaction patterns that in turn result in diminished community cohesion.

An alternative interpretation of this stratification picture posits that the emerging new social class commonality among Jews and the distinctiveness of Jews relative to others may themselves become important sources of cohesion of the Jewish community. Jews are both marked off from others and linked with other Jews by their resources, networks, and lifestyles and connected by family and kinship networks. These are the obvious implications of their occupational-educational distinctiveness and their high levels of attainment. To the extent that community is based on both shared interaction among members and a common set of values and lifestyles, these occupational and educational transformations among American Jews suggest significantly stronger bases of communal cohesion than in the mid-twentieth century, when there was greater educational and occupational heterogeneity generationally. The mobility of Jews away from the occupations and education characteristic of the immigrant generation has been a dominant theme in research. Missing has been an emphasis on the new forms of educational and occupational concentration that have emerged among the third and fourth generations and, by inference, the social networks and institutions that potentially sustain community in a voluntary and open society.

These two alternative outcomes of the educational and occupational transformations that Jews have experienced in twentieth-century America are often presented in oversimplified and extreme forms. Clearly, American Jews cannot be characterized either as a totally assimilated community (in the sense of the loss of communal cohesion) or as an isolated, totally cohesive community. Nevertheless, both perspectives capture part of the processes associated with the transformation of the stratification picture. In part, they address different segments of the community and capture the reality of different segments characterized by different forms of ethnic/religious identity. These interpretations should be viewed as complementary and not necessarily conflicting. And just as ethnic-immigrant assimilation has been described as "segmented,"[7] so I would apply this analytic description to the Jewish community as a whole in both senses: in the sense of group diversity (different segments of the Jewish community have become more assimilated, or in a positive sense they are characterized by greater continuity/cohesion) and in terms of the multiple dimensions/indicators of group continuity (Jews assimilate in some ways and not others).

There are more direct ways to assess the impact of stratification changes on the quality of Jewish life than by inference. National data on selected aspects of Jewish life can be linked to the educational and occupational patterns that I have outlined. A review of some analytic explorations along these lines is useful. Measures of Jewishness that tapped the multidimensional ethnic and religious expressions of Jews in 1990 and 2000–2001—including seasonal ritual observances (Passover and Hanukkah); traditional rituals (kashruth and Shabbat observances); organizational participation (Jewish educational and organizational activities); associational ties (Jewish friends and neighbors); philanthropy (contributions to Jewish charities); and intermarriage attitudes—were related statistically to the occupational and educational characteristics of households in multivariate models (but without data on social class networks or kinship networks). Not surprisingly, the results are complex. Several results are revealing.

First, many of the education and occupation measures are only weakly related to contemporary indicators of Jewishness. What this means is that Jewishness reflects the context of the family life course (e.g., age, family structure, and presence and ages of children) rather than simple measures of educational or occupational attainment. Second, the data reveal that for earlier age cohorts (growing up in the 1930s and 1950s), occupational mobility and educational attainment were linked to disaffection from the ethnic community (as measured by these contemporaneous indicators of ritual and religious behavior, friendship patterns, and Jewish organizational affiliation), and that is no longer the case. Although in the contemporary period measures of ethnic economic resources, ethnic networks, and ethnic business connections are not available to test these arguments fully, it may be that occupational ties have the potential to promote Jewish interaction and Jewish networks.

The situation is somewhat clearer for education. The evidence using several indicators of education shows that higher levels of education reinforce and strengthen Jewish expressions, particularly those tied to participation in Jewish communal activities, and are dependent on age and marital status. College education seems to promote Jewish-related activities for the younger age-groups (below age forty-five), although this is less the case among older cohorts. In this sense, the negative relationship between attending college and Jewishness in the early and middle decades of the twentieth century changed significantly by the end of the twentieth century. The Jewish alienation presumed to be associated with higher levels of educational attainment occurs when higher education is an exceptional group feature characteristic of the few. When exposure to college and university education is an almost universal experience, its negative impact on ethnic and religious identity becomes minimal or is reversed.[8] In short, there is no systematic evidence that the changed stratification profile of the American Jewish community results uniformly in the abandonment of the Jewish community in terms of the wide range of Jewish expressions. The same set of findings characterize the relationship between intermarriage and stratification—in the past there was a clear association between higher education and out-marriage; today that association is weak at best.[9]

The commonality of social class among American Jews and their very high levels of educational and occupational reconcentration are not likely to be sufficient to generate the intensive in-group interaction that characterized the segregated Jewish communities in some areas of Eastern Europe and the United States a century ago. The benefits of these stratification transformations in terms of networks and resources have not recreated the cultural and social communities of Jews of a different era. At the same time, and this is the critical point, the evidence indicates that the emerging social class patterns are not a threat to Jewish continuity in the transformed pluralism of American society. The educational and occupational transformations of twentieth-century America clearly mark Jews off from others and connect Jews to one another. The distinctiveness of the American Jewish community in these stratification patterns has become sharper.

When these stratification profiles are added to the residential concentration of American Jews, the community features become even more convincing. Many have noted the move away from areas of immigrant residential concentration, the residential dispersal of American Jews, and the reshaping of new forms of residential concentration for the second and later generations of American Jews.[10] But new forms of residential concentration have emerged. So the national data on residential concentration combined with educational and occupational concentration tell the story of new forms of community interaction, at least for significant segments of the community. The occupational concentration of Jews, attendance at selective schools and colleges away from home, and work in selected metropolitan areas have resulted in new, powerful forms of Jewish networks and institutions. The geographic concentration of American Jews is astonishing for a voluntary ethnic white group several generations removed from foreignness and not facing the discrimination characteristic of other American minorities. Jews continue to be regionally concentrated in the Northeast and less concentrated in the South or the Midwest when compared to the white non-Hispanic population. In addition there are significant state-level concentrations of Jews, disproportionate to their numbers in the population, and areas within metropolitan communities (neighborhoods) with significant Jewish concentrations.[11]

What might be most "Jewish" about Jews in the twenty-first century is their secular educational achievement. While secular education put Jews into close social contact with gentiles and was once seen as a threat to maintaining the boundaries of Jewish communal life, parents encouraged (and invested in) their children to obtain a high level of education in the United States.[12] Education has not disrupted Jewishness but transformed its meaning. The larger significance of two generations of college-educated Jews becomes not simply a source of group congratulations and pride but a set of generational characteristics. Far from disrupting family and ethnic cohesion, college education constitutes an increasingly shared common experience and a foundation for Jewish social networks. An analysis of educational attainment points to the increased power of families, the creation of increased resources, and the promotion of common lifestyles that, far from dividing families, create new bonds between college-educated parents and college-educated children.

Education has helped solidify social networks among Jews. By binding the generations, education has become a family value. And education and achievement, and an emphasis on family cohesion and values, have become group associations that have raised the status of the Jewish group in the eyes of non-Jews. Unlike in the past, when interaction and marriage between Jews and non-Jews were often mechanisms of escape from Jewishness and foreignness, today non-Jews who find Jewish educational achievements attractive may be inclined to seek out Jewish partners and may seek to convert to Judaism for the purposes of intermarriage. Hence, like education, intermarriage does not necessarily have the same meaning in the new context of generational relationships as it did in the older context of rejection and escape.

Clearly, these stratification changes may result in the disaffection of some individual Jews from the community and exposure to options for integration and assimilation into the non-Jewish mainstream. Even when most Jews are sharing similar educational experiences and are heavily concentrated in a select number of colleges and universities, secular higher education implies exposure to conditions and cultures that are more universalistic than and removed from ethnic-based education. On college campuses, as elsewhere, there are forces that pull Jews toward one another, sharing what is called community—families, experiences, history, concerns, values, communal institutions, religious commitments and rituals, and lifestyles—and forces that pull Jews away from one another in a dynamic often referred to as "assimilation." These alternatives suggest that the boundaries have become porous in both directions (entering and exiting), and the boundaries themselves have become fuzzier as they have widened. The new patterns of education and intermarriage may result in a greater incorporation within the Jewish community of some who were not born Jewish, increasing the general attractiveness of the community to Jews and to others.[13] Thus the factors that maintain porous boundaries in the end of the twentieth and the beginning of the twenty-first centuries are different than they were in the past.

Recent Immigrants in North America

Did these changing factors involved in boundary maintenance in the United States also characterize other historical periods and national contexts? It is likely that the issues discussed here are neither uniquely American nor particularly Jewish. Different contexts shape boundary maintenance among Jews, and these contexts change over time. Thus it is untenable sociologically to search for universal patterns of stratification among Jews or to use explanations of stratification that do not relate to the specific context of the lives of Jews in their communities.

As a way of demonstrating the diversity of stratification contexts, I briefly review some evidence about two groups of relatively recent Jewish immigrants to Canada and the United States, since the 1970s. The goal is to demonstrate the variety of paths different Jewish groups have taken in the stratification processes and the diversity of ethnic/ religious responses to those processes among Jews. Comparisons of Jews in the United States and Canada from Russia and from Middle Eastern countries reveal the diversity among Jews who have come from different places of origin, are characterized by different cultures and social contexts in these places, are immigrating to countries at somewhat different periods, and are entering two societies with different immigration policies, patterns, and cultures. Even the designations "Jew" from "Russia" and from the "Middle East" imply easily definable populations and places that, on reflection, are anything but simple. The results of these comparisons will demonstrate the role of diversity in ethnic distinctiveness, the role of institutions to reinforce distinctiveness, and the broader impact of immigrant transnationalism and networks characteristic of contemporary Jewish communities.

Briefly, my goal is to explore whether the processes associated with the multiple forms of stratification of these Jewish communities have a connection to the cohesion of their communities. What factors sustain the distinctiveness of these communities in the absence of overt discrimination and disadvantage? What structural and cultural contexts sustain continuity in the face of pressures toward disintegration of the uniqueness and distinctiveness of these communities? The short answer to these questions for Russian and Middle Eastern Jews both in the United States and Canada is communal institutions and social and family networks that are the core elements sustaining communal continuity and distinctiveness and maintaining boundaries between communities. Institutions construct new forms of Jewish cultural uniqueness that redefine the collective identity of Jewish culture and values that are anchored in the structural underpinnings of communities.

In making multiple comparisons I emphasize several themes: first, the role of the socioeconomic, cultural, and family background selectivity of immigrants and the role these factors play in creating the social-cultural baggage of the newcomers; second, the role of the phenomenon of immigration, particularly the contexts of moving in terms of refugee status and policies and the role of the state and Jewish institutions in facilitating immigration, settlement, and integration; and third, the role of social capital and networks in generating ethnic communities in the transition from immigrant status. These are not the only themes that could be explored, but they appear to me to be the most central theoretically and empirically.

Recent Jewish immigrants to Canada and the United States from Russia and the Middle East had very different demographic profiles. Russians came in much larger numbers and with a consequent larger impact and more conspicuous presence. They joined an already established community of Jews and, except in a few regions and communities, remain the primary immigrant-ethnic community within these Jewish communities. At the same time, both Russian and Middle Eastern immigrants are often secondary migrants, with Middle Eastern migrants coming from France and Israel and Russians coming from

Western Europe and increasingly from Israel. These secondary migrants have networks and communities that can characterize them as "transnational" migrants. These multiple networks reinforce the cohesion of these communities. And while Canada and the United States were historically the recipients of large numbers of immigrants from Russia and Eastern Europe at the turn of the twentieth century (and in the decades after World War II), relatively fewer Jewish migrants from the Middle East had come in the earlier period. There are also significant differences in the degrees of Jewish cultural cohesion among Russian and Middle Eastern Jewish immigrants. While the Russians had little or no connections to Jewish culture and religion, Moroccan, Iranian, and Syrian Jewish immigrants were raised in communities that had a rich Jewish culture. Although many of the migrants themselves have been exposed to secular economies and cultures, they had a very different exposure to Judaism and Jewish culture than the Russian migrants did in the contemporary period. Most of those from the Middle East had strong Jewish family and kinship networks that were also economic networks. By contrast, Russian Jews, in particular the most recent migrants, are more likely to have formed families with non-Jewish persons and use education as the key path to occupational mobility and integration. Hence, in North America, the connections of the Russian immigrants to the Jewish communities and to Judaism are unlike the connections of Jews from the Middle East.

Together these observations suggest that the stratification profiles of these two Jewish groups are significantly different from each other, and the connections to Jewish identity and boundary maintenance are likely to be different as well. Recent Jewish immigrants of Moroccan, Syrian, and Iranian origins have developed extensive networks and institutions in various communities in the United States and Canada; Moroccans are the largest of the immigrant Sephardic communities in Canada that have formed their own ethnic communities, with local institutions, rabbis, and communal assistance programs. For the Moroccans, many of the institutions are centered around religion, but more accurately on culture (including food, family/kinship rituals, and economic ties). As for other immigrants, the results of integration tend to be twofold and heterogeneous. On the one hand, there are those who abandon their ethnic origin, move to areas of residential integration, engage in occupations that are not part of the ethnic network, join no ethnic associations, and minimize their kin and extended family contacts and have weak cultural ties to Jewishness and Judaism. Some of these are "assimilated" and become simply "American" or "Canadian"; others join some other ethnic group through marriage or through some cultural melting (such as in the American Jewish community). Many of these changes occur generationally.

On the other hand, there are those who, in the process of integration, link to others of similar ethnic background and join kinship, social, and occupational networks and follow marriage patterns that connect to their ethnic origins. They, too, are integrated into American or Canadian society, but their integration has reinforced a sense of ethnic community and shared culture. Whether these networks and their associated institutions will characterize their children as they attain greater and newer forms of social and economic integration remains an open question.

Social, family, and economic networks have played a powerful role among Jewish Middle Eastern immigrants in both the United States and Canada. These Jews have redefined their communities along ethnic lines, developing their own schools, neighborhoods, and informal networks and economic enterprises, most powerfully in cities where they have been heavily concentrated, such as Montreal, Toronto, New York, and Los Angeles. For Moroccan and Iranian Jewish immigrants these networks and institutions assume cultural features for at least two generations. They have at the macro level diversified American and Canadian Jewish life and added important new cultural dimensions to communal institutions. The key is that economic networks, occupational and educational patterns, and strong kinship bonds reinforce ethnic communal distinctiveness.

Unlike the immigrants from the Middle East, the recent wave of Russian immigrants did not come to America and Canada from established Jewish communities. Their Jewishness was a burden, but an inescapable burden, in Russia. They came with the assistance of the organized formal Jewish community. These Jewish institutions were successful in making them not "Jewish Americans" or "Jewish Canadians" but Americans and Canadians of Russian origin. With improvements in English and with economic success, Russians became simply

American or Canadian. The second generation born in America or Canada went to public schools and developed, along with their parents, informal networks that were economic and social and somewhat cultural, and they remained marginally distinctive. They were immigrants in America but distinctive from the majority of non-Jewish immigrants in the United States and Canada, particularly from Asian and Latin American countries. Altogether, the experiences of these recent Jewish immigrants have developed similarly, in many ways, on both sides of the national border. However, there have been important differences in the different national contexts. I look now at what has been distinctive to the United States.

Approximately three hundred thousand Jewish immigrants and their household members from the former Soviet Union (FSU) were living in the United States according to the 2000-2001 National Jewish Population Survey (NJPS).[14] They appear to have very strong ethnic ties but weaker religious ties than the American Jewish population as a whole. This is not surprising given the background the immigrants brought with them from their country of origin and the higher secular but ethnic ties that were formed there. Along with ethnic residential concentration, FSU Jews are more connected to other Jews through marriage and friendships. Fully 91 percent are married to other Jews from the FSU (compared to 68 percent of non-FSU Jews who marry within their own ethnic group in the United States). Moreover, 71 percent report that half or more of their close friends are Jewish (compared to 51 percent among American Jews generally); and 47 percent date only other Jews (compared to 18 percent of American Jews generally). Data suggest that, compared to American Jews generally, Russians of Jewish origin have even more powerful networks since more of their friends are also of Russian origin.[15]

The real puzzle is how much these patterns are peculiar to the first generation foreign-born and what patterns will characterize the second and third generations. I suggest (not as a prediction but as a reasonable set of expectations) that the second generation of Russian Jews in America will be less likely to live in areas of Russian concentration, will be bilingual (having grown up in Russian-speaking households), will be well educated, and, unlike their parents, will use their educational attainment to more successfully respond to job opportunities. It is unlikely that the adult children of Russian immigrants will be anything but secular in their religious practice. I suspect that kinship networks, transnational ties, and some economic networks will reinforce ethnic distinctiveness. Further, I suspect that some of the exposure to Jewish institutions (schools, Jewish organizations, and, for a small minority, synagogues) will reinforce the ethnic component of the second generation. They are more likely than their parents to be integrated into the Jewish community and the general American community.

Based on evidence from other white ethnic groups in America, I would expect bifurcation or segmentation of the second generation. By this I mean that some will be assimilated ethnically and religiously into the American mainstream, especially among those whose parents are already interreligiously married and successful economically. A second group will be those who remain attached ethnically in terms of kinship, transnational ties, and perhaps economic networks. They will be ethnic Russians of Jewish origins. And a third group may be likely to merge with the American Jewish community, losing more of their ethnic origins and becoming secular American Jews. The relative proportions of these sections of the second generation are anyone's guess. In the longer run (i.e., by the third generation), I doubt whether ethnic ties will remain strong. Most will be Americans of Eastern European origins (merging the variety of ethnic groups within the category called "Russian"). Some will identify as American Jews and many will not. The role of transnational ties is considerably stronger among both Russian and Middle Eastern immigrants than among earlier Jewish immigrants, and the consequences for the second and later generations are difficult to assess.

I turn now to the case north of the border. Will similar patterns characterize Russian Jews in Canada? The answer is both yes and no. Many of the early Russian Jewish immigrants follow the general pattern of Russian immigration to the United States. After the collapse of the Soviet Union in 1991, an increasing flow of Soviet Jews entered Canada, part of a larger wave of immigration from the former Soviet Union to Western countries that was economically motivated. More than one million Jews migrated to Israel, the United States, and Canada. About one-half of the Jews from the former Soviet Union who entered Canada came in through Israel. Residential concentration in the Canadian mosaic of ethnic groups is the norm. This is likely different from many of the ethnic communities in the United States, including the Jews after three generations.

The two-step immigration, to Israel and then to Canada, contributes to the transnational nature of the Russian Jewish community as part of a diverse international diaspora. From the immigrants' perspective, they were a group of Jews looking to improve their material opportunities, part of a Canadian transnational Russian Jewish community with branches in the United States, Germany, and Israel. Compared to the last period of immigration, however, the proportion of those who came through Israel increased from 70 to 75 percent.

In some communities in Canada, for example, Montreal, many of the Jews of Russian origins came by way of Israel and tend to reside in Jewish neighborhoods. They have their own Jewish institutions, providing both religious and educational services, and special programs are available for Russian youth and older persons. The community has several Russian newspapers and a small Russian Jewish supplementary school, which operates on weekday afternoons and on Sundays. General institutions also offer students of Russian origins advanced courses in math and courses in Russian language, literature, and history.

A similar pattern characterizes Russian Jews in Toronto, where most live in Jewish neighborhoods and where Jewish organizations play a central role in coordinating services, including English as a second language (ESL) classes. Older immigrants tend to be more predisposed to ethnic and cultural retention. They are more likely to speak only Russian, and they have a lower potential for social, cultural, and professional integration. Russian language maintenance and ongoing interest in Russian-Soviet literature and culture characterize the Canadian Russian community. There are stores that carry Russian-language newspapers, magazines, and newsletters and also video stores that specialize in Russian-speaking movies. Local radio stations offer daily news and music broadcasts in Russian, and the multicultural television station offers weekly programs in Russian.

Complicating the picture is the fact that between one-quarter and one-third of the immigrants are partly Jewish or non-Jewish. After decades of atheist indoctrination in the Soviet Union, assimilation and intermarriage became very common among Soviet Jews. More than 90 percent of these Jews are completely secular, and their Jewish identity is defined as ethnic rather than religious. Non-Jews and assimilated Jews are not likely to develop or transmit a Jewish identity or to integrate into the synagogue-centered Jewish community. For the children of Russian Jewish immigrants, the rate of participation in the Jewish education system is relatively low. Religious Jewish education was found to be the most important variable predicting Jewish identity and community affiliation. Canadian Jews take pride in their relatively high rate of participation in Jewish education. A recent Toronto study documented that, despite an increasingly high rate of drop-off in early adolescence, 90 percent of all Jewish children in metropolitan Toronto have experienced some form of Jewish education, and 58 percent were enrolled, at the time of the study, in a Jewish school.[16] By comparison, only 40 percent of Russian Jewish children experienced some form of Jewish education, and this was usually for a shorter period of time. It is clear that Russians receive high levels of general education in Canada, and some at younger ages receive this education in Jewish contexts. But that occurs in the short run and does not guarantee that they will identify as "Russian Jews" in Canada rather than as Canadians of Russian origin. Their education is likely to distinguish them from others, but in ethnically divided Canada, they are likely to retain their national origin identity—likely, in other words, to describe themselves as "Russian" rather than "Jewish."[17]

The key to understanding the Russian Jewish ethnic community in Canada is to focus on its extensive networks of relatives and friends in Israel, the United States, Europe, and Russia. Cities outside Canada (e.g., Tel Aviv and Ashqelon, Los Angeles, New York, Boston, Berlin, and St. Petersburg) have become attractive tourist destinations and arenas for business. Many immigrants kept their citizenship in the post-Soviet republics. Some even kept their apartments there so they could return for extensive visits. With the emergence of new economic opportunities in the former Soviet Union, a number of Canadian Russian Jews have developed international businesses with affiliate companies in their home countries. Canadian research confirms the high rate of interethnic relationships and a high rate of insularity from non-Soviet Jews.[18] With recently increased possibilities for international exchange through the Internet and e-mail, as well as transnational travel, the idea of a former Soviet, worldwide Jewish community assumes practical dimensions.

As immigrants with a particular linguistic, national, and cultural heritage, Russians create their own ethnocultural enclaves in Canada. Russian Jewish communities in Canada are transnational communities, expressed in the economic and social-cultural domains. Russian Jews cherish their identity and their culture, considering it to be superior to what they view as the shallow North American culture. Moreover, many members of the Russian Jewish community, a high propor-tion of them elderly and unemployed, are discouraged from learning English and integrating into the local social dynamics and politics. Many immigrants from the former Soviet Union can be described as physically living in one country while mentally belonging to another.

The historical experience of the organized Canadian Jewish com-munity clearly demonstrates a trend in which immigrants establish themselves economically and only later take up positions in the orga-nized Jewish community. This was typical of the English and German Jews of the nineteenth century, the Russian Jews of the late nineteenth and early twentieth centuries, and the post–World War II immigrants from Europe and North Africa. Contemporary Jews from the former Soviet Union will probably follow a similar path. The question is not whether Russian immigrants will be involved in the Jewish commu-nity but rather how this involvement will be shaped. The research has found ample evidence of social and community cohesiveness and solidarity among Russians. It remains to be seen whether they will amalgamate into the existing organizations of the host community or whether they will create their own brand of Jewishness and Jewish community life.

Conclusions

What can one conclude about these recent Russian and Middle East immigrants in the United States and Canada? The immigrant groups are different in their historical backgrounds, settlement, transnationalism, the education of children, as well as in their Jewishness. Nevertheless, their Jewishness is a reflection of both secular and religious origins. It is social and cultural, not only "spiritual" and ideological. I suggest the following: Jewishness differs in Canada and the United States because the nature of these larger communities differs, especially in that ethnicity is stronger in Canada, whereas ethnic origin (at least among white ethnics) fades over time in the United States. Furthermore, language remains an important marker in Canada; in this case, Russian and French are the predominant languages of the new immigrants, rather than the Yiddish that characterized earlier generations of Russian Jews. One should keep in mind, too, that the new migrants are forming new communities that are transnational—some with residential segregation, institutions, and organization that are ethnically based—and that they rely on powerful kinship and economic networks. Finally, the profiles of stratification and social mobility among the Jewish communities of Russian and Middle Eastern origin are quite different for many of the reasons that I have already suggested. Some of the processes of change they undergo are similar, albeit beginning from different starting points. But the paths to economic integration are quite different. For the Russians, the path is largely through secular education. For those of Middle Eastern origins, it is through family and economic networks. Clearly and most obviously one cannot examine the stratification and assimilation processes or boundary maintenance as a uniform process among Jews in contemporary communities. There is diversity in the processes and in the outcome. Any theory of stratification applied to the Jewish community and the identity of Jews must begin with this diversity in origins, in processes, and in outcomes.

What will characterize the next generation as new forms of Jewishness emerge, new connections to places of origin emerge, and new cultural and social ties are formed and reinforced by networks and institutions? This is the primary question that remains. As new international ties emerge, new conflicts arise, and other minorities compete, new forms of ethnic and religious identity (both redefined in new contexts) will likely emerge. Just as my generation's grandparents could not have envisioned what the lives of their grandchildren would become, we should take that powerful lesson and refrain from assuming that we know what will be the forms of integration of the next generation. One thing is clear from this brief review: the contours of the next generation of Russian and Middle Eastern immigrants in the United States and Canada are unlikely to be anything that we can imagine. The contours of the American Jewish community and its connection to stratification may be altered as well. How the boundaries between Jews and others (and among Jews by ethnic origins) will be maintained requires further study that we have yet to design and investigate.

Notes

1. See Carmel Chiswick, The Economics of American Judaism (New York: Taylor and Francis, 2008).

2. See, among others, Sidney Goldstein and Calvin Goldscheider, Jewish Americans: Three Generations in a Jewish Community (Englewood Cliffs, N.J.: Prentice-Hall, 1968); Nathan Glazer, American Judaism (Chicago: University of Chicago Press, 1957); and Calvin Goldscheider, Jewish Continuity and Change: Emerging Patterns in America (Bloomington: Indiana University Press, 1986).

3. The details of this pattern are presented elsewhere, particularly in Calvin Goldscheider, Studying the Jewish Future (Seattle: University of Washington Press, 2004). Others have documented these patterns of Jewish stratification. See Harriet Hartman and Moshe Hartman, Gender and American Jews: Patterns in Work, Education, and Family in Contemporary Life (Waltham, Mass.: Brandeis University Press, 2009); and Moshe Hartman and Harriet Hartman, Gender Equality and American Jews (Albany: State University of New York Press, 1996). See also Paul Burstein, "Jewish Educational and Economic Success in the United States: A Search for Explanations," Sociological Perspectives 50, no. 2 (2007): 209–28.

4. See Goldscheider, Studying the Jewish Future, chap. 6.

5. This corresponds to sociologist Milton Gordon's notion of "eth-class" as the conjunction between social class and ethnicity. See Gordon, Assimilation in American Life: The Role of Race, Religion, and National Origins (New York: Oxford University Press, 1964).

6. For an analysis, see Frances Goldscheider and Calvin Goldscheider, Leaving Home before Marriage: Ethnicity, Families, and Generational Relations (Madison: University of Wisconsin Press, 1993).

7. On segmented assimilation, see Rubén Rumbaut and Alejandro Portes, Ethnicities: Children of Immigrants in America (Berkeley: University of California Press, 2001), chap. 10.

8. See, e.g., Esther Wilder, "Socioeconomic Attainment and Expressions of Jewish Identification: 1970 and 1990," Journal for the Scientific Study of Religion 35, no. 2 (1996): 109–27. For similar patterns, see Hartman and Hartman, Gender Equality; using the 2000–2001 National Jewish Population Survey, see Hartman and Hartman, Gender and American Jews.

9. See Calvin Goldscheider, "Are American Jews Vanishing, Again?" *Context* 2, no. 1 (2003): 18–24; Goldscheider, *Studying the Jewish Future*, chap. 2.

10. Sidney Goldstein and Alice Goldstein, *Jews on the Move: Implications for Jewish Identity* (Albany: State University of New York Press, 1996).

11. These have been systematically documented in the *American Jewish Year Books* over many decades. See also Goldstein and Goldstein, *Jews on the Move*, chap. 2.

12. On the earlier period, see Susan A. Glenn, *Daughters of the Shtetl: Life and Labor in the Immigrant Generation* (Ithaca, N.Y.: Cornell University Press, 1990).

13. Externals also play a role in shaping the identity of Jews and the changing boundaries of the community. The presence of other minorities (Asians and Muslims, for example, as well as religious fundamentalists among Protestants) who compete in the marketplace (broadly defined) with Jews often serves as a basis for group cohesion. One can treat this in the context of globalization and the impact of events external to the United States on group cohesion. For Jews, this reflects the impact of Israel. It can also be seen in the growing legitimacy of diverse ethnic and religious groups within a multicultural North America. See Calvin Goldscheider, *Israel's Changing Society: Population, Ethnicity, and Development*, 2nd rev. ed. (Boulder, Colo.: Westview Press, 2002), chap. 12.

14. See the NJPS home page, at www.jewishfederations.org/content display.-html?ArticleID=60346.

15. The materials on Canada were derived from Rina Cohen, "The New Immigrants: A Comparative Profile," in *From Immigration to Integration: The Canadian Jewish Experience; A Millennium Edition*, ed. Ruth Klein and Frank Dimant (Toronto: B'nai Brith and Malcolm Lester, 2001), 213–27; Morton Weinfeld, *Like Everyone Else . . . but Different: The Paradoxical Success of Canadian Jews* (Toronto: McClelland and Stewart, 2001); Robert Brym, William Shaffir, and Morton Weinfeld, eds., *The Jews in Canada* (Toronto: Oxford University Press, 1993); and Charles Shahar and Howard Magonet, *Immigration and Language*, pt. 5 of *2001 Census Analysis: The Jewish Community of Montreal* (Toronto: United Israel Appeal Federations Canada, May 2005).

16. Weinfeld, *Like Everyone Else . . . but Different*, chap. 8.

17. Ibid.

18. Roberta Markus and Donald Schwartz, "Soviet Jewish Émigrés in Toronto: Ethnic Self-Identity and Issues of Integration," in Brym, Shaffir, and Weinfeld, *The Jews in Canada*, 402–20.

7

Good Bad Jews

Converts, Conversion, and Boundary Redrawing in Modern Russian Jewry, Notes toward a New Category

SHULAMIT S. MAGNUS

> It is of no use to Your Majesty to pour holy water on the Jews and call them Peter or Paul . . . Know, Sire, that Judaism is one of the incurable diseases.
>
> —Solomon ibn Verga, *Shevet Yehuda*, Spain / Italy, 16th century

One of the more interesting questions about a group's behavior is its boundary drawing: how, when, and why a group literally defines itself, by marking who is in and who is out. What criteria are used to designate insiders and outsiders, and who decides? Who enforces lines that are drawn, with what measures and authority? What role do self-conscious elites, articulate leaders in processes of boundary drawing—in the Jewish case, rabbinic and communal authorities—play, and what role is played by social forces and popular consensus, expressed in folk tales, the press? When are lines drawn—when and why do groups feel the need to do this? And when are lines redrawn, why, and by whom? Such questions are particularly germane in the study of Jewish society since, until the creation of the State of Israel, Jews were everywhere a minority, lacking linguistic uniformity, a state, or even geographic contiguity, yet despite and indeed because of this, with a pronounced sense of self and other. While defining "Jew" was not solely a behavior of Jews—it was very much also an activity of non-Jews, of Christian and Muslim authorities, and of Jew-haters—clearly, Jews have actively engaged in boundary drawing and maintenance.

Contrary to popular assumption, Jewish lines have been debated, contested, and shifted many times over in Jewish history since the articulation of the matrilineal principle in rabbinic law after 70 CE.[1]

This essay examines one case of Jewish boundary-line redrawing: the creation in late nineteenth- and early twentieth-century Russia of a category of people I call "good bad Jews": Jews who converted to Christianity opportunistically or for personal reasons and who used their positions as both former Jews and current members of the majority religion to help Jews and Judaism in situations of extreme duress. My focus here is not the motivations, voices, and experience of such converts, though such an inquiry is much needed.[2] Rather, it is the response of Jews and of Jewish society to this type of convert. For not only were these converts not deemed treasonous or malevolent; they were considered good and even heroic and saintly, a determination made by popular opinion, but also enjoying Jewish organizational and even Orthodox rabbinic sanction. Such attitudes, even for a few, exceptional cases, constitute an effective revision of the definition of "Jew," and of "good Jew," whatever the formal status of converts was under halakha or in established custom that carried over to modern times to punish conversion, even as boundary lines were being redrawn to accommodate good bad Jews. This essay is but an opening inquiry to a subject whose dimensions and significance can be assessed only with much further research in the periodical literature, memoirs, and archival records of individuals and institutions of Russian Jewry in this period. But I hope that it points to a phenomenon worthy of study.

To appreciate the departure that a phenomenon of good bad Jews represents, it is important to note the traditional Jewish stance toward converts in law and social attitudes. As is known, some of the worst oppressors of Jews were apostates who turned vehemently on their former coreligionists, the corporate representation of the Jewish self they sought to eradicate. Among the better known such converts in the medieval world are Nicholas Donin, Paolo Christiani, and Geronimo de Santa Fe, who alleged anti-Christian teachings in the Talmud and instigated church and state persecutions of Judaism, in the form of forced theological disputations and sermons, discriminatory clothing, and mass burnings of the Talmud.[3] There was a long half-life to medieval apostate anti-Jewish incitement; Martin Luther used the writings of such converts in his sixteenth-century tirades against Jews and Judaism.[4] But this sort of convert was a modern type as well. In sixteenth-century Italy, anti-Jewish works by apostates provided the basis for church condemnation of the Talmud and other rabbinic works, thousands of copies of which were seized and burned in 1553. Such accusations led to church censorship of Jewish books and the decline of Jewish printing in Italy, where it had previously flourished. As Robert Bonfil states, "The history of polemical diatribe against the Jews and the censure of Jewish books in Italy is studded with the names of neophytes, who, once baptized, dedicated their . . . Jewish learning to the cause of Christianity."[5]

An extreme expression of apostate persecution of Jews and Judaism is the case of the Frankists, followers of the Sabbatian pseudo-messiah Jacob Frank in eighteenth-century Poland, several thousand of whom converted. The Frankists several times instigated forced disputations between church authorities and Jews, in the aftermath of which, in 1757, cartloads of Talmud folios were burned. Frank and his devotees offered the church verification of the blood libel at a time when several such accusations had been leveled. In the second of the disputations the Frankists provoked, the Jews were forced to debate the blood libel, giving credence, even in denial, to the very possibility of such a ritual. Significantly, the Frankists offered as proof of the libel statements of earlier apostates to Christianity.[6]

As is known, there is no halakhic way to undo Jewishness, to unbecome a Jew. Conversion out has no status, no efficacy, in Judaism. Jews who convert of their own volition are very bad Jews, but they remain Jews under rabbinic law, going back to the Babylonian Talmud's discussion (Sanhedrin 44a) of a biblical case of transgression from which came the foundational dictum, *yisrael af al pi she'hata yisrael hu:* "a Jew, though he has sinned, remains a Jew."[7] To Jews, converts were "heretics": the Hebrew account of Donin's persecution of French Jewry states, "Since he joined himself to the Gentiles, he was called Nicholas the heretic"—the very use of which term confirms Donin's continued status as a Jew (Christians were not heretics, just Christians).[8] Donin and others like him, obviously, were terribly bad Jews, but they were Jews, whatever they considered themselves or the church considered them. Indeed, the very ineradicability of Jewishness in Jewish eyes, which of course these converts knew very well, may well have been a potent source of their rabid, if Sisyphean, persecution of it. As the quotation that opens this essay might indicate, Jews may well have taunted converts precisely with assertions of the futility of their act.

Apostasy, of course, was a theological betrayal of Judaism and, regarding Christianity, considered not just an abandonment of true for false belief but an embrace of idolatry, a separate and egregious offense, worse for being public by definition.[9] But conversion was also a sociological and psychological crime against the persecuted Jewish group, a treasonous going over to the camp of the oppressor. The terms *mumar* and *meshumad / meshumed*, for "apostate," conveyed utter opprobrium, contempt, and revulsion in Hebrew and Yiddish. Converts were considered deceased, for whom families were to observe all the mourning rites save burial itself, completely and irrevocably cutting off contact with them. As Elisheva Carlebach notes, "Medieval Jews erected mighty cultural barriers to conversion," setting martyrdom, passive or self-inflicted, as the preferred alternative to it, seeing conversion even under duress as a terrible failure.[10] Writing of medieval apostates, Jeremy Cohen notes their marginality in both their erstwhile and new communities, "spurned by their former coreligionists," while unable to integrate into the Christian laity, an isolation ("bitter loneliness") that Carlebach notes about early modern converts as well.[11] Anathematization was to serve as a deterrent, lest the manifold benefits of conversion—immediate exemption from anti-Jewish discrimination and possible additional financial and occupational rewards—tempt Jews over the line.

While the degree of such shunning declined as incidents of conversion increased in modernity, it is known to have continued not only among the rigorously observant but among acculturated and secular Jews as well. Thus the parents of Joseph von Arnsteiner, purveyors to the Austrian court, "drove him from their house," disinherited him, and refused to see him or his child or even respond to his letters after his conversion in 1778.[12] A "scrupulously observant" uncle of Martha Bernays, Sigmund Freud's wife, sat shiva for a brother who had converted to attain a professorship.[13] Some in the moderately observant family of the convert Edith Stein shunned even intermarried members.[14] A Jewish soldier in the tsarist army in the second half of the nineteenth century, who was a member of a Jewish guildlike group formed to support and enforce observance of rabbinic law, had his name excised from the group's minute book for being baptized or otherwise behaving "non-Jewishly."[15]

But such behavior was by no means confined to religious circles. Late nineteenth-century Russian Jewish cultural nationalists—intellectuals educated in Russian schools and universities but dedicated to the creation and perpetuation of a modernized, secular Jewish culture—held very negative attitudes about and were extremely critical of the "many converts among them, perhaps even more so than . . . the Orthodox," according to Yehuda Slutsky.[16] Such attitudes were pronounced in the Russian-language Jewish periodical *Voskhod*, which advocated a dual stance of acculturation and loyalty to Russia, along with continued Jewish cultural distinctiveness. They were also expressed in some circles of Russian Jewry's communal organization, the Society for the Promotion of Enlightenment among the Jews of Russia, known by its Russian acronym, OPE. The mass-membership self-defense organization of German Jews, the Central Association of German Citizens of the Jewish Faith (Centralverein deutscher Staatsbürger jüdischen Glaubens), led overwhelmingly by secular Jews affiliated, if at all, with Reform synagogues, mounted a vehement campaign against apostasy as "the most abhorrent form of cowardice," denouncing converts in terms Ismar Schorsch likens to their medieval precedents, as "renegades who sacrifice . . . honor and conviction to win recognition."[17] For secular Jewish nationalists, apostasy was the ultimate betrayal, beneath contempt, some Zionists pathologizing conversion as a "primary symptom of . . . mental instability" and converts as "manifestly diseased," bearing the sign of a "baptismal hydrocephaly."[18]

This historical background of traditional—and quintessentially modern—Jewish revulsion for converts is what makes the emergence of a discourse and markedly changed behavior toward good converts in Russia in the second half of the nineteenth and the early twentieth centuries so striking. While the emergence of changed attitudes to certain converts, who were not written out of Jewish public consciousness but were claimed with ambivalent pride (Heinrich Heine comes most readily to mind), marked Jewish modernity elsewhere, the Russian cases were more sharply etched for coming against the more extreme tsarist context and for utterly lacking ambivalence.[19] Alan T. Levenson notes two cases of "apostate[s] as philosemite[s]" in Germany, Selig Cassel and Edith Stein, but theirs were different from the ones I examine in several ways.[20] Unlike the good bad Jews of this essay, Cassel and Stein were sincere, religious converts. Both attempted to convert other Jews, with some success. Levenson tells us that Cassel did not "dwell on his Jewish roots," but the good bad Jews of this essay earned the "goodness" of their attribution precisely by public, non-Jewish, awareness of their Jewish origins and the fact that they continued Jewish associations, in friendships and even organizational memberships, and in formal ties in extremely public situations—sensational trials of Jews accused of ritual murder—all of which means, of course, that other Jews maintained these ties to them, in private and public. The good bad Jews of this essay are thus also distinguished from missionizing converts in nineteenth-century England who, Todd Endelman notes, defended Judaism or Jewish rights but were disconnected from the Jewish community.[21] There were some medieval converts who, like the modern ones Levenson and Endelman describe, defended Jewish customs against Christian distortions, some even rebutting the blood libel.[22] But again, what makes the cases considered here significant is the Jewish *response* to the converts in question, with Jews portraying and treating them as *ohavei yisroel*, "lovers of Jews."

I was first drawn to the question of nineteenth-century Russian Jewish converts from my work on Pauline Wengeroff, two of whose children, she relates in her *Memoirs*, converted when faced with anti-Jewish educational quotas (in fact, a third, whom Wengeroff omits from the *Memoirs*, also converted, and not opportunistically).[23] Several substantial works about apostates were produced during Wengeroff's lifetime by two prominent Russian Jewish writers: Shmuel Leib Zitron, and Shaul Ginzburg. Zitron wrote a four-volume, Yiddish-language work titled *Avek fun folk, tipn un silueten funm noyenten ovor* (Gone from the People, Types and Silhouettes from the Recent Past), published by the Ahiasaf house in Warsaw in 1920. He later produced a second, Hebrew-language work on this subject, titled *Me'ahorei hapargod: Mumarim, bogdim, mitkhahshim* (From behind the Screen: Converts, Traitors, Deniers), published in Vilna in 1925. Ginzburg wrote a Yiddish-language work titled *Meshumodim in tsarishn rusland* (Apostates in Tsarist

Russia) as the second volume of his *Historishe verk* (Historical Work), the first volume of which focuses on the Jews of St. Petersburg. The book about converts is more than three hundred pages long and carries the same subtitle as its partner: *Farshungen un zichroynes vegn yidishn lebn in amolikn rusland* (Researches and Memoirs of Jewish Life in Russia of Former Times), thus including converts explicitly in a study of Jewish history. It was published posthumously in New York in 1946 (Ginzburg died in 1940; he wrote the book in the 1930s).

Both Zitron's *Avek fun folk* and Ginzburg's *Meshumodim* are heavily anecdotal, contain few notes, and have no indexes or bibliographies, though of the two, Ginzburg's is far more scholarly: it contains far more references, expressed in the text and in occasional notes; it makes occasional, general citations of archival sources, some of which Ginzburg possessed (a handwritten Hebrew letter by Daniel Khvolson is reproduced in the volume), and it cites occasional names of informants or written sources. Both authors cite or seem to rely on contemporaries with direct knowledge of the people and events they describe, whom they, the authors, knew. Sometimes, the authors themselves had direct knowledge of the converts they describe—an invaluable perspective when the focus is contemporaneous Jewish perceptions and attitudes. Both works are extremely rich precisely for their lack of detachment from their subjects and audience.

Clearly, for two such substantial works to be written and published, there had to have been significant Jewish interest in apostasy in Russia in the first decades of the nineteenth century, and there is much to indicate that this was the case: the serialization over several months in 1909 in the Warsaw Yiddish-language newspaper, *Di neye velt*, of a "new, large, original novel of M. Spektor," titled *Di meshumedet'te* (The [Woman] Convert); the publication of Jacob Lestchinsky's article, "Ha-shemad be-aratsot shonot" (Apostasy in Various Lands), in *Ha-olam* (vol. 5, no. 10 [1911]); and A. N. Frenk's *Meshumodim in poyln* (Apostates in Poland; Warsaw, 1923), a reflection of interest in the "unusually high [incidence of conversion] for eastern Europe" that Raphael Mahler notes about Poland in the nineteenth century.[24]

Of particular note is Ahiasaf's publication of Zitron's work. This Hebraist-Zionist publishing house, founded in 1893 at the initiative of Ahad Ha'am and other leaders of the Hibbat Zion movement, was one of the most venerable in Eastern Europe, publishing in its thirty years of existence many works by prominent nationalistic authors—Simon Bernfeld, Ahad Ha'am, Hayim Nahman Bialik, and Sha'ul Tchernichowsky. It was a major institution of cultural Zionism.[25]

What is one to make of this robust interest in apostates among the Yiddish and Hebrew reading public of this period? Zitron gives a short introductory section in the first volume of his Yiddish work, which does not address this question. Ginzburg's work lacks any introduction, so there is nothing from either author about their motivations and intended audiences. But the lack of such statements would itself indicate that the interest this subject held for its intended public was considered self-evident, requiring no explanation or justification. The chapters in these works are neither overtly didactic nor hand-wringing communal assessments of what had gone wrong in Jewish society. They are biographical sketches, describing their subjects, sometimes with unveiled antipathy that readers are clearly assumed to share, sometimes with astonishing sympathy and pride that readers are clearly also expected to share.

The total number of conversions in Russia in the nineteenth century, to Russian Orthodoxy, Catholicism, or Lutheranism, was surely a large part of the Jewish public's interest in this subject. Historians estimate the number to have been a stunning 84,500, or 41 percent of all Jewish converts in Europe—albeit, from the world's largest Jewish population, which numbered around 5.8 million in 1880.[26] In his memoirs, Vladimir Medem, one of the leaders of the Jewish socialist movement in Russia and Poland, the Bund, speaks of his parents' generation (born in the 1830s and 1840s) as "engulfed by a veritable epidemic of conversions."[27] One of Ginzburg's chapters is titled, "A Gallery of Converts in Petersburg."

Medem's memoirs, and those of other Jews of this era including Wengeroff, testify that many converts and their Jewish families and wider Jewish circles maintained contact. In Medem's case, it was clearly these very ties, violating halakha and custom, that maintained the awareness of Jewishness that led to his ultimate "return." That ties continued is not surprising given the increased incidence, and the variety of type, of conversion, with most occurring to facilitate opportunity rather than from religious conviction.

Still, conversion continued to shock and scandalize. Wengeroff, who first published in 1908, insistently contextualizes her sons' conversions in the wave of apostasy that followed the imposition of anti-Jewish educational quotas in the 1880s. Yet she characterizes them as the greatest tragedy of her life and devotes considerable space in a narrative that omits much of basic importance to explaining and rationalizing them. Indeed, this very historicization of her sons' behavior testifies to a heavy sense of shame and personal failure she felt at their conversions. Her husband, whom Wengeroff depicts as recklessly abandoning Jewish tradition in favor of material success and acceptance by other modernizing Jews, scolded the first of their sons to convert for having deserted the camp of the besieged.[28] Similarly, the conversion of Lev Kupernik was a "forceful blow" to his father (discussed below), who Ginzburg says suffered over it "for years."[29] Russian Jewish opinion was clearly in flux on the issue of conversion but, even in its most acculturated and assimilated circles, far from jaded about it.

Zitron does not categorize the apostates he writes about. Ginzburg does, creating sections on converts of earlier periods: "Informers and Missionaries," "Careerists," and those he describes in "Between Two Worlds." The oppressor-apostate continued in this period and figures in both men's accounts. Thus Zitron has a chapter about Aharon Yisroel Braiman, who authored a tract supporting the blood libel and was a Hebrew tutor to a Jew-hating priest who taught at the German University of Prague and promoted the libel. Zitron and Ginzburg have chapters on the notorious Jacob Brafman, who served the tsarist government as a censor of Hebrew and Yiddish books, attacked the Jewish communal organization (*kahal*) in Russian periodicals, and described the OPE as a "state within a state," a particularly potent Judeophobic charge.[30] In his best-known work, *The Book of the Kahal* (which one Odessa Jewish intellectual, Menasheh Morgulis, called "the Bible of Russian Judeophobia"), Brafman argued that Jewish communal organization undermined loyalty to the state.[31] Ginzburg and Zitron devote chapters to other apostates who caused grief through missionary efforts or anti-Jewish activity—Asher Temkin, Josef Rabinovitch, and Jacob Priluker—and give details about other oppressor-apostates in other chapters.[32] Indeed, Zitron's introductory remarks to his first Yiddish volume open, without explanatory comment, on the oppressor-apostate, stating that some of the worst oppressors of Jews came from their ranks, which implies his sense that the existence of bad-bad Jews was a prominent question in his readers' minds.[33]

Not surprisingly, I have found in these works only a few converts who qualify as good bad Jews; one would not expect minions of such people. But the focus here is not this type of convert per se but *Jewish perception that some meshumodim were good*, precisely when the vast majority of converts abandoned Judaism for personal gain, and some did vicious harm. To appreciate the significance of Zitron's and Ginzburg's depictions, it is important to know something about these men.

Shmuel Leib Zitron (1860–1930) was a prolific Hebrew and Yiddish writer of journalistic essays and stories, educated in Lithuanian yeshivas, including its premier academy, Volozhin. He joined Hibbat Zion in its early days, writing Zionist pieces, and, for decades, lecturing and writing on Zionist themes. He translated Leo Pinsker's *Autoemancipation* into Hebrew and was a friend and associate of Peretz Smolenskin. Zitron also translated works of the emerging Yiddish literature into Hebrew. He published serialized and monograph histories of both the Hebrew and the Yiddish presses. Zitron, then, was particularly attuned to the Jewish reading public.[34]

Shaul Ginzburg, born in 1866, was a distinguished author and historian of Russian Jewry. Like Zitron, he came from Minsk and was active in Hovevei Zion. Ginzburg wrote for Russian- as well as Yiddish-language Jewish periodicals; he founded and edited the first Yiddish daily in Russia, *Der fraynd*, which was noted for its high literary standards and played an important role in the development of Yiddish journalism. Ginzburg served for decades in the OPE, as secretary and as a member of various commissions for special projects; in the 1890s he was among a group of young nationalists in the organization, a continuation of a tendency begun in his student days at the University of St. Petersburg, where he drew police attention for involvement in a society of Jewish students. His populist leanings led him to Yiddishism (rather than to the support of Hebrew, for example, as the language of instruction in Jewish schools), Yiddish, of course, being the language of the Jewish masses. Ginzburg became devoted to documenting Russian Jewish cultural history, a focus that led to his pioneering, landmark collection *Jewish Folk Songs in Russia*, coproduced

with Pesach Marek, his associate in the OPE. Ginzburg cofounded the
Jewish Literary and Scientific Society, continuing his work even after
the Bolshevik Revolution made such work dangerous. Fearing arrest,
Ginzburg fled Russia in 1929.[35]

Both Zitron and Ginzburg, then, were active cultural nationalists,
as well as journalists closely attuned to the Jewish street, which makes
their focus on converts, and their positive remarks about "good" ones,
all the more interesting.

The best known of the good bad Jews they depict is Daniel
Khvolson, the distinguished orientalist noted in all reference works
on Russian Jewry: Lucy Dawidowicz's classic collection of translated
primary sources, The Golden Tradition (1966); the Encyclopaedia Judaica; The
YIVO Encyclopedia of Jews in Eastern Europe; as well as Zitron's and Ginzburg's
works. Wengeroff, too, mentions him, though not by name. Born in
1819 to impoverished parents in Vilna, Khvolson was a Solomon
Maimon–like figure: an iluy (child prodigy), and rabbinical matmid
(prodigious student), married against his will, desperate for European
learning (unlike Maimon, divorcing his wife before departing for
Germany in his search for enlightenment). Like Maimon, Khvolson
taught himself the Latin alphabet from store signs and the rudiments
of German, Russian, and French, from dictionaries. He fled on foot
to Riga, then to Breslau, Germany, where he was befriended by Max
Lilienthal (appointed by the government under Nicholas I to reform
Russian Jewish education) and especially by the German Jewish religious reformer Abraham Geiger, who helped guide his education in
classical and modern European languages and in navigating German
university education in Semitic languages, through to completion
of his doctorate. In 1850 or 1851, Khvolson returned to St. Petersburg, where the minister of public enlightenment offered him the
chair in Hebrew, Syriac, and Chaldaic philology in the newly established department of Oriental Studies at the university, on condition,
according to all accounts I have seen but Zitron's, that he convert (no
Jew could occupy a professorship), which Khvolson did in 1855, for
this purpose. Three years later, he was appointed to a similar position at the Russian Orthodox and Catholic theological academies in
that city, something clearly unimaginable for an unconverted Jew. In
these capacities, Khvolson taught virtually every scholar of Semitics

in Russia in the second half of the nineteenth and the early twentieth centuries, Jew and Christian alike.

Probably the best-known "fact" about Khvolson is his reputed response when asked if he had converted out of conviction, to which Khvolson was said to have replied, "Yes, I was convinced it was better to be a professor in St. Petersburg than a *melamed* [a teacher of young children] in Eyshishok [a tiny suburb of Vilna]." This bon mot is produced in every treatment of Khvolson I have seen—except Zitron's and Ginzburg's.[36] According to Zitron, Khvolson resolutely refused to discuss his conversion, even when asked. Zitron also offers a very different version of how Khvolson's conversion came about, one that is consistent with his extremely sympathetic overall treatment of him. According to Zitron, Khvolson came to the attention of Nicholas I after having been appointed—while still a Jew—to teach Oriental languages at the University of St. Petersburg—made possible because the minister of enlightenment, A. S. Norov, was both deeply impressed by Khvolson's erudition and singular expertise and very fond of him. Nicholas summoned Khvolson to an audience, a prospect that terrified Khvolson, who was well aware of the tsar's reputation for depraved cruelty, Zitron says. The first thing the tsar asked him was, "Ours?"—meaning, "Christian?"—which Khvolson, however, understood as asking if he was Russian—to which he responded affirmatively. The tsar then expressed his desire for Khvolson to teach "our" priests, a statement that, according to Zitron, Khvolson did not even understand (his Russian was always poor, both Zitron and Ginzburg attest). Norov, however, informed him that the tsar had issued two orders: that Khvolson truly become one of "ours," that is, convert to Russian Orthodoxy, and that he become a professor in the church's seminary. Khvolson's reaction to this, says Zitron, was speechless shock. The tsar's orders, however, Norov said, were to be implemented immediately, with Khvolson now assured a brilliant career (no one but Khvolson, apparently, concerned about the absence of religious sincerity and the seemingly crass materialism of the conversion).[37]

What is significant about this account is less its veracity than its fulsome sympathy for Khvolson, who, contrary to the other myth of him as a cynical opportunist, behaving with self-evident self-interest (if given the choice, the myth asserts, who wouldn't choose being a professor over being a *melamed*—in a backwater?), is here the utter, hapless victim of the evil tsar's Jew-hating, conversionist, designs—an image that fit popular Jewish stereotype of both Jew and Nicholas.[38] The tale Zitron relates brings Khvolson "down" to the level of the ordinary Jew in tsarist Russia, making him a victim and his conversion forced, not opportunistic. While Zitron does not cite his source for this tale, it and much else of his treatment would seem to emanate from certain Orthodox circles, elite and popular, which were particularly close to Khvolson. Even the other myth, however, is sympathetic to Khvolson.

Khvolson went on to become what might be called the archetypal good bad Jew. I do not know whether he served as an explicit model for other such Jews, but that is certainly possible. In any case, he stands out for the treatment he receives in Jewish sources. Ginzburg opens his chapter on Khvolson, the largest in his book (Zitron's is similarly substantial), saying that Khvolson was the best known of all converts and, astonishingly, that "in the smallest and most provincial Jewish shtetlach people would speak of the *vunder mayses* [miraculous deeds] of this Lithuanian poor yeshiva boy."[39] *Vunder mayses*—the same term applied to wonder-working Hasidic rebbes!

Khvolson earned this adoration because, in stark contrast to bad-bad Jews, who incited persecution and in particular supported the blood libel, including in cases Khvolson was involved in—bad-bad Jews and good-bad ones arrayed against each other—he used his stature to deny publicly and vehemently any basis for the libel. Khvolson returned to Russia at the time of a blood libel trial in Saratov (1852). He served as an expert witness for the defense (meaning of course that the Jewish side had invited him to do so) and gave a ringing, extensive denunciation of the libel. According to an account written on the occasion of Khvolson's eightieth birthday by Baron David Gintsburg, head of the OPE for more than forty years and one of Khvolson's students, when the court ignored his testimony, Khvolson declared: "With my hand on the heads of all who are dear to me in this world, I swear before the Almighty Creator of heaven and earth that this is a lie, a lie, a lie! Jews never used Christian blood for any religious or any other purposes, so may God help me, my dear wife, and my only child. Amen, amen, amen."[40] Some years later, he published a scholarly tome denouncing and disproving a host of antisemitic charges, including this one. Not content with reacting to incidents, Khvolson used his position at the Catholic theological seminary to deliver a yearly lecture demonstrating the fraud of the blood libel, pointedly noting that it was first directed at early Christians, who then turned it against Jews. Following another blood libel case, in Kutais, Khvolson wrote a richly documented study of the libel that was published in an edition of ten thousand copies—obviously, he was working with Jews, and they were relying on him—and met with the tsar's brother in a vain effort to undermine the grand duke's convictions (shared by the tsar) about the libel.

What was Russian Jewish reaction to Khvolson during his lifetime? Following the vindication of Jews in Kutais accused of ritual murder, Zitron relays (based, it seems, on Baron Gintsburg's account), that Khvolson was escorted into the brilliantly lit synagogue of the town, led by the head of the congregation. The *aron hakodesh* holding the Torah scrolls was opened, an act reserved for sacred liturgical moments, and a special mi-sheberakh (prayer on behalf of an individual) was chanted by the cantor, while the rabbi delivered a fervent Hebrew sermon extolling him. For a long time after this, Zitron states, a special Khvolson mi-sheberakh was recited during the Torah reading in "many congregations" on behalf of "*morenu ha-rav* Daniel," "our teacher and rabbi, Rabbi Daniel" (with the blessing using Khvolson's baptismal name, Daniel, rather than Joseph, the name given him at circumcision). Since, of course, Khvolson's pro-Jewish efficacy derived entirely from the fact that he was a Christian—no Jewish authority, rabbinic or secular, would have been credible in defending Judaism against the ritual murder charge—one can only conclude that all this, the extraordinary communal reception and the telling of Khvolson myths, is powerful evidence that if "good" conversion was not being valorized *ab initio* (le-khat'hila), it was certainly valorized as such post factum (bedi'eved), by *stam yidn*—average Russian Jews, but also by the rabbi and other religious officials of the Kutais synagogue.

But Khvolson had other explicit and prominent rabbinic connections and endorsements. Zitron writes that, following Khvolson's actions in the Saratov affair, he was deluged with telegrams and letters from "the greatest rabbis and scholars [geonim] from the most important communities," expressing "love and respect" for him and promising him the afterlife in highest paradise. While Khvolson had disagreements with various *gebildeten* (secular-scholarly) Jews (of whom Shaul Ginzburg was one), Zitron says that he was particularly close to great rabbis, including Isaac Elhanan (Spektor) of Kovno (one of the greatest rabbinic authorities of the time, whose influence was enormous in Russia and beyond); the head of the Volozhin yeshiva; and others of their stature. There was not a rabbinic or communal leader who came to St. Petersburg (where the OPE was based and all Jewish affairs before the government were processed) without paying a lengthy visit to Khvolson, both Zitron and Ginzburg state; at these visits, Khvolson, Zitron says, would tearfully inquire about his old rabbinic teacher and other former associates in Vilna. These visitors, in turn, would return to their towns full of Khvolson *mayses* (tales), telling of the man with the "holy Jewish spark," Zitron says, whom "divine Providence had made an intimate of the government *in order to position him to be able to protect the Jewish people in time of trouble*" (emphasis added). An extraordinary understanding of Khvolson, therefore, had developed: that, like Queen Esther of the Purim story, Khvolson had been put in his peculiar position by the hand of God, so that he could save Jews when they needed it; indeed, Zitron says, in the Jewish shtetlach, people engaged in Talmudic disputations (*pilpul*) about whose soul had been reincarnated in Khvolson: Judah Maccabee? Mordechai (Queen Esther's uncle and co-hero of the Purim story)? Provincial Jews, Zitron says, considered Khvolson a *melits yosher*, a defense advocate on behalf of traditional, unacculturated Jewish schools (heders, talmud torahs, yeshivas), which were the particular target of government hostility. Khvolson, depicted in Zitron's account as shell-shocked after his conversion, had his *pintele yid* ("his little speck of Jewishness"—an enormously popular Jewish folk belief, a version of which is expressed by Solomon ibn Verga in this essay's epigraph) awakened by none other than the evil tsar himself, when he called on Khvolson's expertise in a government commission to assess Judaism's stance on the ritual use of human blood.[41]

While the treatment of Khvolson is extraordinary by any measure, there is another remarkable account in Ginzburg's work of another, less-well-known good bad Jew, Lev Kupernik, who receives affectionate, even adoring treatment, about whom Zitron, too, writes, though in less detail. The best way to describe Kupernik (1845-1905) is as a brilliant, outrageous rogue, with a passion for justice. Kupernik was the son of a Jewish communal worker, *maskil*, adherent of Hovevei Zion, a cofounder of the OPE, and author, who contributed to Hebrew periodicals and wrote a history of the Jews of Kiev, where he was a wealthy businessman and banker. His father, educated in Volozhin, gave his gifted son a secular and a basic, if not (according to the demanding standards of that day) an extensive, Jewish education. Kupernik went to gymnasium and then to university in Moscow, where he studied and began to practice law. Kupernik, however, had an avid love of theater and in Moscow joined the company of famous actors. He fell in love with one of the stars of the day, who also happened to be the daughter of an important justice official, and converted to Russian Orthodoxy to marry her (no intermarriage was possible in Russia, since civil marriage did not exist; all marriages were under religious auspices. Most conversions for marriage went from, not to, Judaism, conversion to which was a punishable offense until 1905).[42] Kupernik then moved to Kiev to accept a position as a defense attorney in the new Russian justice system (created in 1864), quickly earning a reputation as one of the most brilliant lawyers in Russia. He was involved in major cases, but assiduously also accepted more typical, small-town cases, of Jews and peasants alike, earning him enormous popularity as a wandering dispenser of law and justice; in Ginzburg's words, he was beloved in all of southern Russia. Kupernik, says Ginzburg, became the model and ideal of law students, a very disproportionate number of whom were Jews—meaning, of course, that Kupernik's conversion hardly impeded his stature among them. Indeed, Ginzburg describes Jewish law students idolizing him.

Aside from being a brilliant speaker, Kupernik was also a successful journalist, writing weekly in the main newspaper of the Kiev region, *Zharieh*—which happened to have a Jewish editor. Kupernik, Ginzburg writes, often raised the Jewish question in his articles and attacked antisemitic writers who published in anti-Jewish newspapers.

Ginzburg relates many humorous anecdotes about Kupernik, who had an impish, mischievous personality and enjoyed pranks. It is very clear from his presentation that Ginzburg adored the man, whom he likens to Heine, and reveled in relating his exploits. It is also clear that Kupernik continued to have Jewish friends as well as colleagues. Tellingly, Ginzburg notes such associations as simple facts, indicating that he, and apparently the intended readers of his work, saw nothing remarkable, much less objectionable, about this. Ginzburg does go out of his way to assure his readers that Kupernik, who was at least a religious skeptic if not an outright atheist, did not, as Ginzburg puts it, *khalilo* (God forbid), believe in Christianity. Indeed, he gleefully cites the text of Kupernik's terse, Caesar-like, rhyming telegram to his father announcing his conversion and marriage: "I fell in love, I converted, I got married" (*Vlyubilsya, krestilsya, zhenilsya*)—for which Kupernik himself or someone very close to him (his father?) had to have been the source—and insists that Kupernik knew that there was no getting away from history and birth and that, indeed, he had no such intention. Instead, he became an "outspoken Jew," because "baptism could not alter anything." Jews ("everyone," in Ginzburg's words) knew that "[Kupernik] did not undertake apostasy for the sake of career or material need" (a comment that betrays Jewish resentment against those who converted for gain). Jews, says Ginzburg, held Kupernik as "one of their own" (*yidn hobn im gehaltn far zeyer*). And when ordinary Jews would joyfully recount his wonderful legal triumphs, Ginzburg says, there "would always be a feeling of pride in *our* famous Kupernik" (emphasis added).[43]

Like Khvolson, Kupernik undertook the defense of Jews accused of ritual murder, in a case arising in 1878 in Satshneri, in the Kutais region. Despite, of course, any evidence, but also the exonerating testimony of a doctor who examined the body of the dead girl in question, the town's Jews were accused collectively, with a guilty verdict considered certain.

Alexander Tsederbaum, the editor of the Hebrew newspaper, *Hamelits*, perceiving in the case a grave danger to the Jews of the whole country, convinced Abraham Zak, a Jewish banker in St. Petersburg (and, I would note, Pauline Wengeroff's brother-in-law), to fund a vigorous defense. They signed "the famous Russian lawyer, Aleksandrov," and Kupernik for the job, with Zak underwriting costs.[44] Kupernik, however, took the case pro bono, refusing any pay for a trial that lasted more than a year. The two lawyers split the tasks between them, Aleksandrov addressing the specifics of the case, and Kupernik taking on the absurdity and fabrication of the ritual murder charge itself. His presentation aimed at demolishing the charge for all time, Ginzburg writes; he did a historical survey of the charge from the Middle Ages to the present to illustrate its baselessness. Justice eventually prevailed and the Jews were acquitted. Both lawyers made a triumphal return to St. Petersburg, greeted and feted along the long route back with banquets in their honor, celebrated, according to Ginzburg, in all Jewish towns and shtetlach.

Kupernik also argued on behalf of Jews in the wake of pogroms: in 1882 and especially after the Homel pogrom of 1903, when Jewish self-defense, organized by the Bund, the Jewish socialist party, first emerged. The Jewish defenders were charged with hooliganism, and Kupernik undertook their defense. He failed, but not for lack of effort. When Kupernik died in 1905, Ginzburg ends, "all the Jews of Kiev" (in great contrast to Khvolson's funeral, according to both Zitron and Ginzburg) turned out for his massive funeral, held, of course, according to Russian Orthodox rites.[45]

What is one to make of the phenomenon of these good bad Jews? First, clearly, the dimensions of the phenomenon remain to be determined, though to the two examined here, several more could readily be added. Victor Nikitin, one of the cantonists kidnapped into Russian military service under Nicholas I, converted under the pressures exerted on Jewish conscripts.[46] In a time of anti-Jewish violence and official discrimination, he wrote a substantial, favorable history of Jewish settlement in Russia, published serially in the Jewish journal *Voskhod* and then separately, in expanded versions, in the 1880s—that is, initially and repeatedly under Jewish auspices.[47] Vladimir Fedorov (Grinboim) was the censor of Jewish books in Kiev and later in Warsaw, a position rife with malevolent potential (fully realized by Brafman). He converted after being turned down for a position in one of the planned government Jewish schools and later spoke of having become a Christian "in spirit." Yet, far from becoming "one of those who speak ill [of Jews] to the authorities," he wrote to Russia's leading *maskil*, Isaac Ber Levinson, as he suspected "some Jews" believed of him, "God forbid!" he said; "how can I look upon [Jewish] pain indifferently?" Like Khvolson, Fedorov maintained active ties with leading *maskilim*—Levinson, Avraham Ber Gottlober, and Leon Mandelstamm—

and they, obviously, with him. He translated the Talmudic tractate San-hedrin (dealing with judicial matters, such as standards for testimony) into Russian, in order, he wrote to Levinson, "to refute all the slanders that have been cast upon it . . . I hope that both Jews and Christians will read it and exclaim, 'What a treasure we have discovered!'" His introduction to the work was a detailed defense of the Talmud, the focus of much Judeophobic attack and the pretext for denying Jews expanded rights. Fedorov also translated into Russian Moses Mendels-sohn's *Jerusalem*, a vigorous defense of Judaism and a plea to decouple religion and civil status, an act whose meaning, as Jewish civil status in Russia was being debated, is obvious. In this and in his attempts to intercede with Kiev authorities on behalf of the Jews, Fedorov behaved as a *shtadlan*, the traditional Jewish intercessor before the authorities, except that he, like Khvolson, derived his usefulness from the fact that he was a Christian. Like Khvolson, Fedorov served in the OPE.[48] Vilna-born Avraham Uri Kovner was a *maskil* who sharply criticized *haskalah* (Jewish enlightenment) literature and became a pioneer of modern Hebrew literary criticism. He converted for love at the age of fifty-one but thereafter, as previously, openly challenged antisemites, including Fyodor Dostoevsky and writers for the antisemitic Russian journal *Novoe Vremya*.[49] There was a Polish-born good bad Jew, as well, who made efforts on behalf of Russian Jewry: Jan Bloch converted as a young man but remained devoted to Jewish interests, producing a massive study of Jewish living conditions in the Pale and arguing forcefully against tsarist anti-Jewish policies. For the extensive statis-tical work on this project, Bloch, a wealthy businessman and financier, employed several very Jewish Jews: Nahum Sokolow and Isaac Leib Peretz. He had ties with Theodor Herzl, too, and declared in his testa-ment, "I was a Jew my whole life and will die a Jew."[50] The lives and communal reception of all these converts merit close examination.

Of the extraordinary Jewish response to Khvolson and Kupernik, one can say that it emerged at a time of grave danger and needs, nothing new of course in Jewish history. What was new was that tradi-tional norms anathematizing converts were no longer intact, not only among acculturated and assimilated Jews but among the traditional masses and some leading Orthodox figures, and not only by individ-uals but in Russian Jewry's communal organization, the OPE. Further, the extraordinary receptiveness to these men was not confined to situations of dire threat. The inclusion of Khvolson and Fedorov, and of another apparent good bad Jew, Nicholas Bakst, in leadership positions in the OPE's cultural projects is extremely striking, singular in Jewish communal history, as far as I know, and cries for full examination.[51] Khvolson proposed that the OPE sponsor a translated collection of excerpts from the Talmud and other rabbinical writings, for internal use, as a primer in Judaism and as a substantive response to the anti-Talmudic calumnies of Brafman and others. His proposal was accepted and eventuated in three volumes in 1874-76 titled *The Worldview of the Talmudists*, whose materials were selected by two prominent, conservative Vilna *maskilim*, Sh. Y. Fuenn and H. L. Katzenellenbogen, and whose annotations and bibliographical notes were done by Yehuda Leib Gordon, Russian Jewry's foremost cultural leader, who served as secretary of the OPE.[52] According to Brian Horowitz, Khvolson (whom Horowitz simply lists with the others as "the very best scholars among the *maskilim*") edited the volume. Khvolson and another member of the OPE proposed ways to increase literacy in German among the overwhelmingly Yiddish-speaking Russian Jews.[53] Responding to an appeal by Gordon to prominent *maskilim*, Khvolson advocated before the government for permission to publish a collection of Jewish fables Gordon had prepared.[54] Khvolson corresponded with and had letters published in Gordon's newspaper, *Ha-melits*.[55] He seems to have been treated in this world like an eminent *maskil*, while in most of the traditional world, like a saint, a messenger of God.

Ginzburg's account of Khvolson shows that such regard and inclusion were not universal: his antipathy to Khvolson is undisguised—and Ginzburg stresses that he knew him personally from their time in the OPE, on which, Ginzburg notes, he served as secretary (after Gordon). Ginzburg more than suggests that Khvolson's Christianity was sincere to the point of exaggeration—either this, or that he fawned over Christian symbols for effect with powerful authorities. Ginzburg was a member of a circle of young nationalists in the OPE who were incensed at the involvement of a *meshumed* in Jewish internal cultural affairs (a proposed Russian-language Bible translation, a proposed curriculum for modern rabbinical training). Khvolson, Ginzburg pointedly notes, did not avail himself of the license to return to Judaism when this became legal, after the Revolution of 1905, even though he was by then an established professor, with a pension. "He died a *meshumed*," Ginzburg writes scornfully, alienated in his last years from the Jewish world of St. Petersburg, his funeral attended by almost no Jews. Ginzburg's account confirms what Zitron says about Rabbi Spektor and other prominent rabbis' support of Khvolson, as well as his popular adoration, particularly "in the provinces." The latter, however, Ginzburg characterizes as "poshete frumakes," simpleminded religious fanatics (the irony: Jewish religious fanatics, fervently adoring a convert), and pointedly notes that other very eminent rabbis—Naftali Zvi Berlin, Eliyahu Chaim Meizl, Chaim Soloveitchik—a minority, he admits, would have nothing to do with Khvolson, their opposition expressed in contemptuously biting rabbinic similes.[56]

Still, it is clear from Ginzburg's own account that hostility to Khvolson and his standing and involvement in Jewish life were exceptional. Indeed, Ginzburg's chapter appears, in part at least, to be an attempt to unseat Khvolson's popularity. Rather, what stands out about both Khvolson and Kupernik is the unbroken contact with members and even leaders of the Jewish community, the friendships and the professional and communal collaboration that persisted. For all his hostility to Khvolson, Ginzburg states that he does not consider Kupernik to have been anything but a Jew (perhaps because Kupernik's advocacy was legal, not cultural, because he did not presume to take a role in the self-definitions of Jews). Zitron pointedly notes that Khvolson spoke and wrote to his dying day of "we Jews," wondering, clearly disappointed, why Khvolson did not "correct the old mistake and return" to Judaism when he was able (Ginzburg knows why; Zitron is baffled). Zitron relates, as noted, that Khvolson refused to speak of his conversion, but also that he would deflect questions about this with biblical and Talmudic references. "Particularly popular with the people," Zitron cites the following delicious bit of Khvolsonalia on the subject of his ethnic and religious affiliation. Commenting on the central words of Yom Kippur liturgy, *ad she'lo notsarti, eini kedai, ve' akhshav she'nostarti, ke'ilu lo notsarti* (Before I was created, I was not worthy, and now that I have been created, it is as if I had not been created), Khvolson, Zitron says, punned on the similar-sounding Hebrew words "created" and "converted to Christianity," to say: "Before I converted, it was as if I had not converted, and now that I have, it is as if I had not converted"—then asserting that there was nothing further to discuss.[57]

Whether Khvolson actually said this, one cannot say. The point here is what Jews *thought, or even invented,* as well as how they behaved on the subject of these converts, and this clearly, was extraordinary. This essay has looked at what traditional Jewish attitudes to converts were, and why. But the Jews discussed here were *good* bad Jews, deemed so by Jewish society, from the streets of the shtetlach, to elite publishing houses, to synagogues and great rabbinic authorities, people not shunned and ostracized, but a part of society, in life-threatening emergencies but also in the more prosaic ordeals, hopes, and plans, of being Jewish in tsarist Russia.

Given the disruptions of the twentieth century—the Bolshevik Revolution and the Shoah—and the destruction in those cataclysms of the society and culture that had begun to elaborate new criteria and definitions of membership, it will never be known how this dynamic would have played out. Unlike some strains of converso-Jewishness, "good bad" Jewishness does not appear to have transmitted across generations: Khvolson's children did not maintain contact with Jews or identification as such (though Ginzburg reports, with obvious glee, that they all looked very Jewish); the same was true of Kovner's children.

One sees from both Ginzburg's and Zitron's works that Russian Jewish culture had begun to differentiate types, and a taxonomy, of *meshumodim*: bad ones, who converted and did harm (Zitron even designates one, Semyon-Efron-Litvinov, a prize student of Brafman, as one of the worst and most corrupt converts—worst bad Jews?); less bad but still bad ones, who converted for personal gain and drifted away, leaving Jews as a whole to their fate; still less bad ones, like Kupernik (and Kovner), who converted for love; and, finally, good, saintly ones—Kupernik kicked himself way up in this taxonomy—who used their position precisely as apostates to save Jews under mortal threat and to uphold the honor of Judaism. For such, Jewish society held out its most cherished reward: inclusion.[58]

Notes

Warm thanks to Breindl Billet and Mordechai Billet for speedy help obtaining some of the Zitron material.

1. On the problematics of even conceptualizing boundary drawing in Jewish society before the rabbinic articulation of the matrilineal principle, and on this principle becoming the rabbinic norm, see Shaye J. D. Cohen, *The Beginnings of Jewishness: Boundaries, Varieties, Uncertainties* (Berkeley: University of California Press, 1999). On the problems of boundary drawing regarding forced converts from Spain and Portugal and their descendants, see Yirmiyahu Yovel, *The Other Within: The Marranos' Split Identity and Emerging Modernity* (Princeton, N.J.: Princeton University Press, 2009).

2. Some important studies of converts are Guido Kisch, *Judentaufen: Eine historisch-biographisch-psychologisch-soziologische Studie besonders für Berlin und Königsberg* [Jewish Converts: A Historical-Biographical-Psychological-Sociological Study, Particularly for Berlin and Konigsberg] (Berlin: Colloquium Verlag, 1973); Peter Honigmann, *Die Austritte aus der Jüdischen Gemeinde Berlin, 1873–1941* [Departures from the Jewish Community of Berlin, 1873–1941] (Frankfurt am Main: Peter Lang, 1988); Nathan Peter Levinson, *"Ketzer" und Abtrünnige im Judentum: Historische Porträts* [Cutting off from Jewish Society: Historical Portraits] (Hannover: Lutherisches Verlagshaus, 2001); Elisheva Carlebach, *Divided Souls: Converts from Judaism in Germany, 1500–1750* (New Haven, Conn.: Yale University Press, 2001); Carlebach, *Divided Souls: The Convert Critique and the Culture of Ashkenaz, 1750–1800*, Leo Baeck Memorial Lecture 46 (New York: Leo Baeck Institute, 2003); Deborah Hertz, *Jewish High Society in Old Regime Berlin* (New Haven, Conn.: Yale University Press, 1988); Hertz, *How Jews Became Germans: The History of Conversion and Assimilation in Berlin* (New Haven, Conn.: Yale University Press, 2007); Marsha L. Rosenblit, *The Jews of Vienna, 1867–1914: Assimilation and Identity* (Albany: State University of New York Press, 1983); and Steven M. Lowenstein, *The Berlin Jewish Community: Enlightenment, Family, and Crisis, 1770–1830* (New York: Oxford University Press, 1994). On conversion in modern Jewish history, see Todd Endelman, "Conversion as a Response to Antisemitism," in *Living with Antisemitism: Modern Jewish Responses*, ed. Jehuda Reinharz (Hanover, N.H.: University Press of New England, 1987), 59–83; Endelman, *Radical Assimilation in English Jewish History: 1656–1945* (Bloomington: Indiana University Press, 1990); and Endelman's introduction and his "Social and Political Context of Conversion in Germany and England, 1870–1914," in his *Jewish Apostasy in the Modern World*, ed. Todd Endelman (New York: Holmes and Meier, 1987), 1–19, 83–107.

3. On these cases, see Robert Chazan, ed., *Church, State, and Jew in the Middle Ages* (West Orange, N.J.: Behrman House, 1980), 255–76; Jacob Rader Marcus, *The Jew in the Medieval World: A Source Book*, rev. ed. (Cincinnati: Hebrew Union College Press, 1999), 163–68; Jeremy Cohen, "The Mentality of the Medieval

Jewish Apostate: Peter Alfonsi, Hermann of Cologne, and Pablo Christiani," in Endelman, *Jewish Apostasy*, 20–47; and Cohen, *The Friars and the Jews: The Evolution of Medieval Anti-Judaism* (Ithaca, N.Y.: Cornell University Press, 1982). On Jewish apostasy in Spain, see Yitzhak Baer, *A History of the Jews in Christian Spain*, vol. 2, *From the Fourteenth Century to the Expulsion*, trans. Louis Schoffman (Philadelphia: Jewish Publication Society of America, 1971); and Jane S. Gerber, *The Jews of Spain: A History of the Sephardic Experience* (New York: Free Press, 1992). On medieval Jewish apostasy in general, see Jacob Katz, *Exclusiveness and Tolerance: Studies in Jewish-Gentile Relations in Medieval and Modern Times* (New York: Schocken, 1962), 67–76.

4. On convert persecution of Judaism in general and the connection with Luther in particular, see Sander L. Gilman, *Jewish Self-Hatred: Anti-Semitism and the Hidden Language of the Jews* (Baltimore: Johns Hopkins University Press, 1986), 22–67; Heiko A. Oberman, *The Roots of Anti-Semitism in the Age of Renaissance and Reformation*, trans. James I. Porter (Philadelphia: Fortress Press, 1981) (chapter 3 is titled "Johannes Pfefferkorn: The Shrill Voice of a Convert"); and R. Po-Chia Hsia, *The Myth of Ritual Murder: Jews and Magic in Reformation Germany* (New Haven, Conn.: Yale University Press, 1988).

5. Robert Bonfil, *Jewish Life in Renaissance Italy* (Berkeley: University of California Press, 1991), 119. See also Marcus, *The Jew in the Medieval World*, 191–94.

6. On the Frankists, see Gershom Scholem, "Frank, Jacob," in *Encyclopaedia Judaica* (Jerusalem: Keter, 1972), 7:55–72; and Pawel Maciejko, "Frankism," in *The YIVO Encyclopedia of Jews in Eastern Europe*, ed. Gershon David Hundert, 2 vols. (New Haven, Conn.: Yale University Press 2008), 1:540–44, and the literature cited there.

7. On the development and application of this principle, see Jacob Katz, "Yehudi af al pi she'hata yehudi hu" [Though He Sinned, He Remains an Israelite], *Tarbiz* 27 (1958): 203–17; and Katz, *Exclusiveness and Tolerance*, 67–81.

8. Quoted in Chazan, *Church, State, and Jew*, 225.

9. Compare two very different examples, from different eras and regions, cited in, respectively, Katz, *Exclusiveness and Tolerance*, 23; and Dan Ben-Amos and Jerome R. Mintz, eds. and trans., *In Praise of the Baal Shem Tov (Shivhei ha-Besht): The Earliest Collection of Legends about the Founder of Hasidism* (Bloomington: Indiana University Press, 1970), 35.

10. Carlebach, *Divided Souls: The Convert Critique*, 5, 4.

11. Cohen, "Medieval Jewish Apostate," 23; Carlebach, *Divided Souls: The Convert Critique*, 10.

12. See Hilde Spiel, *Fanny von Arnstein: A Daughter of the Enlightenment, 1758–1818*, trans. Christine Shuttleworth (New York: Berg, 1991), 52–56.

13. Yosef Hayim Yerushalmi, *Freud's Moses: Judaism Terminable and Interminable* (New Haven, Conn.: Yale University Press, 1991), 47.

14. Alan T. Levenson, *Between Philosemitism and Antisemitism: Defenses of Jews and Judaism in Germany, 1871–1932* (Lincoln: University of Nebraska Press, 2007), 137.

15. Yohanan Petrovsky-Shtern, "'The Guardians of Faith': Jewish Traditional Societies in the Russian Army; The Case of the Thirty-fifth Briansk Regiment," in *The Military and Society in Russia, 1450–1917*, ed. Eric Lohr and Marshall Poe (Leiden: Brill, 2002), 415–16n1.

16. Yehuda Slutsky, *Ha-itonut ha-yehudit rusit ba-me'ah ha-t'sha esreh* [The Jewish Russian Press in the Nineteenth Century] (Jerusalem: Mosad Bialik, 1970), 8. Unless otherwise noted, all translations in this chapter are mine.

17. Ismar Schorsch, *Jewish Reactions to German Anti-Semitism, 1870–1914* (New York: Columbia University Press, 1972), 139. See also Jehuda Reinharz, *Fatherland or Promised Land: The Dilemma of the German Jew, 1893–1914* (Ann Arbor: University of Michigan Press, 1980).

18. Quoted in Hertz, *How Jews Became Germans*, 14.

19. On Heine's and Ludwig Boerne's conversions and conversionist rhetoric, see Gilman, *Jewish Self-Hatred*, 148–87; on Heine, see Ritchie Robertson, *Heine* (New York: Grove Press, 1988); and Paul Mendes-Flohr, *German Jews: A Dual Identity* (New Haven, Conn.: Yale University Press, 1999). There is no full treatment of Jewish reception to these converts, to Heine in particular, but it is clear that German Jews took great pride in his works and in his cynicism regarding his baptism.

20. Levenson, *Between Philosemitism and Antisemitism*, 132–41.

21. See Endelman, *Radical Assimilation*, 164–67.

22. See Carlebach, *Divided Souls: The Convert Critique*, 12–13.

23. See Pauline Wengeroff, *Memoirs of a Grandmother: Scenes from the Cultural History of the Jews of Russia in the Nineteenth Century*, trans. with introduction, notes, and commentary by Shulamit S. Magnus, 2 vols. (Stanford, Calif.: Stanford University Press, in press), vol. 1.

24. Raphael Mahler, *Hasidism and the Jewish Enlightenment: Their Confrontation in Galicia and Poland in the First Half of the Nineteenth Century* (Philadelphia: Jewish Publication Society of America, 1985), 208.

25. On the Ahiasaf house, see Kenneth B. Moss, "Ahi'asaf," in *YIVO Encyclopedia*, 1:22. On Ahad Ha'am's relationship to Ahiasaf, see Steven J. Zipperstein, *Elusive Prophet: Ahad Ha'am and the Origins of Zionism* (Berkeley: University of California Press, 1993).

26. Michael Stanislawski, "Jewish Apostasy in Russia: A Tentative Typology," in Endelman, *Jewish Apostasy*, 190. One missionary source cited an estimated combined total of 224,000 Jewish conversions in Europe and the United States in the nineteenth century, a figure Endelman finds reasonable. Endelman, introduction to *Jewish Apostasy*, 18n6; see also Magda Teter, "Conversion," in *YIVO Encyclopedia*, 1:348–51. For differing estimates of conversion in medieval Ashkenaz and the ability to assess rates, compare Katz, *Exclusiveness and Tolerance*, 67–68; and Avraham Grossman, *Pious and Rebellious: Jewish Women in Medieval Europe* (Waltham, Mass.: Brandeis University Press, 2004), 205.

27. *The Life and Soul of a Legendary Jewish Socialist: The Memoirs of Vladimir Medem*,

trans. Samuel A. Portnoy (New York: Ktav, 1979), 2. Medem's parents converted, at different times and for different reasons; he and all his siblings were converted, though he alone at birth, and to Russian Orthodoxy. This hardly qualifies as an "involuntary" conversion; see Teter, "Conversion," 350. Rather, one must consider it "pre-voluntary." Indeed, Medem experienced a childhood attraction to Christianity, then a growing, seemingly inexorable, identification with (working-class) Jews, until he finally classed himself as one, his "conversion" self-effected, while under arrest in a police station, when he was asked his nationality and declared it "Jewish." Medem, *Memoirs*, 179. Medem did not serve Jews as a convert, from the position and with the advantage of a Christian, and so does not qualify as a "good bad Jew." Rather, his journey "home," as he puts it, shows the operation of forces of dissimilation in modern Jewish history, on which, see Shulamit Volkov, "The Dynamics of Dissimilation: *Ostjuden* and German Jews," in *The Jewish Response to German Culture: From the Enlightenment to the Second World War*, ed. Jehuda Reinharz and Walter Schatzberg (Hanover, N.H.: University Press of New England, 1985), 195–211.

28. Pauline Wengeroff, *Memoiren einer Grossmutter Bilder aus der Kulturgeschichte der Juden Russlands im 19. Jahrhundert* (Berlin: Poppelauer, 1910), 2:182–83, 192–93. On Wengeroff's memoir and her narration of modern Jewish assimilation, see Shulamit S. Magnus, "Pauline Wengeroff and the Voice of Jewish Modernity," in *Gender and Judaism: The Transformation of Tradition*, ed. T. M. Rudavsky (New York: New York University Press, 1995), 181–90; Magnus, "Kol Ishah: Women and Pauline Wengeroff's Writing of an Age," *Nashim: A Journal of Jewish Women's Studies and Gender Issues* 7 (2004): 28–64; and Magnus, introduction to Wengeroff, *Memoirs*, vol. 2. Shmuel Leib Zitron, *Me'ahorei hapargod: Mumarim, bogdim, mitkhahshim* (Vilna: n.p., 1925). Zitron's chapter on Semyon Vengerov, one of Wengeroff's converted sons, differs radically from Wengeroff's account of the home environment and Semyon's conversion. While Semyon does not qualify as a good bad Jew—he went on to have a brilliant career as a pioneer of Russian literary history, not a champion of Jewish causes—Zitron's account is remarkable for its sympathy to him and his extreme hostility to Wengeroff, whom he blames for creating the home atmosphere that led to Semyon's conversion—effectively, absolving Semyon. On the disparity between these two accounts, see Magnus, introduction to Wengeroff, *Memoirs*, vol. 2.

29. Shaul Ginzburg, *Meshumodim in tsarishn rusland: Farshungen un zichroynes vegn yidishn lebn in amolikn rusland*, vol. 2 of *Historishe verk* (New York: Tsiko Bikher Farlag, 1946), 270.

30. Cited by Brian Horowitz, *Jewish Philanthropy and Enlightenment in Late-Tsarist Russia* (Seattle: University of Washington Press, 2009), 79.

31. Ibid. On the impact of Brafman's book, see Steven J. Zipperstein, *The Jews of Odessa: A Cultural History, 1794–1881* (Stanford, Calif.: Stanford University Press, 1985), 115.

32. On Rabinovich, see Steven J. Zipperstein, "Heresy, Apostasy, and the Transformation of Joseph Rabinovich," in Endelman, *Jewish Apostasy*, 206–31.

33. In these introductory remarks, Zitron relates, uncritically, what would seem to be a popular if bizarre theory of the origins of high-ranking bad-bad Jews in Russia: to counteract an anti-Jewish decree of Nicholas I, the Jews decided to turn ("sacrifice") some of their most brilliant, Volozhin-yeshiva-educated men (members of its *kloyz* [intensive study hall]) into double agents, who would infiltrate the Russian regime, whence they could exercise influence to help Jews. This strategy failed catastrophically, and these gifted converts became highly placed oppressors. Almost as bizarre as this tale is Zitron's seeming attribution of it to Reuven Kulisher, an intellectual from Odessa and influential member of the OPE, who, one must assume, cannot have put it forth as other than folk belief. See Zitron, *Avek fun folk, tipn un silueten funm noyenten ovor*, 4 vols. (Warsaw: Ahiasaf, 1920), 1:3–5; on Kulisher, see Horowitz, *Jewish Philanthropy*, 34, 44.

34. On Zitron, see Yehuda Slutsky, "Zitron, Samuel Leib," in *Encyclopaedia Judaica*, 16:1186; Avner Holtzman, "Zitron, Shemu'el Leib," in *YIVO Encyclopedia*, 2:2133–34.

35. *Jewish Folk Songs in Russia*, photo reproduction of 1901 St. Petersburg ed., ed. and annotated by Dov Noy (Ramat Gan, Israel: Bar Ilan Press, 1991). On Ginzburg, see Yehuda Slutsky, "Ginsburg, Saul," in *Encyclopaedia Judaica*, 7:582–83; the references to Ginzburg in Benjamin Nathans, *Beyond the Pale:The Jewish Encounter with Late Imperial Russia* (Berkeley: University of California Press, 2002); and Horowitz, *Jewish Philanthropy*.

36. See, e.g., Christoph Gassenschmidt, "Khvol'son, Daniil Avraamovich," *YIVO Encyclopedia*, 1:890; and Lucy Dawidowicz, *The Golden Tradition: Jewish Life and Thought in Eastern Europe* (New York: Holt, Rinehart and Winston, 1967), 335. Dawidowicz calls this tale "Khwolson folklore" and notes that the remark is reputed.

37. Zitron, *Avek fun folk*, 1:35.

38. See Michael Stanislawski, *Tsar Nicholas I and the Jews* (Philadelphia: Jewish Publication Society, 1983). On popular Jewish hatred of Nicholas, see Magnus, introduction to Wengeroff, *Memoirs*, vol. 1.

39. Ginzburg, *Meshumodim*, 119. Subsequent quotations from Ginzburg's chapter on Khvolson are from *Meshumodim*, 119–56; subsequent quotations from Zitron regarding Khvolson are from *Avek fun folk*, 1:3–38.

40. Quoted in the excerpt of Ginzburg's document in Dawidowicz, *Golden Tradition*, 336. On the relationship between Ginzburg, magnate, philanthropist, intercessor with the Russian government on behalf of Jews, and Khvolson, and his writing on the latter's eightieth birthday, see the very negative account in Ginzburg, *Meshumodim*, 147–54. Khvolson's wife was a Jew; they married before his conversion. See Zitron, *Avek fun folk*, 1:11–13; and Ginzburg, *Meshumodim*, 123. She, too, surely converted, since the church

would not have tolerated an ongoing marriage to a Jew by a teacher of its seminarians, but Zitron says nothing about this, though he otherwise blames her for being alienated from Judaism and influencing Khvolson to this end (without success, it would seem, according to Zitron's depiction of Khvolson, but compare this with Ginzburg's [*Meshumodim*, 154–55]).

41. Zitron, *Avek fun folk*, 1:14–17, 23–24, 29.

42. Nathans, *Beyond the Pale*, 97.

43. Quoted passages are all from Ginzburg's chapter on Kupernik in *Meshumodim*, 269–70.

44. Zitron, *Avek fun folk*, 1:33.

45. Ginzburg, *Meshumodim*, 278 (on the Jews of Kiev and Kupernik's funeral). On another Jewish lawyer who served as defense attorney in a ritual murder trial, the infamous Beilis case of 1913, see O. O. Gruzenberg, *Yesterday: Memoirs of a Russian-Jewish Lawyer*, ed. Don C. Rawson (Berkeley: University of California Press, 1981). The traumatic event is evoked in Sholom Aleichem's novel, *The Bloody Hoax*, trans. Aliza Shevrin (Bloomington: Indiana University Press, 1991).

46. On this chapter in Russian Jewish history, see Stanislawski, *Tsar Nicholas*, 13–34.

47. See Slutsky, *Ha-itonut*, 286; and Olga Litvak, "The Literary Response to Conscription: Individuality and Authority in the Russian-Jewish Enlightenment" (Ph.D. diss., Columbia University, 1999), 39n45, 39n47.

48. On Fedorov, see Ginzburg, *Meshumodim*, 251–63; Zitron, *Avek fun folk*, 1:143–42; Eli Lederhendler, *The Road to Modern Jewish Politics: Political Tradition and Political Reconstruction in the Jewish Community of Tsarist Russia* (New York: Oxford University Press, 1989), 105–6; Litvak, "Literary Response to Conscription," 98; Horowitz, *Jewish Philanthropy*, 34; and, in some detail, Stanislawski, *Tsar Nicholas*, 144–46.

49. On Kovner, see Yehuda Slutsky, "Kovner, Abraham Uri," *Encyclopedia Judaica*, 10:1230–32; Ginzburg, *Meshumodim*, 157–93; and Dawidowicz, *Golden Tradition*, 338–43.

50. Quoted in the excerpt about Bloch from Nahum Sokolow's memoirs, in Dawidowicz, *Golden Tradition*, 344.

51. Brian Horowitz, in *Jewish Philanthropy* (34), mentions that several founding members of the OPE were converts but does not identify these as Khvolson and Fedorov or explore their inclusion in that organization, nor does he note it when recording Khvolson's subsequent cultural involvement in the OPE. Horowitz (69) identifies Bakst as a non-Jew (not as a convert), but Michael Stanislawski, in *Tsar Nicholas* (107), says that Bakst was a graduate of one of the Crown rabbinical schools. The entry for Bakst in *Jewish Encyclopedia.com* says nothing about his religious status. See Herman Rosenthal, "Bakst, Nicolai Ignatyevich," http://www.jewishencyclopedia.com/view.jsp?artid=158&letter=B (accessed June 2009).

52. See Michael Stanislawski, *For Whom Do I Toil? Judah Leib Gordon and the Crisis of Russian Jewry* (New York: Oxford University Press, 1988), 118; and Horowitz, *Jewish Philanthropy*. On the history of the OPE and its increasing promotion of a nationalist agendum, see Horowitz, *Jewish Philanthropy*; and Nathans, *Beyond the Pale*. One must wonder why Khvolson's seminary overseers tolerated his pro-Jewish involvements.

53. Horowitz, *Jewish Philanthropy*, 39. This proposal did not eventuate as Khvolson proposed, but that is irrelevant here.

54. Stanislawski, *For Whom Do I Toil*, 32–33.

55. Ginzburg, *Meshumodim*, 138–39.

56. Ibid., 132–46, 152–56.

57. Zitron, *Avek fun folk*, 1:35.

58. This taxonomy is evident too in Aleichem's *Bloody Hoax*, with its clear antipathy to the convert, Lapidus. One also gets a sense of the limits of inclusion of converts in the radically changed circumstances of a postwar Jewish state, in the "Brother Daniel" case, adjudicated before the Supreme Court of Israel in the 1960s. Born a Jew, Oswald Rufeisen converted to Catholicism while in hiding from the Nazis in Poland and became a priest. Passing as a Pole, he risked his life numerous times to save Jews in Mir. See Nechama Tec, *In the Lion's Den: The Life of Oswald Rufeisen* (New York: Oxford University Press, 1990); and Levinson, *Ketzer*, 139–45. Rufeisen applied for Israeli citizenship as a Jew under the state's Law of Return. He clearly differs from the good bad Jews of this essay by having been a religious convert and for continuing to consider himself a Jew not only by descent but by religion, seeing his conversion not as a breach with Judaism but as its realization and fulfillment—the archposition, of course, of the church about Judaism. To admit the validity of such a claim would have been not to redefine but to obliterate Jewish lines, against a highly charged history (as glimpsed in this essay) of Christian attempts to convert Jews. Rufeisen's clear halakhic status as a Jew and his heroic behavior to Jews during the Shoah were acknowledged during the deliberation of his case, but the chief rabbinate of Israel nonetheless opposed his petition, which the Court ultimately denied. See Tec, *In the Lion's Den*, 230. By contrast, the good bad Jews of this essay were not seeking official Jewish validation of their Christianity; by all accounts but Ginzburg's about Khvolson, they were not sincere Christians and were not seen as such by Jews. Rufeisen's attempt to separate Jewish descent from Jewish belief was not unprecedented: Nathans, in *Beyond the Pale* (97), notes that "apostate Jews often reported Yiddish as their native tongue [on censuses], either because it literally was or because they thereby sought to express the possibility of being a Christian of Jewish ethnicity." Indeed, on the censuses of 1890 and 1897, members of the Orthodox Church were broken down into ethnic groups, including "Jewish."

8

"Jewish Like an Adjective"

Confronting Jewish Identities in Contemporary Poland

ERICA LEHRER

The purpose of poetry is to remind us
how difficult it is to remain just one person,
for our house is open, there are no keys in the doors,
and invisible guests come in and out at will.

—Czesław Miłosz, "Ars Poetica?"

The identity of any man or woman is, after all, or often is, a palimpsest
composed of fragmentary memories, imprints, of those he or she has
loved.   —Bernard Harrison, "Talking Like a Jew"

One is of the nation one can feel ashamed for.

—Adam Michnik, quoted in
Konstanty Gebert, "Jewish Identities in Poland"

Dekalog 8: Thou Shalt Not Bear False Witness (1989) was a highly praised
segment in a ten-part film series by the esteemed Polish director
Krzysztof Kieślowski, each part of which references one of the ten
biblical commandments.[1] *Dekalog 8* grapples with the problem of
Polish-Jewish reconciliation vis-à-vis the Holocaust.[2] The film tells the
story of choice in an ethical hell. Zofia, an ethics professor in late
1980s Warsaw, meets Elisabeth, the New York–based translator of her
work who has come to audit Zofia's classes. In 1943, in the thick of the
Nazi occupation of Poland, Elisabeth, a six-year-old Jewish child, had
been refused shelter by the Catholic Zofia on the grounds that Zofia
could not break the eighth commandment by pretending the child
was a Christian. Elisabeth, now grown, seeks an explanation from the
woman who denied her refuge so many years before.

The film presents this confrontation in the context of Zofia's under-graduate ethics class, where Elisabeth offers her own story (made anonymous) in response to Zofia's request for examples of ethical dilemmas, in this way revealing herself (to Zofia only) as the Jewish child the professor once rejected. A student responds to the case presented, easily pointing out its central flaw—had the woman truly been acting according to Christian ethics, there would have been no dilemma at all. Rejecting the Jewish child on grounds of bearing false witness would have meant unjustifiably stressing the letter of the law over its spirit. The problem seems solved. Yet the film has just begun, and viewers are to be drawn deeper into a consideration of bearing witness and to a realization that witnessing remains a central problem that separates and binds Jews and Poles today.

This essay is an attempt to understand bearing witness as a kind of moral remembering that, as many Poles I have met illustrate, is deeply intertwined with individual and group identification. Just as Kieślowski's *Dekalog* presents stories loosely related to each commandment, my task here is to stimulate thinking around "bearing witness" as a metaphor with multiple valences. The question at the center is, who can remember for whom?

The Demand for Witness

In the postsocialist era Poles have been confronted with previously suppressed aspects of their nation's history concerning Jews. Poland has also been scrutinized by the West (and by the Jewish establishment in particular) for its willingness and ability to re-reckon its collective *rachunek sumienia*, or "bill of conscience," and to revise its national self-image accordingly.

These confrontations have sent shocks through Polish society, and the public response has been notable for the intensity of debate about the extent of Polish responsibility for historical events, both in terms of complicity and in terms of present-day recollection and reconciliation.[3] Outcomes have included substantial revision in the presentation of Nazi extermination camp memorial sites, especially Auschwitz (in Polish, Oświęcim). Not only were mortality statistics radically revised, but the narrative presentation was reoriented to clarify that the vast majority of the victims in these camps were Jews—a reality that was grossly elided during the Communist era in favor of an "internationalist" perspective, though one that nevertheless catered to strong ethnonational discourse highlighting Polish suffering.[4] The "War of the Crosses" that began in 1989 (and included the 1992 vacating of the Carmelite convent at Auschwitz) "ended" in 1999 with something of a stalemate and awaits a next move or a sociopolitical rumble.[5] Finally, Jan Gross's book *Sąsiedzi (Neighbors)*—a "revelation" regarding Polish complicity in Jewish genocide, recounting the massacre of the Jewish half of the small eastern Polish town of Jedwabne by their non-Jewish neighbors—has ignited a particularly fervent wave of national self-scrutiny (and self-defense) and has forced a reconsideration of the core myth of Polish "martyrology" that has yet to subside.[6] On the diplomatic level, Jedwabne was dealt with unequivocally in an international commemoration that included a speech of collective national contrition by the Polish president (accompanied by a protest from some Polish groups against the idea that there was anything to apologize for).[7]

Throughout these upheavals the notion of "witness"—false or otherwise—has been prominent and has in some ways come to define the public discourse on Polish-Jewish reconciliation. The term *witness* (or alternately *bystander*) is widely used to categorize the Polish position regarding the Holocaust, as distinct from *perpetrators* (Nazis/Germans) or *victims* (Jews).[8] Polish-Jewish sociologist Zygmunt Bauman and Polish-Jewish writer Henryk Grynberg have emphasized the trauma experienced by Poles because of what they were witnesses *to*.[9] Regardless of the specific terminology or perspective, the *problem* of bearing witness has taken center stage.

Dekalog 8 artfully registers the problematic. While the translator—the source of the demand for the professor to bear witness—represents in many significant ways an insider (shared Polish language, dress, tastes, intellectual milieu, biblically based ethical context), she is depicted as coming from elsewhere, from outside. Thus the return of Jewishness to Polish consciousness is presented as the motivating factor in Polish witnessing/introspection. And the film suggests that an encounter of moral ideologies, a clash of narratives or deep logics about the past, accompanies this return.

Indeed, Jewish travel to Poland today enacts a constant repetition of this confrontation. The Jewish demand for Poles to own up to their past choices—individual and societal—and thus to see themselves for who they "really" are, often accompanies Jewish visits to Poland, whether or not it is made explicit. As the "accused" professor in the film states to the translator she once turned away, "And you traveled so far to watch my face when you told the story."

Kazimierz as "Cultural Appropriation"

Enter Kazimierz. Until the early 1990s it was a largely empty, dilapidated part of Kraków where the many crumbling synagogues and the door frames with visible impressions of mezuzahs wrenched away during the Nazis' brutal removal of the Jews were the most obvious evidence of hundreds of years of Jewish habitation. Kazimierz's proximity to Auschwitz, the major Jewish travel destination in Poland, has transformed the quarter into a kind of way station through which Jews pass, leading up to and descending from the pivotal experience of visiting the Holocaust's central symbol. At present, fashionable Jewish-themed cafés and shops line the main square in Kazimierz; beckoning customers with signs in Hebrew and Yiddish (as well as English and Polish), they offer Jewish food, decor, and music, with the occasional waiter or musician wearing Jewish ritual garments, like a yarmulke or tzitzit. Kazimierz is a special place in which to consider the theme of bearing witness to the Polish-Jewish past. Due to a constellation of forces, Kazimierz has engendered a particularly robust spectrum of individuals whom I describe as "Jewish-identified": culture brokers, local entrepreneurs, public intellectuals, and assorted fellow travelers who have taken as their task the perpetuation of Jewish heritage. While for many, engagement with Jewish heritage is a way of making a living, the "industry" is not singularly commercial but rather, as Richard Kurin suggests of culture-brokering projects elsewhere, "an honor, a responsibility, and something that can sometimes be turned to personal advantage and profit."[10]

Among those involved in Jewish cultural work, tour guides form a kind of "front line" in relation to Jewish visitors in Kazimierz. Their experiences reveal both the Jewish demand for and the Jewish incredulity toward positive Polish engagement with Jewishness: for bearing witness. Janina, a twenty-five-year-old tour guide for the Jarden Jewish Bookshop at the time of our interview (today she holds a Ph.D. in Polish-Jewish history from a major U.S. research university), told me that when and why she started to be interested in Jewish history are "question[s] I've heard a hundred times [from Jewish tourists]," and she laughed. She talked about how some Jews "don't really listen to me, they don't treat [as] serious what I'm saying, because they think I can't know what I'm saying because I'm not Jewish." Marta, a graduate student in ethnology and a colleague of Janina, said:

> Basically there is a difference between Jewish and non-Jewish [tour-ists] . . . I think non-Jewish tourists, they basically listen to me, what-ever I tell them. They believe it. . . . And [with] Jewish tourists . . . very often, especially people from Israel, and America, Jewish people, they're very anti-Polish. And the only thing they "know" [she gestures scare quotes] about Poland, or they think they know, is Polish anti-semitism, and those Poles collaborating with Nazis through the whole war.[11]

The experiences recounted to me by Polish tour guides, and similar tourist-guide interactions I witnessed directly, illustrate a Jewish sense of ownership of Jewish heritage and history in Poland and reveal sus-picion or indignation or both toward what are perceived as ethnic Polish attempts to interpret this history in a way that might be at odds with the collective memory of Poland that Jews bring with them. Such sentiments can be seen as rejections of the possibility of a legitimate Polish engagement with or perspective on Jewish heritage.

"Cultural Appropriation" as False Witness

For many Jewish visitors, the mere participation of non-Jewish Poles in commerce relating to Jewish tourism is distasteful. But beyond the common accusation of crass, mercenary self-interest—that Poles are now profiting from Jewish tragedy toward which they were inad-equately empathetic to begin with—there is a more abstract level, a particular kind of discomfort caused by the confusion that occurs when Poles step into what is seen as ethnically Jewish territory. The sense among visiting Jews that doing "Jewish things" is something only Jews *do*, and further that doing such things is something that only Jews *should* do is both deep and widespread. This was revealed in the remarks of a thirty-five-year-old Californian convert to Judaism (and the daughter-in-law of a Polish Holocaust survivor). Referring to wooden figurines of Jews traditionally made by non-Jews in Poland, she commented, "Did you see the figurines? The little, mournful-looking fiddlers with long sad faces and beards? It's just sick! These people are dead, were killed! And you want to buy a little statuette? It makes my stomach turn! I mean, *unless there's some Jewish person making these in some artistic way.*"

The sense of ethnic boundaries—of memory, of representation, of identity—is a central challenge confronting those who participate in Kazimierz. Who owns the Jewish past, Jewish culture, the right to mourn Jewishness lost, the right to act Jewish, to feel Jewish, to define Jewish, to "be" Jewish? The constraints individuals would impose on others through their answers to these questions are a matter of daily concern in Kazimierz. Exploring the answers some local people in Kazimierz are formulating has implications regarding not only what we understand Jews to be but also how we understand the concept of "identity." But my immediate goal is to consider how these ethnic boundaries are asserted or transgressed in relation to bearing witness, an act that Poles stand accused of being unable to do faithfully.

I use "witnessing" here to highlight two interconnected functions of identification: namely, that performances of "identity" can be both ways of grappling with history—or the work of remembering—and attempts at truth telling about subjectivity—that is, about the self, relative to history. This process of engaging with the past has both ethical and historical dimensions. Performances of identity can be seen as acts of witnessing because they make claims to historical truth. Coming to terms with history, I suggest, requires bearing witness to the subjective truth of one's felt identity as much as to the categories of identity proposed or imposed by official and unofficial sources external to the self.[12] Witnessing, then, involves a commitment to the truth both about oneself and about history. And identification, inversely, can be a form of witnessing.

Dekalog 8 also suggests this subtler, while no less significant, tie between witnessing and identity. Not incidentally, in two separate scenes, the film implies that the identity of Elisabeth, the translator (who speaks fluent, accentless Polish), has been deeply affected by her wartime experiences. In the first scene, she prominently fingers her gold chain, on which hang two charms: a gold cross and a somewhat smaller (and shadowed) gold *chai* (the Hebrew word for "life" and a common charm). In the second scene, Zofia catches a glimpse of Elisabeth at bedtime, leaning on the mantle in her guestroom praying, hands clasped and eyes shut in what appears to be a characteristically Christian pose of prayer. The film viewer learns only that the Jewish girl had finally been sheltered by another Polish family, but it is never stated that the adult translator she became is now a Jewish woman— her identity as a grown woman is not portrayed as a simply "Jewish" one. Thus Elisabeth seems to represent a kind of disquiet, a Polish alter ego returning to confront a more comfortable, familiar, and unprob- lematic identification of Polishness and Catholicism.

This ambiguity opens onto my central concern. Especially given the profound wartime pressures to conceal, assert, demand allegiance to, suffer from, and resist the attribution of certain Jewish identities, how could a person's sense of self with respect to Jewishness not be influenced in the process? This leaves palimpsests far richer than the conventional, seemingly unitary and historyless identity categories of "Pole" and "Jew" would seem to proclaim. Testifying to these layers, honoring and representing their coexistence, bears witness to what history has wrought with the self.

"Thou Shalt Not . . .":
Ethnicity, the Self, and the Grounds of Legitimate Witness

Claude Lanzmann's documentary film *Shoah* makes clear the accusation of Polish false witness and connects it to the problematic Polish = Catholic equation.[13] In a scene in which Lanzmann asks Polish villagers assembled outside their church to recount their memory of a wartime event, during which the local Jews were herded into the same church before being gassed in vans waiting outside, he lets the Poles appear to condemn themselves as unreliable or tainted witnesses. They offer two fantastical "recollections." The first is that the Jews, in their agony, "called on Jesus and Mary and God"—a clearly Christian evocation. The second is that the confiscated suitcases of the Jews—though unseen by these Poles—had been filled with gold.[14]

In Shoshanna Felman's tour de force analysis of the film, she describes how in this scene "the Poles in effect bear false witness." She states that "out of empathy in the first case, with respect to the imagined moaning of the Jewish prisoners of the church, out of hostile jealousy and of competitive aggression in the second case, with respect to the imaginary hidden treasures and envied possessions, the Poles distort the facts and dream their memory."[15] The message here is that even when Poles attempt to empathize with Jewish suffering, they are trapped by their own mythology. Felman continues, reaching a deeper problematic. She interprets the Polish failure to bear faithful witness as "exemplifying both their utter failure to imagine Otherness and their simplified negotiation of the inside and the outside, by merely projecting their inside on the outside. It is to their own fantasy, to their own (self-) mystification that the Poles bear witness, in attempting to account for historical reality."[16]

What traps Poles, then, is their utter "outsiderness," the profundity of their difference from Jews. With this, Felman seems to suggest that there are constraints to witnessing based on subject position or group identity that encumber the attempt to imagine a position apart from one's own—in this case, to the extent that the attempt to witness for the other is false.

But proprietors of Jewish-themed establishments in Kazimierz tend to be Poles, who have a sense of being caretakers of Jewish heritage in the absence of a robust local Jewish community. And here this sense of being an outsider custodian of Jewishness at times begins to blur with a sense of insiderness—of having, attempting to have, or being relegated to the status of group member. Indeed, as I illustrate, many of the "non-Jewish Poles" involved in Jewish cultural production in Kazimierz are not quite as "non-Jewish" as they may first seem to be. They fall between conventional categories of "Jew" and "Pole," either in their self-representations or as others identify them.

"Jewish Like an Adjective":
Truths of Jewish Identity in Contemporary Poland

The question of Jewish identity in Poland is tortured and often tangled, and the now-grown Jewish girl in *Dekalog 8* is a familiar type in the postwar (and more publicly in the post-Communist) Polish social landscape. The number of Polish Jews who survived the war was slim (about 10 percent of the prewar population of 3.5 million), and many Poles have mixed heritage that, for some, is just now coming to light (i.e., the "Madeleine Albright syndrome").[17]

One of the more striking is the Catholic priest Romuald Weksler-Waszkinel (he changed his name in 1992 from Romuald Waszkinel). Only twelve years after he entered the priesthood did his mother reveal to him that he had been born to a Jewish couple, Yaacov and Batya Weksler, and was adopted by the only parents he had known, the Catholic Piotr and Emilia Waszkinel, just before his Jewish birth parents were deported to the Vilna ghetto. A shelf in his home displays a scale and a samovar that belonged to his biological parents, along with a picture of his adoptive parents, a set of tefillin, a Hanukkah menorah, and the text of the fundamental Jewish prayer "Shema Yisroel"—along with a picture of Jesus, bleeding on the cross.[18] Despite deep and abiding stereotypes, intolerances, and essentialism regarding Jews in Poland, the *logic* of Jewish identity in Poland allows for the existence of particular types of "hybrid" or nonnormative Jewishnesses that the larger—that is, the non-Polish—"Jewish world" does not. As Weksler-Waszkinel puts it, "I can be a Jew in Poland, but as a priest, I cannot be a Jew in Israel."[19]

Kazimierz is a place to which many such "Jewish-identified" people gravitate, as it offers a conducive atmosphere for exploring and identifying with Jewishness. The quarter draws category-defying individuals, people "sort of 'on the edge' between being Jewish and not-Jewish," as Jarden Jewish Bookshop owner Zdzisław designated himself and his wife, Lucyna.[20] Such in-between, "Jewish-identified" people find their own ways to represent their sense of self. Marta, an employee in the bookshop and the tour guide to Jewish Kazimierz introduced briefly above, has dyed-black hair and a large Hebrew *chai* tattooed on her right shoulder.[21] She told me:

The first question [tourists] ask me is if I'm Jewish. And recently, since I wear [the] *chai* [tattoo], they usually don't ask me this question anymore. They think that I'm Jewish; they figure it out from my *chai*. So instead they say, "Since you're Jewish, what are you doing here? Why didn't you move to Israel or America? Why are you still here? What is your family doing, and how did they survive the war?" And then I really don't know what to answer. Because sometimes I'm so sorry for them, because they're so sure that I'm Jewish, so sometimes I just don't want to tell them, "You know, listen, it's not that simple, I'm not really Jewish." I try to get out of this question somehow, because I feel like they would feel, kind of like hurt if I told them I'm not Jewish.

Marta suggests that if she were to tell visitors she's *not* Jewish, they might perceive her as somehow traitorous, as falsifying her identity. But her wording also suggests that she feels this answer would be not merely wrong but *inadequate*, that it would be too facile to capture the complexity of her situation. "It's not that simple," she says.

Marta has a long-standing involvement with Jewishness:

It's been probably half of my life—I'm twenty-three—that I remember I've been interested in that. And I remember my biggest dream was going to Israel and learning Hebrew, for the longest time. And there was always this something that was pulling me to Judaism and Jews, and there was always this deep feeling inside of me that I couldn't explain. And I finally managed to go to Israel when I was nineteen, and right before I was going there, really it was maybe two days before that, my grand-mother, my mother's mother, she told me, "Oh, you know, it could be interesting for you; I never told you that before because I thought it was nothing important, but since you're going to Israel, I guess it could be interesting for you, but you see your grandfather was Jewish."

This sense of being unconventionally Jewish, while prevalent in Kazimierz, is also delicate. To the extent that such different kinds of Jewishness make themselves public, they are likely to be overwhelmed by the inroads of mainstream categories of Jewishness imported by Jewish tourists and Western Jewish foundations dedicated to resur-recting Jewish life in Eastern Europe. These work on a model of Jewishness centered on descent and religious practice, with Jewishness through the maternal line and Orthodox observance as the "high bar" for authenticity

Those associated with the high-traffic Jewish bookshop—Marta, as well as Zdzisław and Lucyna—are often called on to articulate their identities, and the sense of self and Jewishness they express has been subject to the ongoing scrutiny and feedback of foreign Jewish visitors. Marta made her statement to me in 1999. When I made a return visit to Kazimierz in December 2003, Marta had converted to Judaism (after a year in New York with an Israeli boyfriend), and by 2007 she had married and moved to an Orthodox enclave in Jerusalem.

But there are yet more deeply hidden forms of Jewishness in Poland—and particularly in Kazimierz—that reveal a logic of Jewishness and of identification very different from that governing either mainstream Jewish or Polish notions of this ethnic category. There is the case of Brother Stefan, a Catholic monk and the director of a shelter and soup kitchen in Kazimierz. I met him through his mother, with whom I struck up a conversation on a city bus in Tel Aviv some months earlier after I noticed her reading a Polish-language magazine. She found out when she was thirty that her father had been Jewish. We met in a café where she told me her story and then suggested I contact her son, Brother Stefan, when I returned to Kraków. Stefan's father had also been Jewish, and Stefan expressed his identity in this way:

> We don't feel like Jews, but rather we feel Jewish. Like an adjective. I feel my mother has a lot of Jewishness in her, but she isn't a Jew. Jewishness—it's different from being a Jew.
>
> We feel an atmosphere, the problems of Jewishness. We feel near, a closeness. As a boy I had an intuitive feeling of connection to Jewishness. It felt like something mine. I read a lot about it. But we grew up Catholic. This can be a dilemma, but also a synthesis. The situation in Poland made many people creative. . . .
>
> Many people involved in the development of Kazimierz have Jewish roots but can't say this aloud because of the intolerant atmosphere [in Poland]. So they work on Kazimierz's development as a way of doing something Jewish. . . .

American Jews have to understand that Polish conditions are different. To be a Catholic doesn't mean to lose one's Jewishness. . . .

[Such people] also carry Jewishness. Such people are also chosen. They feel themselves chosen as Jews. Their hearts are Jewish.

In normal conditions, my family should have lost our Jewishness. But my grandmother spoke well of Jews. And [she said] that we are different, even though we're Catholic. So something must be there. It's a very mystical phenomenon. One cannot scorn this phenomenon. In Poland there are 1 percent real Jews, and 99 percent of these others. A lot of these others developed Catholic culture in Poland—but in a very special way, original, with something of Jewishness. Tuwim, Słonimski, Lechoń [classic Polish authors of Jewish descent]—they were Jews, but built, contributed to Catholic culture. Agnieszka Holland in the United States is a Jew, but also Catholic. Daniel [Oswald] Rufeisen, a Carmelite priest in Israel, wanted to invent Jewish rites within the Catholic liturgy. . . .

I think Polish Jews have a special task. If they survived so much—the Holocaust, Communism—it can't be for nothing. Somehow Kazimierz exists in that current. Maybe thus there is the conflict between American Jews—with their need for speed, for effectiveness. People here have a different pace. Another way. American Jews want to give money, push a button, and see results. I know Polish Jews who gather with their families on Saturday. No Torah. They don't even say it's Shabbat. But it's important.

Brother Stefan suggests a grammar of identity, in which the kind of Jewishness he possesses has the function of an adjective, suggesting that feelings of closeness to and engagement with the "problems of Jewishness" inflect but do not constrain one's self. He contrasts this with the state of being "a Jew," even "a true" or "a real Jew," an alternate identity he attributes to others. This latter state—communicated as a noun—seems to imply something more fundamental. Here identification intersects again with witnessing, in the sense of "truth telling," as Brother Stefan raises the problem of expressing his felt Jewishness in the face of mainstream categories.[22] He also suggests that merely engaging oneself with the reestablishment of life in Kazimierz—a place so intensely coded as Jewish—is itself *a way of being Jewish*.

One might argue that these are "safe" examples of "vicarious" identification with Jewishness. First, both Marta and Brother Stefan seem to have "biological" grounds on which to make a claim to that "one drop of Jewish blood." But what about those truly "pseudo" Jews who cannot make even that claim?[23] My response to such an inquiry would be, simply, that it is the *claim* to blood, not the drop of it, that may or may not course through one's veins (to use the language of the Western popular conception of genetic relatedness) that is significant here. Anyone can *make a claim* to Jewish "blood." Indeed, many people do, and the absence of documentation is a problem only for Orthodox Jewish authorities and the State of Israel—which use different (and evolving) criteria to select and define the aspects of Jewishness that form their boundaries: nationality, religion, ethnicity, and so forth.

Tellingly, it is examples to the contrary—when a Pole attempts to *disavow* even one drop of Jewish blood—that seem doomed to fail in the Polish context. Imputing Jewishness to another—or claiming it for oneself—is an extraordinarily effective way to socially define someone as such. Despite 1990 Polish presidential candidate Tadeusz Mazowiecki's formal documentation of Catholic baptismal certification extending back twelve ancestral generations, the Polish public was not convinced. His opponent, Lech Walesa, had intimated that Mazowiecki was hiding his Jewish ancestry. The suggestion was enough to destroy citizen confidence, and he was forced out of the race. That said—and I return to this problem later in this essay—one might suggest that there is a distinction to be made if the "drop" of Jewish blood one claims ownership of today would have been recognized as sufficient for Jewish racial classification by the Nazis, thus consigning one to the "Jewish" rather than the "Polish" fate.

"Vicarious Identity" as Cultural Critique

The Jewish-identified Poles I met in Kazimierz do not identify themselves *as* Jewish in conventional terms. But they clearly identify with Jewishness in a variety of ways that deserve attention. I would go one step further and suggest that these Jewish-identified Poles, in the confusion and consternation they create (whether actively or passively), also function as a form of cultural education and cultural critique. This notion derives in part from Naomi Seidman's provocative concept of a "politics of vicarious identity." Her concept recognizes that expressions of ethnicity can take unexpected forms, most specifically in asserting the self by "resisting a straightforward identity politics in exchange for participation in the struggle of 'someone else.'"[24]

Here I suggest that Poles identifying with or passing as Jewish work more or less explicitly against both the racist distortions of identity once enforced by the Nazis and the ethnonational constraints still placed on identity by Polish and Jewish national mythologies today. These identifiers/passers use "strategic provisionality" rather than "strategic essentialism" to disrupt entrenched notions of what difference is—and what forms it can take.[25]

While some Jewish-identified Poles may pass as Jewish, and thus only on occasion educate Jewish visitors that their assumptions about Jewishness need revision, other people actively "represent" Jewishness, publicly asserting that they are Jewish as a means of "cultural protest" against exclusivist Polish nationalism and antisemitism. Zdzisław, the owner of the Jewish bookshop, told me that he gave his son a conspicuously Jewish middle name, "David," in 1968 for this reason and that he once proclaimed himself "Żydokomuna" (a Jewish Communist) to a platitudinous priest who presumed both his Jewish ethnicity and an accompanying religious conviction.[26] A similar stance was taken by Krzysztof Czyżewski, the founding director of the Fundacja Pogranicze (Borderlands Foundation) in Sejny, Poland (an organization that uses the arts to support cultural intermingling and dialogue among cultural communities). He told the audience at a recent Jewish conference that, on principle, he does not deny it when Polish people ask him if he is Jewish.[27] He added that he would not, of course, claim this identity among Jews.[28]

Agnieszka, another Jewish-identified Pole and a born-again Pentecostal Christian who is deeply involved in Jewish community life, recounted an activist moment of her own in the following incident:

There is a shop on the corner, a milk shop; they sell all these milk products. And a man came, he was just before me; so he came and he said to this woman, [shouting] "And all these things are because of

Jewish people!" You know, "It is horrible that Jewish people are doing this and this and this!" And he was complaining to this *sprzedawczyni* [salesperson] . . . about the prices, that prices are growing, and something about *butter*, that the price of *butter* was growing . . . Stupid things! Which it usually is . . . in blaming Jews. . . .

And then I said, "Panie! Ma pan cos preczwko Zydom?!" I told him, "Hey! Do you have anything against Jews?" And he was *so* terrified, you know? That he was just *silent*, and the woman who was selling was also—you know, there was just a silence. They didn't say *anything*. [Maybe] they *do* have something [against Jews], or they have *nothing*. But I was so angry, you know, uch . . . I left this shop, and I didn't even *realize* what I did. But then I was *proud*, you know! *What* is this, you know? What, am I going to tell them *nothing*? Because of that, because there was such a silence, so many people died.

Agnieszka represents Poles who are demanding recognition of Jewishness as a legitimate way of being Polish if Poland is to be a democratic polity. Those who take as their task to "represent" Jewish culture are often also "representing" for Jews, in the sense of "speaking for (*and as one of*) those commonly left unrepresented in public forums."[29]

Faithful Witness and the Politics of Identification

If demands to bear witness to history have an impact on (national) self-conception, then perhaps the inverse is also true—that one's self-conception guides and constrains one's latitude to bear witness. As John Gillis suggests, "The core meaning of any individual or group identity, namely, a sense of sameness over time and space, is sustained by remembering; and *what is remembered is defined by the assumed identity*."[30] If who one feels one *is* affects one's ability to *witness*—and if who others believe one to be affects their willingness to accept one's witnessing—then a central problematic in Polish-Jewish reconciliation might be the narrow categories in which one's identity, and thus one's stance toward the past, is so often presumed and encouraged to fit.

In the end, then, it may be that Felman is not entirely wrong in her suggestion that who one is—or perhaps better, who one thinks one is—constrains one's ability to bear witness. This possibility is illus-

trated by Adam Michnik, Polish former dissident, journalist, parlia-
mentarian, and current editor of *GazetaWyborcza*, one of Poland's major
newspapers, in a widely republished meditation addressing the recent
revelations about the Polish wartime slaughter of Jews at Jedwabne:

> By coincidence I am a Pole with Jewish roots. Almost my whole
> family was devoured by the Holocaust. My relatives *could have* perished
> in Jedwabne. Some of them were Communists or relatives of Com-
> munists, some were craftsmen, some merchants, perhaps some rabbis.
> But *all were Jews, according to the Nuremberg laws of the Third Reich*. All of them
> could have been herded into that barn, which was set on fire by Polish
> criminals.
>
> I do not feel guilty for those murdered, but I do feel responsible.
> Not that they were murdered—I could not have stopped that. *I feel guilty
> that after they died they were murdered again, denied a decent burial, denied tears, denied
> truth about this hideous crime, and that for decades a lie was repeated*. . . .
>
> Writing these words, I feel a specific schizophrenia: I am a Pole,
> and my shame about the Jedwabne murder is a *Polish shame*. At the same
> time, I know that if I had been there in Jedwabne, *I would have been killed
> as a Jew*.
>
> Who then am I, as I write these words? Thanks to nature, I am a man,
> and I am responsible to other people for what I do and what I do not
> do. Thanks to my choice, *I am a Pole*, and I am responsible to the world
> for the evil inflicted by my countrymen. I do so out of my free will, by
> my own choice, and by the deep urging of my conscience.
>
> *But I am also a Jew* who feels a deep brotherhood with those who were
> murdered as Jews [italics added].[31]

Michnik does not hide the difficulty of witnessing he faces as a
result of the fluidity, the time-sensitive nature, and the resulting historical discontinuity in the ascribed aspects of Jewish identity. He is a
Pole, but he feels a "brotherhood" with Jews—even that he *is a Jew*—
by virtue of the Jewish identity he would have been ascribed by the
Nazis.[32] Perhaps this kind of open struggling with the shifting circumstances that make us who we are is a form of witness itself—to the
injustices of history perpetrated by those who would remove choice.
Yet even a categorical identity that one chooses (to the extent that

any such category is ever freely chosen) can be a constraint on bearing faithful witness. I asked Lucyna, the non-Jewish co-owner of the Jarden bookshop, how she feels when visiting the ruins of Polish Jewish cemeteries that she helps a Jew from London, Max Rogers, restore. Her response eloquently expresses the bonds of singular identity:

> Oh, it's a very difficult question. . . . Inside I feel a mixture of feelings, because I'm very sorry for everything that happened. And I know why mostly these cemeteries are looking like this. Not because of the Second World War time and German occupation here. They look like that because of everything that happened after the war [at the hands of Polish people].
>
> But this is from one side. On the second side, because of my knowledge, I understand what happened, and how it worked, [so] that it looks like this now. That World War II completely destroyed people's morality. Jewish life [wasn't worth] anything. And people got used to that Jews could be killed anytime and that Jewish property doesn't belong to [Jews]. It belongs to Germans and the rest for Poles.
>
> I think for people who were born after the war, it's very difficult to understand what the wartime meant, how people lived, especially in Poland, you know. Where if you wanted to help a Jew, you should be very strong, and very . . . it was a big responsibility to help a Jew to survive. It was like a game, gambling, you know. You play not only on your life but on the life of your neighbors, your family. It was a big responsibility. And I don't think people can understand what heroes these [Polish] people were who were trying to help Jewish people. And even nowadays, you know. How many people like them can you find? It's impossible. People are rather afraid; they are cowards.
>
> And this is the second feeling that I have. I'm mostly sorry because I'm looking at Max's face. I'm trying to understand what *he* is feeling, exactly. What I could feel if it happened to a cemetery where my parents' graves are. And this is very difficult even to describe. This is the very sad part of this work. *Because as a Pole I'm trying to find an excuse. As a human sometimes I cannot find any excuse. This is very difficult.*

It is this kind of witnessing that Jews demand from individual Poles, the only kind that will be taken as faithful and thus fulfilling: Polish acceptance of some responsibility for the fate of the Jews during the war, a Polish statement that, "yes," as Jan Błoński plainly put it, "we are guilty."[33] And yet precisely at issue is the content of that "we."

Brian Porter suggests a framework in which the attempt to blur identity categories between "Poles" and "Jews" can indeed be central to a Polish "apology" for historical wrongs against Jews.

> For Poles to say, even with the most heartfelt sorrow, "we did it," might sound very nice, and indeed this is probably an important part of any process of historical reconciliation. But ultimately the apology needs to go something like this: "we did it, because the very conception of ourselves that pervaded Poland in the interwar and war years drew sharp lines around "us" and "you," and made it impossible for us to perceive you as neighbors and compatriots, and equally impossible for you to view us in this way. Instead we saw you—and you saw us—as aliens, and at best we watched silently as you were killed, at worst participated in the killing. But we recognize that these self-conceptualizations, these cultural forms of identity, are mutable—that they arose in a specific time, under specific circumstances—and we are working to change them. We recognize that these forms of identity are not the only ones available to us. They never were. And we are working towards a new fluidity of identity, which will allow us to start to blur the lines between "us" and "you," to recognize that in many ways "you" are also "us."[34]

Jewish rejection of "Jewish-identified Poles"—and thus a Jewish attempt to constrain or impose identity categories on Poles—may make Jews appear regressive and, indeed, almost perversely embracing of the very identity categories under which Jews suffered in the past. But such rejection must be understood in the context of a seminal event of identification—the Holocaust—during which the boundaries were inflexible, utterly imposed from without, and determined who would live and who would die. And not only that, as Jews today live within a consciousness of the centuries before the Holocaust, throughout which Jewish identity was not only not chosen, but at times imposed with particular force and narrowness—and often with cruelty, humiliation, and persecution. In Poland in particular, any Jewish attempt to become Polish, to blur identity when *Jews* themselves desired, was, when at all possible, available only at the total resignation from one's Jewishness. The unevenly distributed privilege to assume and cast off identities at will lacks the burden of *inalienability* that typically accompanies a socially stigmatized identity.

Still, Jews also experience and "use" their Jewishness situationally, and their Jewishness changes according to the social and political context in which they find themselves. And if, as it seems it must be, the right to self-definition is centrally at issue (for Jews as well as for everyone else), then Jewish employment of racialist logic of identity as the measure of a person's "true" Jewishness—an "if you had been in Europe during the war, would you have been killed?" measure of Jewish authenticity—seems like a particularly cruel irony of history.

A final explanation of the lure of Jewishness for contemporary Poles is offered by Anna, a twenty-three-year-old Polish woman who had been studying religious practice and participating intensively in the Lauder Foundation's Jewish youth club in Kazimierz. She had begun by pursuing a university degree in Jewish religion and culture but became convinced that her interest and identification were not only intellectual but spiritual as well. While she herself was sure she was of Jewish ancestry—"I'm 80 percent certain that I'm Jewish, but the papers were burned. . . . I can't document it"—she felt compelled to convert. Despite pursuing the most traditionally enshrined trajectory for identification with Jewishness—namely, the halakhic procedures for conversion to Judaism—Anna's self-explanation seemed to center on precisely the "escapist" motivation that troubles scholars who consider the appropriate limits to empathy and identification. For Anna told me, "There is a wise saying: A Jew after WWII said if Christians died in gas chambers, he would have felt morally compelled to convert to Christianity. *I feel most strongly that I'm not on the side that was bad.*"

It seems that Anna, in her relation to her (real or imagined) Jewish ancestry, has made the opposite choice from the one Michnik described above—she seeks to escape, rather than embrace, a "Polish shame" in exchange for a kind of Jewish valor. The behavior of many Polish "new Jews" I observed seems to reflect this desired exchange,

and in engaging in such escapism they risk replicating the deep identification of Polishness with Christianity (and its counterpart vision of
Jewishness as a kind of anti-Polishness).[35]

"Empathy," it has been said, "is not complete identification, the
unconditional 'sympathy' in which, no matter how noble the intention,
the subject is usually lost—replaced by the sympathetic [bystander]
himself, who unconsciously appropriates the subject's voice and attributes."[36] Empathy, rather, is a form of "attention and respect" accompanied by an "awareness that another's tragic experience may never
become our own."[37] Perhaps in this historical context, conversion
to Judaism constitutes, via total incorporation, a more troublesome
"refusal of loss" than the other, more ambivalent identifications that
are common in Kazimierz.[38] As Judith Butler suggests, when a particular set of identifications is "threatened by the violence of public
erasure . . . the decision to counter that violence must be careful not to
reinstall another in its place . . . to [instead] make use of a category that
can be called into question, made to account for what it excludes."[39]

Polish antisemitism, perhaps like every antisemitism, is deeply
based in concepts of self and other, of rejection and desire present
in the very attempt to delineate the borders that separate self from
other. To the extent that "new Jews"—or any Jews—attempt to reject
what is Polish in them in pursuit of some idealized, pure Jewishness,
they set the stage to replicate what has been perpetrated against them.
It is the opposite of what I understood the late Cracovian Jew Rafael
Scharf to have meant when he advised Jews to embrace the accusation
of "dual-loyalty" that has been so often flung at them—indeed, he
said, they should even multiply those identifications, for these allow
the bounds of one's empathy for others to expand.[40] Ultimately, it is
when the bookshop owner Lucyna steps temporarily outside of her
Polishness—indeed, outside of any category smaller than the one that
contains us all—that she seems able to bear unambiguous witness.

That many Christian Poles who helped Jews during the war (or even
those who attempt to memorialize Jewish suffering today) are reticent
about being identified and celebrated for their actions in front of their
neighbors unfortunately illustrates that once a Pole has allied himself
or herself with Jewishness in some way—blood or no blood—he or
she is already suspect. Again, the presence of Jewish "blood" is not the

significant element in being treated as marked by Jewishness. Jewish identification in Poland is a risk for *all* who engage in it.

Simple, yet crucial, missing facts and misinterpreted motivations can produce lifetimes of often misplaced emotion around history. As the viewer comes to learn in *Dekalog 8*, young Elisabeth's rejection was based on information Zofia had received that the girl's planned custodians were working with the Germans. Passing the girl to them would have endangered key links in the Polish resistance, so Zofia—who had saved other Jews during the war—offered the (false) excuse about bearing false witness to prevent this possibility. At the end of the film the viewer is confronted with one more victim of mistaken identity and the moral, as well as the interpersonal, agonies that resulted. The accusation of collaboration leveled against Elisabeth's would-be custodians—for which Zofia's resistance cell had almost executed them— had itself been false. The man, now a tailor, will not indulge Elisabeth's desire to work through the past, and one is left with a hall of mirrors, a complexity of wartime choices and their woeful effects that both prefigure and echo the problems of witnessing I have taken up here.

Extreme trauma, Dominick LaCapra recognizes, may "exceed existing modes . . . of mourning," and the ghosts such trauma produces "are not entirely 'owned' as 'one's own' by any individual or group. If they haunt a house (a nation, a group), they come to disturb all who live in . . . that house."[41] In Kazimierz the need for bearing witness to the tragedies of others comes face to face with what Daniel Boyarin calls "our terrifying bleedings into each other."[42] Whatever else may be said about Kazimierz, in important ways it should be recognized as the product of a Polish desire to bear witness to Poland's own Jewishness, through the creation of what bell hooks calls a "cultural space where boundaries can be transgressed, where new and alternative relationships can be formed."[43]

Notes

1. The numbering of the commandments varies according to faith tradition. While the Polish film *Dekalog*, unsurprisingly, follows the Catholic numbering, in Judaism the prohibition against false witness is assigned the number nine.

2. That all of the ethical quandaries of the *Dekalog* series are "distilled in this particular story" is noted in Paul Coates, "Walls and Frontiers: Polish

Cinema's Portrayal of Polish-Jewish Relations," *Polin: Studies in Polish Jewry* 10 (1997): 240.

3. See especially the special issue of the Polish Catholic monthly *Wieź* (Warsaw) titled "Thou Shalt Not Kill: Poles on Jedwabne," ed. Jacek Borkowicz, Israel Gutman, and William Brand, 2001, http://wiez.free.ngo.pl/jedwabne/main.html. For a comprehensive overview of the history of the debate about the Polish *rachunek sumienia* in relation to Jews, see Antony Polonsky and Joanna B. Michlic, eds., *The Neighbors Respond: The Controversy over the Jedwabne Massacre in Poland* (Princeton, N.J.: Princeton University Press, 2003).

4. According to figures provided by the Auschwitz-Birkenau State Museum, the overall number of victims of Auschwitz in the years 1940–45 is estimated at between 1.1 million and 1.5 million people. Of these, 90 percent—more than a million—were Jews from across Europe. Among the dead at Auschwitz were 140,000 ethnic Poles (mostly political prisoners). Waclaw Dlugoborski and Franciszek Piper, eds., *Auschwitz, 1940–1945: Central Issues in the History of the Camp* (Oświęcim, Poland: Auschwitz-Birkenau State Museum, 2000), 49.

5. Geneviève Zubrzycki, *The Crosses of Auschwitz: Nationalism and Religion in Post-Communist Poland* (Chicago: University of Chicago Press, 2006).

6. Jan Gross, *Neighbors: The Destruction of the Jewish Community in Jedwabne, Poland* (Princeton, N.J.: Princeton University Press, 2001). These revelations were of information that had been a kind of "public secret" since the events took place. Joanna Tokarska-Bakir has called the process the revelations provoked "an explosion of 'post-traumatic psychosis'" centrally involving efforts on the part of historians to *discredit* the new revelations and thus to maintain and protect Poland's identity as victim, not perpetrator. Joanna Tokarska-Bakir, "Poland as the Sick Man of Europe? Jedwabne, 'Post-memory,' and Historians," *Eurozine*, May 30, 2003, http://www.eurozine.com/article/2003-05-30-tokarska-en.html (accessed September 1, 2009). Other commentators have proposed somewhat more sanguine assessments of the process. See Michael Steinlauf, *Bondage to the Dead: Poland and the Memory of the Holocaust* (Syracuse, N.Y.: Syracuse University Press, 1997); and Polonsky and Michlic, introduction to *Neighbors Respond*, 30–31, 39.

7. See Aleksander Kwasniewski, "President Kwasniewski's Speech at the Jedwabne Ceremony," Dialog, July 10, 2001, http://www.dialog.org/hist/kwasniewski.html (accessed September 1, 2009).

8. The messy reality behind these apparently clean categories extends, of course, not only to Jewish public sentiment, which has been given new fuel by the discussions around Jedwabne. Indeed, as Jack Kugelmass states, "Jews see Poles as witnesses, if not outright accomplices, to murder; Poles see Jews as ingrates." Jack Kugelmass, "Bloody Memories: Encountering the Past in Contemporary Poland," *Cultural Anthropology* 10, no. 3 (1995): 295. The canonized Polish self-image, in turn, sees Poles as "heroes and victims" (Polonsky and Michlic, *Neighbors Respond*, 33), and Polish judgment of Jews can even

extend as far as accusing the Jews themselves of being perpetrators, whether through the Judenrat's wartime collaboration in the ghettos or Jewish participation in the postwar, Polish Communist government.

9. Zygmunt Bauman, review of *A Social Analysis of Postwar Polish Jewry*, by Irena Hurwic-Nowakowska, *Polin: A Journal of Polish-Jewish Studies* 3 (1989): 440–41; Henryk Grynberg, "Poles Inherited Some of the Jewish Tragedy," in *The Best of Midrasz 1997* (New York: American Jewish Committee, 2008), 37–38 (first published in *Midrasz* 2 [1997]).

10. Richard Kurin, *Reflections of a Culture Broker: A View from the Smithsonian* (Washington, D.C.: Smithsonian Institution Press, 1997), 39. There are clearly more and less superficial ways of enacting identification with Jewishness, and some are more temporary, situational, and "low cost" than others. I became interested in those individuals who revealed to me identifications that seem intensive or long-standing.

11. Most names used herein are pseudonyms. The conversations took place during fieldwork I conducted in Poland in 1999-2000.

12. I in no way mean to suggest that the subjective and the external are hermetically, or even substantially, separate. Indeed, as I discuss later in this chapter, Jewish tourists' expectations are, among other things, one source defining the senses of self of the "Jewish-identified" individuals I am discussing. Charles Taylor speaks eloquently on this point: "We are expected to develop our own opinions, outlook, stances to things, to a considerable degree through solitary reflection. But this is not how things work with important issues, such as the definition of our identity. We define this always in dialogue with, sometimes in struggle against, the identities our significant others want to recognize in us. And even when we outgrow some of the latter—our parents, for instance—and they disappear from our lives, the conversation with them continues within us as long as we live." Charles Taylor, *The Ethics of Authenticity* (Cambridge, Mass.: Harvard University Press, 1991), 33.

13. *Shoah* was released in Poland in 1985 after earlier government accusations that it was an anti-Polish provocation. "Most Poles rejected Lanzmann's division of European society during the Holocaust (particularly in Poland) into the murderers, their victims, and the bystanders, largely unsympathetic to the fate of the Jews. Yet many were shocked by his interviews with Polish peasants living in the vicinity of the death camps, which revealed the persistence of crude anti-Semitic stereotypes in the Polish countryside. For Catholics, which of course meant the overwhelming majority of Poles, Lanzmann's argument that Nazi anti-Semitism was the logical culmination of Christian anti-Semitism was also unacceptable. But it, too, forced a reexamination of many strongly held attitudes." Polonsky and Michlic, *Neighbors Respond*, 14.

14. Shoshanna Felman, "The Return of the Voice: Claude Lanzmann's *Shoah*," in *Testimony: Crises of Witnessing in Literature, Psychoanalysis, and History*, ed. Shoshanna Felman and Dori Laub (New York: Routledge, 1992), 260.

15. Ibid., 261.

16. Ibid.

17. Ari Goldman, "Albright Finds Her Place among History's Victims," *New York Times*, February 9, 1997. For the general phenomenon, see Ian Baruma, "Poland's New Jewish Question," *New York Times*, August 3, 1997.

18. These observations are taken from *The Secret*, DVD, directed by Ronit Kertsner (Tel Aviv: Belshir International, 2001). The film is in English, Polish, and Hebrew, with English subtitles.

19. Roger Cohen, "For a Priest and for Poland, a Tangled Identity," *New York Times*, October 10, 1999.

20. While the notion of an "edge" recognizes the social solidity/existence of the normative categories of Pole and Jew (and thus in a way validates them), it also insists that this binary does not capture the full range of experience.

21. Tattooing of any kind is generally considered to be forbidden by halakha. (See Leviticus 19:28: "You shall not scrape your flesh for a [dead] soul, and tattoos do not put upon you, I am the Lord.") It has accrued a further, negative valence for Jews because of the Nazis' practice of tattooing concentration camp inmates. None of this, of course, prevents many (especially young) American and Israeli Jews from getting tattoos or even using tattoos to proclaim their Jewishness. See, e.g., Dora Apel, "The Tattooed Jew," in her *Memory Effects: The Holocaust and Acts of Secondary Witnessing* (New Brunswick, N.J.: Rutgers University Press, 2002).

22. As Konstanty Gebert notes, "Jews who are Christians often find themselves in a void between two communities. They often experience mistrust or hostility from Christians as well as an equally painful rejection from Jews." Konstanty Gebert, "Divided by a Common Book," in *Best of Midrasz 1997*, 21. To avoid being overly sanguine about the expansive possibilities of Jewishness, it is important to note the history of (and present) Christian attempts to convert Jews, with the argument that they can *stay Jewish* (culturally). All they need to do is accept the divinity of Jesus (which, in normative Jewish terms, would nullify one's Jewishness). The problem here is that it removes the legitimacy of Judaism as a distinct faith.

23. I thank Dorota Glowacka for raising this question.

24. Naomi Seidman, "Fag-Hags and Bu-Jews: Toward a (Jewish) Politics of Vicarious Identity," in *Insider/Outsider: American Jews and Multiculturalism*, ed. David Biale, Michael Galchinsky, and Susannah Heschel (Berkeley: University of California Press, 1998), 266. Other scholars, too, have proposed arguments in favor of cultural cross-identifications that see identification with an "other" as an ethically desirable approach to injustice. Adrian Piper raises the issue in the context of white racism against blacks in the United States and the social acceptance of the "one-drop rule," stating that "for whites to acknowledge their blackness is, then, much the same as for men to acknowl-

edge their femininity and for Christians to acknowledge their Judaic heritage. It is to reinternalize the external scapegoat through attention to which they have sought to escape their own sense of inferiority." Adrian Piper, "Passing for White, Passing for Black," *Transitions* 58 (1992): 21. Finally, Daniel Boyarin ponders the possibility that "we can transform transgressive desires for the proscribed other . . . into something like what the best love should be, a psychic . . . situation in which one seeks the good of another out of the autonomy and security of a self." Daniel Boyarin, "Interrogate my Love," in *Wrestling with Zion: Progressive Jewish-American Responses to the Israeli-Palestinian Conflict*, ed. Tony Kushner and Alisa Solomon (New York: Grove Press, 2003), 203–4.

25. Judith Butler, "Imitation and Gender Insubordination," in *The Second Wave: A Reader in Feminist Theory*, ed. Linda Nicholson (New York: Routledge, 1997), 305.

26. In 1968 a notorious, government-sponsored antisemitic campaign led to the forced emigration of more than half of Poland's remaining postwar Jewish population of 25,000. Some Polish sociopolitical history is necessary to grasp the particular negative valence of the term Żydokomuna—and thus the particular mocking and daring quality of Zdzisław's comment. Żydokomuna refers to the widespread, nationalistic Polish notion that communism is a Jewish plot. While used already in the interwar years, it gained force around the notion that Jews collaborated with Soviets to oppress Poles in eastern Poland in the early war years (where Jews were said to have "welcomed the Soviets with bread and salt") and in the harsh security forces (Urząd Bezpieczeństwo [UB]) of the early Polish postwar Communist regime.

27. The international conference "The Future of Jewish Heritage in Europe" was held in Prague, May 24–27, 2004. The foundation's Web site is http://pogranicze.sejny.pl.

28. A rabbi in the audience replied, demanding in a tone of profound discomfort that identities be more discrete. He began in Yiddish, "Vos, bistu meshuge gevorn?" (Have you gone crazy, or what?), and continued in English that, just as he does not want synagogues to lose their identity, he does not want people to mix their identities. "I want people to be comfortable in their identities. I am comfortable with who I am, and I want you to be comfortable with who you are," he said.

29. John L. Jackson Jr., "The Soles of Black Folk: These Reeboks Were Made for Runnin' (from the White Man)," in *Race Consciousness: African-American Studies in the Next Century*, ed. Judith Jackson Fossett and Jeffrey A. Tucker (New York: New York University Press, 1996), 179 (italics added). Introducing his experimental ethnographic writing about African Americans in Harlem, Jackson makes the connection between "representing" as depicting and "representin'" as in the street vernacular for standing up/in for. Jackson, "Soles of Black Folk," 179. In the wake of 9/11, non-Muslim women at the University of Michigan participated in an action in which they donned headscarves, using passing as

Muslim as a display of solidarity with Muslim women who might feel ostracized and, it seems, as a lesson for other onlookers in the complexity of identity.

30. John R. Gillis, "Memory and Identity: The History of a Relationship," *Commemorations: The Politics of National Identity*, ed. John R. Gillis (Princeton, N.J.: Princeton University Press, 1994), 3 (italics added).

31. Adam Michnik, "Poles and the Jews: How Deep the Guilt?" trans. Ewa Zadrzynska, *New York Times*, March 17, 2001.

32. Indeed, Michnik's Jewish identity is ascribed by many Poles today. Despite his lack of identification as a Jew throughout most of his life, the newspaper of which he is editor is often identified by right-wing elements in Poland as "Jewish" or controlled by Jews, in large part because of the assumption that he is Jewish.

33. Jan Błoński, "The Poor Poles Look at the Ghetto," in *My Brother's Keeper? Recent Polish Debates on the Holocaust*, ed. Antony Polonsky (London: Routledge, 1990), 44 (first published in *Tygodnik Powszechny*, January 11, 1987).

34. Brian Porter, "Explaining Jedwabne: The Perils of Understanding," *Polish Review* 47, no. 1 (2002): 26.

35. For many "new Jews," like Anna, reinventing themselves as Jews in this way means distancing themselves from most of their life experiences. As Anna explains, "I spent my youth as a *Pole*, so I didn't have to deal with being different. I have no experience with that." Their discovery of, identification with, and cultivation of Jewishness are also often accompanied with expressions of disgust with Poland and Polish culture. "This is a disgusting country," I've heard some say, pointing at dirt, dilapidation, poor customer service, or delinquency. Similarly, a Jewish-identified Catholic woman told me that Polish, which I was studying, was "a language without a future" and recommended that I study Hebrew instead.

36. Tokarska-Bakir, "Poland as the Sick Man of Europe." bell hooks suggests that this kind of practice likely "assuages the guilt of the past," "denies accountability and historical connection," and "establishes a contemporary narrative where the suffering imposed by structures of domination on those designated Other is deflected by an emphasis on seduction and longing where the desire is not to make the Other over in one's image but to become the Other." bell hooks, *Black Looks: Race and Representation* (Boston: South End Press, 1992), 22. There is also no shortage of criticism of what has come to be called "philosemitism" (or occasionally "Judeophilia" or a Jewish-oriented "xenophilia"), generally defined as an exaggerated love for Jews on the part of non-Jews and often accompanied by a pathological overidentification with Jews that is rooted in unresolved post-Holocaust guilt. See Thomas Altfelix, "The 'Post-Holocaust Jew' and the Instrumentalization of Philosemitism," *Patterns of Prejudice* 34, no. 2 (2000): 41–56; Helga Embacher, "Belated Reparations? Philosemitism in the Second Generation" (paper presented at the

Fourth European Social Science History Conference, The Hague, February 27–March 2, 2002); and Joachim Schlör, "From Remnants to Realities: Is There Something beyond 'Jewish Disneyland' in Eastern Europe?" *Journal of Modern Jewish Studies* 2, no. 2 (2003): 148–58.

37. Tokarska-Bakir, "Poland as the Sick Man of Europe."

38. Thanks to Butler's discussion of Freud's "melancholic incorporation" for this idea in her "Imitation and Gender Insubordination," 310–11.

39. Ibid., 305.

40. Scharf communicated this to me in the early 1990s, during one of our conversations in Krakow.

41. Dominick LaCapra, *Writing History, Writing Trauma* (Baltimore: Johns Hopkins University Press, 2001), 215.

42. Boyarin, "Interrogate my Love," 203.

43. hooks, *Black Looks*, 36.

9

Conversos, Marranos, and Crypto-Latinos

The Jewish Question in the American Southwest
(and What It Can Tell Us about Race and Ethnicity)

JONATHAN FREEDMAN

A few years ago I found myself with a seat at the table where most of
the real intellectual work gets done at the contemporary university:
on a hiring committee. This committee faced a more interesting challenge than most; we were charged with hiring a junior person, in any
department, who specialized in any aspect of Jewish cultural or social
life in America. Needless to say, the jockeying among representatives
of the various fields was intense (I am happy to say that we literature
folks prevailed). But the meta-jockeying was equally intense, or so I
discovered to my doubtless naive shock when I proposed that we consider hiring someone whose specialization was Jews in the Americas
of Sephardic descent, that is, peoples who traced their descent to the
Diaspora from Spain in the wake of the political and social persecution
spearheaded by the Inquisition and consummated by the Expulsion of
1492. Such an appointment, it seemed to me, might profitably widen
the field of Jewish American Studies itself. For it promised to open
up the kind of dialogue I was interested in fostering and have tried
to continue to foster in my book *Klezmer America*: a dialogue between
work in Jewish Studies and that done under the heading of "Latino" or
"Ethnic" or even "Atlantic" Studies. But my suggestion, I found, was
not met with universal applause; indeed, I was the only person who
supported it. As an older, very distinguished colleague informed me,
"The Sephardim are of no importance, in the United States. None. At
best—they're a footnote."[1]

Despite his salty language, my colleague may have had a point:
although the first Jews in the United States were Sephardic, they were
rapidly supplanted in numbers and influence by Ashkenazi Jews from

Germany in the mid-nineteenth century and then by a second, larger influx of Ashkenazim from the collapsing Russian Empire in the later years of that century. But nevertheless, I persisted in thinking that the experience of the Sephardim might give us an opportunity to ask a new set of questions about some very familiar issues. For one thing, integrating the Sephardic experience would complicate a number of the narratives commonly ascribed to the Jewish experience—rapid assimilation to Americanness, upward mobility, even the accession to whiteness. In the 1880–1925 period, those Sephardim who emigrated to the United States (largely from Greece, Turkey, Rhodes, and the Balkans) were by and large neglected, marginalized, frequently more impoverished, and less mobile than their Ashkenazi peers—and tensions between Sephardim and Jews within the dominant Ashkenazic culture sometimes took on a racially or ethnically tinged spin. "They used to call us black Jews," said Morris Calderon, an eighty-two-year-old volunteer at the Brooklyn Sephardic Home for the Aged. "They called us *Zigazuk*, which is how Yiddish sounded to us."[2]

Indeed, considered in the context of the American experience at large, the Sephardic experience has even greater consequence, for it offers a different genealogy for the very ideas of race and ethnicity that so powerfully define the contours of our experience than the ones we are used to invoking do. The notion of race in the United States, for example, is (commonsensically enough) painted in hues of black and white: grounded in the experience of slavery, the continuing oppression of African Americans in the post-Reconstruction era, the maintenance of the color line, and, more recently, the recognition (articulated in brilliant writing by W. E. B. DuBois and James Baldwin, given further expression by Toni Morrison, explored by a host of scholars such as Eric Lott, Michael Rogin, and Matthew Frye Jacobson) that whiteness is itself a distinct racial category. The increasingly influential and consequential ideology of race—intersecting with and buttressing the brute facts of white racial supremacy—is usually traced to the eighteenth-century European enlightenment, which shaped the discourses of anthropology, phrenology, and genetics.[3]

Sometimes lost in our focus on the Enlightenment as an originary site of modern racism is a different history, one that can be traced back to the fourteenth and fifteenth centuries in Spain, where the persecution and expulsion of Jews from Iberia was justified on racial grounds. The persecution and expulsion of the Jews from Iberia launched a new style of racist thought—the defamation of a people as much for what they were as for what they believed in or what nation they belonged to. The influential scholar Werner Sollors has reminded us that the very term *race* "in the physical, visible sense" may well have originated in the Castilian *raza*, "used . . . to describe (and expel from Spain) people 'tainted' by Jewish and Moorish blood." That understanding of race was reified by the passage of laws demanding *limpieza de sangre*, "purity of blood," for civil service and ultimately citizenship.[4] This relocation is not merely of genealogical or terminological importance: "race" so understood also looks startlingly like what we know not as "race" but rather as "ethnicity," in ways that both court and evade the determinism to which racial theory tends. As Sollors puts it: "The list of people to whom the doctrine of purity of blood . . . was applied included descendents of heretics and 'penitenciados' (those condemned by the Inquisition)," which implies that "at this terrible beginning, 'race' was hardly based on perception of 'phenotypal' difference but on a religiously and politically, hence 'culturally,' defined distinction that was legislated to be hereditary, innate, and immutable."[5] Ethnicized "culture" in this account is as grimly destructive in its social work as "race." But as we shall see, it can also bear with it possibilities that the deterministic discourse of race forecloses: the possibilities of telling new stories and crafting new identities amid even the most horrific social circumstances.

This reminder of a different itinerary for Jewish history and identity and of its meaning is consequential. It cuts to the very core not only of what we have come to mean by Jews, Judaism, and Jewishness but also of some of the most powerful fictions that organize our social life. In what follows, I briefly explore examples of the complex work that gets done at the intersection between Jewishness and the construction of ethnoracial identity and parse some of the implications we can derive for redefining the relation between race and ethnicity at the dawn of a new century—implications that, although grounded in some of the most dire circumstances (oppression, persecution, exile, genocide), possess a more benign aspect as well. The case study I consider is the story of the self-proclaimed Crypto-Jews in the American

Southwest, alleged descendents of the Sephardic Diaspora in Colorado, Texas, and especially New Mexico. Their stories—while fascinating in their own right—offer a perfect opportunity to examine less familiar questions of Jewishness, the logic of race, and the possibilities as well as the problems of ethnicity as they come together in surprising and wide-ranging varieties.

Beginning in the 1970s and 1980s, a number of New Mexicans, Coloradans, and even Californians of Spanish-speaking descent emerged from obscurity to tell historians, journalists—basically anyone who would listen—strikingly similar narratives of family practices that seemed mysterious or occult: an aversion to pork, killing chickens à la kashruth by slitting their throats and draining the blood, celebrating family dinners on Friday nights with the windows curtained to protect them from prying eyes. Frequently, these narratives lurched into the Gothic: a dramatic deathbed confession of Jewishness by a father, grandfather, or aunt, disbelieved at first by its recipient. Sometimes, they traced a more banal pattern of origin: a chance remark by a distant relative or a family friend. In either case, the stories continue with the teller putting together the pieces of a family puzzle (relatives with Jewish-sounding names, peculiar signs that look like Stars of David on gravestones, or an odd aversion to the local priest or Catholics in general), leading to a self-identification as a "Jew" that is as mysterious as it seems foundational.[6]

These rediscoveries and self-ascriptions led to the establishment of something of a cottage industry in the study of Crypto-Jewishness. A number of historians, led by Stanley Hordes (formerly the state historian of New Mexico), have joined a host of anthropologists and sociologists in studying the Crypto-Jewish phenomenon, as have members of that community, who have founded a Society for the Study of Crypto-Jews and Anusim (*anusim* being the preferred Hebrew term for the Spanish *conversos*, implying that they were forcibly rather than voluntarily converted, which, to make the matter even more complicated, is not always entirely true). The society has established an excellent Web site, sponsored conferences to share research findings on the phenomenon, organized tours for interested onlookers, and generally served as a resource for the production and dissemination of Crypto-Jewish self-identification. Southwestern Crypto-Jews have also been the subject of literary and artistic representation, including Kathleen Alcalá's excellent novel inspired by her Crypto-Jewish ancestors in Mexico, *Spirits of the Ordinary*.[7]

But this flurry of activity has also led to a vigorous counterresponse. Anthropologist Judith S. Neulander began fieldwork on the Crypto-Jewish community only to find herself doubting many of its claims. While acknowledging that many New Mexicans of Latino descent were interested in proclaiming their hidden or secret Jewish past, she vigorously argued that much of the hard evidence for such a past (e.g., the presence of Stars of David on gravesites and the use of dreidels) and much of the soft evidence as well (family narratives of Friday afternoon housecleanings and Friday night Sabbaths, kosherlike dietary practices, etc.) can be explained either by the presence of Ashkenazi Jews in twentieth-century New Mexico (dreidels are an exclusively Ashkenazic device) or by the influence of Seventh-Day Adventism, which exerted a powerful force in New Mexico at the turn of the century and borrowed literally from Judaism's customs and tropes.[8] Neulander's case was pursued by two reporters for the *Atlantic*, Barbara Ferry and Debbie Nathan, who aggressively questioned (as did Neulander) not merely the conclusions of researchers such as Hordes but also Hordes's ethics and methods. These critics and Michael Carroll, a sociologist, did more than just critique the Crypto-Jewish movement; they posed an alternative explanation for the phenomenon, viewing it as a result of ethnic self-hatred among New Mexico's Latino community.[9] To fantasize a connection to a Sephardic past becomes a way for Latinos to connect themselves directly to Spain, asserting a white European rather than a mixed-race or Mexican-inflected identity. As Ferry and Nathan pithily put it, "What better way to be a noble Spaniard than to be Sephardic, since Sephardim almost never marry outside their own narrow ethnic group?"[10] (This assumption is, I should add here, highly debatable: surely the best way to be a "noble Spaniard" is to claim descent from Spanish nobility or at least the odd conquistador or two!)

The war of words continues, in increasingly symptomatic ways. Hordes has recently weighed in with a book weaving together Inquisition records, personal testimony, and larger perspectives on the history of the U.S. West to produce a powerful circumstantial case for the Crypto-Jewish phenomenon in New Mexico, based at its strongest on the presence of Jewish names mentioned in Inquisition records in early Spanish expeditions to what is now New Mexico and southern Colorado.[11] Meanwhile, ordinary Southwest Americans continue to come forward to proclaim their identity as Jews even though many of them are now fully practicing Catholics (including some priests).[12] They offer testimonies based on family histories, they organize houses of worship like the Iglesia de Dios Israelita (Israelite Church of God), and they even provide genetic evidence to support their case: a group of putative Crypto-Jews from Albuquerque has performed genetic testing and discovered a high incidence of the genetic marker associated with the *cohanim*, the Jewish priestly class.[13] But Neulander has yet more arrows in her quiver. She has uncovered Seventh-Day Adventist roots for many of the Iglesia de Dios Israelita parishioners and has also turned to genetics to contest the claims of not only the would-be *cohanim* but also Hordes and others. Neulander is listed as coauthor of a genetic study on a population of New Mexicans and Coloradans published in the *Annals of Human Biology* that reaches the following ringing conclusion: "Our results indicate that, other than a small American Indian component, the Spanish-Americans of New Mexico and southern Colorado are indistinguishable from Iberians in terms of paternal ancestry. Although Spanish-Americans undoubtedly have some Jewish ancestry, they appear to have no more than do Iberians. The Crypto-Jewish scenario proposed by Hordes . . . is refuted by these results. The criticisms of Neulander . . . are well founded."[14] Neulander has gone on to marshal this and other genetic work to pour cold water on the use of "Jewish" genetic diseases by some proclaimed Southwestern Crypto-Jews as "proof" of their putative Jewish origins.[15]

I have more to say about this turn to the genetic. But first, I want to point out some of the problems inherent in these claims of Crypto-Jewish identity. As Hordes has insisted, this is an identity largely based—one that can only be based—not on any of the institutional markers of historical memory, like communal records of a congregation or diaries, journals, or letters, but rather on orally transmitted conveyance, from generation to generation, of a *secret*, a hidden identity. As a result, the signs that are taken as evidence of Crypto-Jewish identity are susceptible to multiple cultural explanations, since by their very nature, they had to be illegible to a hostile community and/ or the village priest. (Many of the stories that anthropologist Janet Liebman Jacobs has collected of New Mexican Crypto-Jews tell of dire retribution exacted by angry villagers on discovering the hidden Jewishness of their fellow townspeople—of houses burned to the ground in particular, an uncanny echo of the fiery fate that met many recusant Jews who thought they had escaped persecution in Mexico City and Veracruz, only to discover that the Inquisition had followed them to the New World.)[16] That identity is thus by definition fundamentally unverifiable, hence epistemologically unstable. By that same token, it is susceptible to a rigorous skepticism of the sort that Neulander and others bring to bear on the issue: they are not wrong to want more than family narratives by way of proof.

If the Crypto-Jewish phenomenon exists at all—and my position on the matter is resolutely agnostic—it is perhaps best approached via folklore studies or, as anthropologist Seth D. Kunin argues, by structural analysis of oral records.[17] These, however, explain little but suggest a lot—and on both sides of the issue. For example, does the fact that so many of these stories have a similar structure make them more likely to be verifiable? The emergence of so many similar stories is indeed suggestive (and I myself have heard quite a few that comport to precisely this model).[18] But the literary critic in me is compelled to note that these narratives frequently resemble a literary genre, the Gothic novel, in which such narratives of secret family identities, kept hidden to escape some socially oppressive institution but revealed at moments of death or enormous pressuring trauma, are common. Is this deeply suggestive of precisely the cultural cross-contamination that Neulander points to? Or, perhaps, does it point to the reverse: can the Gothicism evident in the narratives of the Marranos of New Mexico and the Southwest remind us more fully of the repressed Jewish subtext of the Gothic genre itself?[19]

Moreover, are New Mexican Crypto-Jews Jews at all? Despite some exceptions,[20] they are not accepted as such by the rabbinate, which insists, as it has since the time of mass conversions to Christianity and the rise of the Crypto-Jewish phenomenon in Spain, on conversions for *anusim* wishing to return to the faith; the rabbis' reasoning is that these individuals' connection to Jewishness is one made without any consequential knowledge of Judaism. Of course, by those standards, many people who consider themselves to be Jewish are not Jewish at all—or are in the same status as children of families of Jewish converts whose conversions are approved not by the Orthodox standards but by those of Reform or Conservative movements. But here we are dealing with a much more extreme example, since many of the Southwestern Crypto-Jews were raised as Catholics and consider themselves practicing Catholics, and some (as I suggested earlier) are even priests.

Crypto-Judaism is best understood as a creative improvisation, a syncretic assemblage of beliefs and practices, remade over time, creating a new pattern of belief that mixes elements of the circumambient Catholic culture to which Crypto-Jews largely subscribed with remembered, or recollected, or reinvented practices associated with Judaism.[21] Indeed, because Jews in the American Southwest (if they were there) possessed no access to a Jewish community, Torah scrolls, prayer books, and so forth; because in fact their own identities could only be maintained as a series of rituals whose meaning was likely unknown to them; or because, to put forward the skeptical side of the case, they can only be inferred by a hermeneutic process that is based on the predication of a hidden religious or cultural identity that underlies and motivates those practices which then validate that identity, Crypto-Jewish identity demands to be understood as an autonomous phenomenon, neither "Jewish" nor non-Jewish but somewhere in between. That identity thus calls attention to the fluid and shifting boundaries that have defined and continue to define Jew and gentile alike.

But neither self-proclaimed Crypto-Jews nor their antagonists are willing to rest in this state of epistemological uncertainty. In search of something more tangible than family narratives or ambiguous cultural artifacts, participants on both sides of the Crypto-Jewish debate have turned to idioms of race—to the language, in this case, of genetic determinism. Consider, for example, the seemingly authoritative genetic study that "confirms" Neulander's skepticism. The conclusions of the study, it should be noted, are somewhat less decisive than they appear, for a number of reasons. Taken on its own terms, the study's claim that "Spanish-Americans undoubtedly have some Jewish ancestry [but] appear to have no more than do Iberians" suggests that

there are many thousands of people of Jewish descent in the Southwest. If, by my rough population estimate, about 10 percent of the
people of Iberia are of Jewish descent—the great-great-great-great
(and so on for ten more generations) grandchildren of conversos and
Marranos—then there ought to be close to ninety thousand in New
Mexico alone, although—and it is a significant omission—we have no
way of knowing how many of these are descendents of Crypto-Jews
or not.[22] The claims of Hordes and others do not come anywhere near
this number. Moreover, Hordes's thesis depends not on the narrative
of a greater number of conversos making the trek from what is now
Mexico to what are now northern New Mexico and southern Colorado
(however piquant and romantic such a narrative might be) but rather
on a greater number of descendents of these conversos being Crypto-
Jews, or, at the very least, as being interested in thinking of themselves as descendents of Crypto-Jews. This, it cannot be emphasized
strongly enough, no amount of genetic testing can reveal. Indeed, the
whole turn to the genetic seems oddly beside the point. The American
Southwest could be teeming with descendents of conversos who have
utterly lost any sense of connection to their ancestral past, and this
would authenticate Neulander's thesis, pace Neulander herself. Conversely, there could only be a few hundred or so descendents of conversos out of the roughly 780,000 or so Latinos in New Mexico, yet
if every single one of them maintained some kind of connection with
a Jewish past, this would more than authenticate Hordes's position.

Meanwhile, the turn to the genetic is also evident in the other
side of the debate, in the experience of those New Mexican Hispanos
who, on the basis of a do-it-yourself genetics kit, are convinced that
they are descendents not merely of Marranos but of the cohanim, the
priestly class, the most exalted of all possible Jewish descents as well as
one that has historically maintained the purest genetic lineage (albeit
on the Y chromosome and hence through the father, surely a problematic ascription given the traditional matrilineal construction of
Jewish identity). In so doing, both the Crypto-Jews and their critics
rely on biological thinking that harkens back to the value placed on
blood purity in fifteenth-century Spain that gave birth to a new style
of thought about race as an essentialized and determining characteristic of identity. Both the authenticators of Crypto-Jewishness and the

skeptics replicate the very logic of *limpieza de sangre* by first demanding
evidence of unbroken or unmediated descent as a sign of identity,
then misreading the ambiguous shards of such evidence as markers of
identity categories that are ultimately cultural in nature and historical
in determination. If nothing else, they remind us of how perdurable a
racialist understanding of identity remains and how essential Jewishness remains to that understanding. The lesson here is that the turn to
the genetic to explain matters that are cultural in nature and meaning
can only remind us of the importance of a perspective which insists
on culture and history as consequential in terms of human identity or
group affiliation.

To claim this is not to slight the importance of the phenomenon
of claimed Crypto-Jewishness in the American Southwest, nor is it to
claim that Crypto-Jews are products of a mass delusion, or even as
one of my colleagues at Michigan, Julian Levinson, has suggested, to
instance their self-ascriptions as a variant of the recovered-memory
phenomenon of the 1990s. To the contrary: it is to assert that the
appearance of self-described Crypto-Jews, whatever the truth or false-
hood of their claims, is of signal importance because it provides a
compelling example of the ways in which Jewishness intersects with
other cultural formations in ways that are richly transformative of
both. Consider, for example, one flashpoint in the controversy over
their authenticity, the case of the dreidel. Although the claims that
Crypto-Jews can be authenticated because of the presence of dreidels
in their households may be problematic as "proof" of origins, these
objects bear with them equally powerful implications. One is to
remind us that people seize on objects and signs in the world around
them to create new narratives about themselves and, in so doing,
transvalue those objects and remake their signification. People in the
American Southwest who wish to affirm their Jewishness for whatever
reason (whether family tradition, cultural needs, desire to find a place
in multicultural America, ethnic self-hatred, class aspiration, or some
combination thereof) can and do actively remake the meaning of the
dreidels that they cite as evidence of their "true" Jewish origins. In
so doing, however, they are also inscribing themselves in an aspect
of the Jewish tradition. The dreidel, after all, is itself an adaptation of
a German folk game put somewhat paradoxically to use in a holiday

that celebrates the maintenance of Jewish national identity. The dreidel is also part of a Hanukkah tradition that is inflated in America into a substitute for a Christian holiday. In short, the dreidel itself has played an important role in precisely the syncretic practices and construction of new identities that we associate not just with the Crypto-Jewish phenomenon but with the complex history of Jewish relations to the cultures in which Jews have lived.

And, just to push the argument even farther, the dreidel song ("Oh dreidel, dreidel, dreidel / I made it out of clay") has become an integral, if ironically deployed, part of the syncretic, sampling work of a Latino performance artist who goes by the name of El Vez—a U.S.-born Mexican American meta-Elvis impersonator whose "real" name is Robert López. Admittedly, the song is not the only example of how El Vez's work persistently draws on a host of discordant cultural materials—white, black, Latino, and Jewish—to bring a sense of Latino difference into the American musical idiom at large.[23] For instance, this singer covers—or perhaps it would be better to say recovers—James Brown's "Say It Loud, I'm Black and I'm Proud" as "Say It Loud! I'm Brown and Proud." The act of recovery here, in other words, involves emphasizing the occluded presence of the Latino in the white-black imaginary that circumscribes race thinking in the United States. By also drawing attention to the presence of Jewishness in the ethnic mix of the United States (on his album of Christmas standards, no less) El Vez's music underscores an important theme of this essay. El Vez's "original" family name, López, is, to square many circles, that of an illustrious family of Sephardim, some who were conversos and some who were not; one member was the doctor executed in the famous sixteenth-century Doctor's Plot in London, and another was one of the first Jews to settle in Newport, Rhode Island. In addition to these, and most relevant to the issue at hand, stands the ambiguous figure of Bernardo López de Mendizabal, governor-general of New Mexico in the seventeenth century, who was successfully prosecuted (on circumstantial evidence at best) by the Inquisition for questionable Sabbath practices—for being, in other words, a high-ranking, subversive Crypto-Jew.[24]

López, or El Vez, or whoever he claims to be may be a descendent of conversos and Marranos, or he may not be; it really doesn't matter.

Whatever his possible origins, his mixing of cultural forms reminds us that all identities are in some respects malleable products of history and personal choice. López's performances that draw on a wide range of ethnic materials and identities suggest that individuals and groups engage in an ongoing process of revisionary remaking that springs from multiple origins and can take on radically different meanings over the course of time and historical location. López / El Vez's example is not really so different from the real or invented stories that the Judeo-Hispanos tell of their origins: for he and they alike suggest how individual subjects can construct new narratives out of the materials that history has bequeathed them—sometimes playfully, sometimes in deadly earnest, always, constantly, testing the limits of authoritative markings of identity, origin, and cultural and social meaning. Controversies about the "truth" of the cultural claims of Southwestern Crypto-Jews will never be settled. But these claims can remind us how rich have been the stories we make out of the cascadings of diaspora and how productively syncretism complicates our conceptual models of difference and ethnicity.

Notes

I would like to thank a number of audiences who have heard talks based on this material—at the University of Washington conference that gave rise to this volume, at the American Jewish Society Conference, and at the University of Pittsburgh, the University of Michigan, and at the University of Southern California—and responded with helpful suggestions and emendations. I have particularly profited from comments by Kathleen Alcalá, Monique Balbuena, Kirsten Silvá Gruesz, Michelle Habell-Pallan, and George Sánchez and the editors of this volume, to all of whom deep thanks are due.

1. For a more extensive discussion of these themes in the Crypto-Jewish identity debate, see Jonathan Freedman, *Klezmer America: Jewishness, Ethnicity, Modernity* (New York: Columbia University Press, 2008).

2. Quoted in Brigitte Sion, "Where Have All the Sephardim Gone?" European Sephardic Institute, http://www.sefarad.org/publication/lm/036/6.html (accessed January 21, 2008).

3. See, e.g., George Mosse, *Toward the Final Solution: A History of European Racism* (New York: Howard Fertig, 1975).

4. Werner Sollors, ed., preface to *Theories of Ethnicity: A Classic Reader* (New

York: New York University Press, 1996), xxv. On the significance of race and blood, see Benzion Netanyahu, *The Origins of the Inquisition in Fifteenth-Century Spain* (New York: Random House, 1995), especially 982–83.

5. Sollors, preface to *Theories of Ethnicity*, xxxv.

6. This process of public self-identification, at least for a national audience, began in 1987 with a program on National Public Radio (NPR), "Search for the Buried Past: The Hidden Jews of New Mexico," produced by Nan Rubin and Benjamin Shapiro and repeated in 1992. This show received, according to Rubin, the largest volume of mail in NPR history and inspired many self-proclaimed Crypto-Jews to come forward. See Barbara Kessel, *Suddenly Jewish: Jews Raised as Gentiles Discover Their Jewish Roots* (Hanover, NH: University Press of New England, 2000), 33. It was followed by an article featuring many personal accounts of (alleged) Crypto-Jewish origins. See Kathleen Teltsch, "Scholars and Descendants Uncover Hidden Legacy of Jews in Southwest," *New York Times*, November 11, 1990. Subsequently, similar narratives have appeared with regularity in books and in the Jewish and the mainstream press alike. For a good summary of these narratives, see Kessel, *Suddenly Jewish*, 17–38; and Theodore Ross, "Shalom on the Range: In Search of the American Crypto-Jew," *Harper's* 319 (December 2009): 76–84. Yet more accounts, in still greater detail, can be found online at http://www.cryptojews.com/personal_stories.html (accessed January 31, 2009).

7. Kathleen Alcalá, *Spirits of the Ordinary: A Tale of Casas Grandes* (San Francisco: Chronicle Books, 1997). Other recent works include Sandy Eisenberg Sasso's children's book *Abuelita's Secret Matzahs* (Cincinnati: Clerisy Press, 2005); Cary Herz, *New Mexico's Crypto-Jews: Image and Memory* (Albuquerque: University of New Mexico Press, 2008); and Ricardo Montoya's play, *Palestine New Mexico* (premiere, Mark Taper Forum, Los Angeles, 2009). See Charles McNulty's review of Montoya's play in the *Los Angeles Times*, December 14, 2009, http://latimesblogs.latimes.com/culturemonster/2009/12/theater-review-palestine-new-mexico-at-mark-taper-forum.html (accessed January 30, 2010).

8. Judith S. Neulander, "The New Mexican Crypto-Jewish Canon: Choosing to be 'Chosen' in Millennial Tradition," *Jewish Folklore and Ethnology Review* 18 (1994): 19–58.

9. Michael Carroll, "The Debate over a Crypto-Jewish Presence in New Mexico: The Role of Ethnographic Allegory and Orientalism," *Sociology of Religion* 63 (2002): 1–19.

10. Barbara Ferry and Debbie Nathan, "Mistaken Identity? The Case of New Mexico's 'Hidden Jews,'" *Atlantic Monthly*, December 2000, 94; Carroll, "Debate over a Crypto-Jewish Presence."

11. Stanley Hordes, *To the End of the Earth: A History of the Crypto-Jews of New Mexico* (New York: Columbia University Press, 2005).

12. For example, Herz (*New Mexico's Crypto-Jews*, 48–49) includes the account of Father William Sanchez, who discovered late in life his Jewish

origins via a DNA kit. Sanchez also figures prominently in Ross, "Shalom on the Range."

13. As described, with some sympathy and little of the animus of her *Atlantic* article, by none other than Debbie Nathan, "Cross Ways: Hispanics Search for the Origins of Their Unique Faith That Fuses Jewish Tradition with the Celebration of Christ," *Houston Press*, January 17, 2002.

14. Wesley K. Sutton, Alec Knight, Peter A. Underhill, Judith S. Neulander, Todd R. Disotell, and Joanna L. Mountain, "Toward Resolution of the Debate regarding Purported Crypto-Jews in a Spanish-American Population: Evidence from the Y Chromosome," *Annals of Human Biology* 33, no.1 (2006): 111.

15. Judith S. Neulander, "Folk Taxonomy, Prejudice, and the Human Genome: Using Disease as a Jewish Ethnic Marker," *Patterns of Prejudice* 40 (2006): 381–98.

16. Janet Liebman Jacobs, *Hidden Heritage: The Legacy of the Crypto-Jews* (Berkeley: University of California Press, 2002), especially 145–46.

17. Seth D. Kunin, "Juggling Identities among the Crypto-Jews of the American Southwest," *Religion* 31 (2001): 41–61. Kunin's expanded version of this argument, *Juggling Identities: Identity and Authenticity among the Crypto-Jews* (New York: Columbia University Press, 2009), was published too late to be consulted for this essay.

18. I have given this essay as a talk five times. After four of these lectures, a male member of the audience came up to me to tell me how he discovered his Crypto-Jewish origins through a family revelation; in three of these accounts, the revelation was made on the deathbed.

19. For the relation between the Gothic novel and Jewishness, see, among others, Judith Halberstam, *Skin Shows: Gothic Horror and the Technology of Monsters* (Durham, N.C.: Duke University Press, 1995); Carol Margaret Davison, *Anti-Semitism and British Gothic Literature* (London: Palgrave Macmillan, 2004); and Matthew Biberman, *Masculinity, Anti-Semitism, and Early Modern English Literature: From the Satanic to the Effeminate Jew* (London: Ashgate, 2004), especially 147–81.

20. Jacobs cites a case in which a rabbi reassures a self-identified Crypto-Jewish woman who believes her Catholic mother's illness had been caused by her Jewish genes that she, the daughter, really is a Jew, despite her lifelong disconnect from that identity. Since this goes against centuries of Jewish teaching, my sense is that he either was ignorant of the tradition or has jettisoned halakhic accuracy for compassionate care. See Jacobs, *Hidden Heritage*, 103.

21. This is the perspective Kunin brings to the subject, with the explicit invocation of Claude Lévi-Strauss's term "bricolage."

22. Here's my logic: roughly sixty-seven thousand conversos survived the Inquisition according to historians versed in census records (the actual number should be larger, given that many conversos successfully veiled their Jewish origins). After ten generations, assuming that each generation produced three surviving children, the number of people of converso descent

would equal 5.7 million out of a total population of roughly 40 million. Subtract for wars, pestilence, and the like, and you still have 10 percent of the population. If anything, this is an understatement: a recent genetic study argues that 20 percent of the Spanish population is of Jewish descent and 11 percent are of Moorish origin. See Nicholas Wade, "Gene Test Shows Spain's Jewish and Muslim Mix," New York Times, December 8, 2008.

23. I am grateful to Michelle Habell-Pallan for this reference, which kicked off the train of thought that concludes this essay. For more on El Vez, see Michelle Habell-Pallan, Loca Motion: The Travels of Chicana and Latina Popular Culture (New York: New York University Press, 2005); and José Saldívar, Border Matters: Remapping American Cultural Studies (Berkeley: University of California Press, 1997), especially 185–98.

24. Henry Tobias, A History of the Jews in New Mexico (Albuquerque: University of New Mexico Press, 1990), 6. Tobias cites France Scholes, "Troublous Times in New Mexico, 1659–1670," New Mexico Historical Review 12 (1937): 380–452. For other Crypto-Jewish Lópezes, see Renée Levine Melammed, Heretics or Daughters of Israel? The Crypto-Jewish Women of Castile (New York: Oxford University Press, 1999). Melammed writes about Maria and Isabel López, who were both burned at the stake for Judaizing in the fifteenth century. See also the account of Albert López, a Tejano, who comes to terms, late in life, with his Crypto-Jewish upbringing, in his "My Crypto-Jewish Self," Kulanu, http://www.kulanu.org (accessed January 21, 2008).

10

The Contested Logics of Jewish Identity

LAADA BILANIUK

"Jewish like an adjective." "Good bad Jews." "Jewishness." With these words we struggle to capture something that does not fit in the simpler naming, "a Jew." Yet even the simple noun "Jew," given here in English, is a field of struggle.[1] Whether we consider the question of who is or is not a Jew, or the possibility of degrees of Jewishness, we come back to the centrality of language in the conceptualization and performance of identity. Language allows us to name, and thus to identify, feelings and practices. Even if we consider identity as physically embodied and genetically determined, the meaningfulness of phenotypes and genotypes emerges only through communication, with language as the unavoidable mediating link between physical and social states of being. Likewise, language mediates our spiritual identity, inasmuch as we must communicate to develop and articulate our individual spiritual selves into a social grouping, into a social historical trajectory. Often we take language for granted, for it is like breathing, and instead we focus on the "content" as somehow separate from, and more important than, the words. But just as breathing is to life, language is to identity; it makes us people and makes a sense of self and group belonging possible. It is worthwhile then to consider the parallels between theories of language and identity in grappling with the paradoxes that being Jewish, or being a Jew or non-Jew, presents.

As the essays in this volume attest, there is a persistent, and perhaps unresolvable, tension between understandings of Jewish identity, some of which view it as predetermined, clearly bounded, and physically embodied and others as ideologically constructed, embodied through performance, and without clear boundaries. This divide parallels that found in studies of language between approaches that consider languages to be natural phenomena, existing as idealized discrete units (labeled with names like "English," "Hebrew," and "Russian"), and those that view them as socially constructed, categorized through discursive and ideological processes, overlaid onto a complex dynamic field of practices. The opposition between these two overarching epistemologies—one that views language and identity as idealized, natural, and essential phenomena and the other that posits them to be ideological, social, and constructed through practice—is the basis for many of the conflicts and paradoxes of identity discussed in this volume.

Idealist/naturalist/essentialist approaches assume that there are, a priori, such things as "languages," entities existing independently from our ideological constructions and acts of labeling. These languages are seen as organic emanations of peoples, who are also seen as forming discrete, idealized entities. Nations, as discrete formations linked to discrete peoples, are understood as natural developments. This nationalist logic pervades contemporary thinking, inasmuch as countless practices are constructed around a belief in the naturalness of national and corresponding linguistic units. Labeled and institutionalized, languages as discrete entities have become deeply ingrained in our ways of knowing the world. However, ideological/social constructivist approaches take the opposite view, namely, that people's beliefs, desires, and struggles are the key forces shaping the meanings and structures of language at the most basic levels. Studies of language ideology have shown that languages are constantly ideologically constructed, but to accept this idea we must struggle against the sense that we know what "English" (or another labeled language) is.[2]

The interdisciplinary essays in this volume suggest that we must also go through a similar process to see identities as something other than given essences. Susan Glenn illustrates this in her essay on the idea of "Jewish" looks when she quotes from a mid-twentieth-century sociologist's observation that "while science 'emphatically denies the popular notion of race,' the public was still more inclined to trust the 'clear-cut evidence' of their own 'senses,' which told them that 'it is often possible to tell a Jew from a Gentile, just by looking at him.'"[3] The evidence of our senses is given meaning through our *habitus*, the lifelong accumulation of predispositions that frames how we interpret what we experience.[4] Through habitus, social constructions are naturalized; they become part of our way of thinking, the window through which we see the world. Through habitus, physical embodiments of Jewishness were not only recognized; they were also learned and performed.

Recurring patterns of physiology, posture, speech, or other behaviors become internalized as stereotypes in our worldview. The structuring powers of habitus not only discipline and constrain us, but they also help us find meaning. Visual stereotypes of Jewishness such as physical traits, facial expressions, and gestures have played a major role in Jewish life by making Jews easily recognizable; this recognizability provided Jews with a sense of kinship and thereby strengthened their sense of security. Even though "Jewish" looks may be in the eye of the beholder, the training of eyes to notice some traits and not others nevertheless establishes another social sphere in which discourses of identity might be played out, in what Glenn refers to as an "anxious ritual of Jewish connoisseurship."

Nevertheless, as Glenn's essay also shows, for decades anthropologists have professed that identity is a social construct and that as such it can be fluid, layered, and shifting—in a word, complex. The idea that identity is not primordial, that it is not controlled by our genes, came both from a rejection of the racial discourses that justified slavery and the Holocaust and from studies of how people actually "do" identity—where and how they experience it, and how they explain it. The latter includes the lived practices that serve to create and maintain boundaries, from what we wear to how we talk. If we study what is actually going on, we find a great deal of complexity and variation in what might otherwise be called "a single identity."

At the same time, these lived practices are interpreted according to an ideology, a logic, and the dominant logic of identity has been a categorical nationalist / racialized logic, in which people are either one thing or another. Gad Barzilai's essay focuses on the conflict between identities as lived and defined by individuals and as officially imposed notions of "who is a Jew" in Israel. He shows that a dominant logic of identity geared toward the perceived needs of the secular state and reinforced by the powerful sway of Orthodox religious leaders has shaped definitions of the term Jew in Israeli citizenship law. In Barzilai's words, the determination of "who is Jewish" for the purpose of citizenship rights amounts to "a sociopolitical legal means to mark boundaries between various communities in ways that discipline community members." These rigid borders are not only ideological; they can become embodied in physical barriers that restrict access and movement of individuals and groups. The physical barriers, then, act as "structuring structures," working in turn to re-create ideological boundaries.[5] A related point about the power of ideology over identity claims also emerges in Susan Martha Kahn's essay on Jewish-assisted reproduction. She points out that belief in a national/racialized logic allows people to interpret the link to one out of more than sixteen thousand ancestors fourteen generations back, as provided by genetic testing of sex-linked genes, as the decisive factor in one's identity, ignoring thousands of other connections. Kahn poses a challenge to this genetic logic when she asks, "Is an identity that is conceptualized as shifting and complex less real than an identity that is reified in genetic terms?"

An identity that we recognize as the product of human actions seems to many people less definitive than an identity that is determined by forces of nature. Those who challenge this naturalist logic by proposing a social constructivist approach evoke even more skepticism when they refer to identity as a product of "imagination," as in the title of Benedict Anderson's influential book *Imagined Communities*, where he argues that languages and nations were socially constructed in tandem.[6] While we can argue that a social constructivist approach does not make identity any less real, when an identity is threatened or challenged, the idea that it is "imagined" provokes considerable anxiety.

The boundaries, the areas where the divisions between us and them are drawn, are key in any categorical logic of identity, and those who reside on those boundaries, in the marginal or liminal area, or who blur them will be seen with distrust, or even as a threat to the identity itself. Looking at the people who are called impure, who are at the margins, can give us a better sense of how identity works in the first place. Fredrik Barth in the late 1960s argued that it is the boundaries, and the functional things that people do, that are much more important than the "content" of an identity.[7] The essays by Erica Lehrer and Jonathan Freedman show us that the very logic of identity is different on the boundaries and that it is potentially revolutionary.

Take the phrase "Jewish like an adjective." One Polish informant interviewed by Lehrer for her research on Holocaust tourism used this language to convey that the term *Jewish* can describe an aspect of identity. This "Jewish" identity is not all-encompassing but is a facet of a more complex identity. Whether resurrected from bits of family history or adopted anew, this partial Jewish identity rejects exclusive categories of Jewishness and Polishness (which entails being Catholic and non-Jewish) and pushes for a more capacious definition of both. Lehrer contrasts the stories told by Poles who pursue a partial Jewishness with those who undertake halakhic procedures for conversion to Judaism and seek what might be called a categorical Jewish identity, sometimes to escape negative connotations of Polish identity.

According to Lehrer, some Jews find the idea of a partial Jewishness problematic and lacking commitment, for many reasons. Jews were killed in the Holocaust because they were Jews, without allowance for degrees of Jewishness. And as Lehrer tells us, historically Jews who tried to become "Polish" had to give up their Jewishness completely—something that many Poles who are aspiring to some degree of Jewishness today are not doing, they are not giving up their Polishness. Nevertheless, as Lehrer explains, an either-or definition of being Jewish or Polish seems to work according to the "very identity categories under which Jews suffered in the past." To Lehrer, it "seems like a particularly cruel irony of history" that some Jews use a strict either-or logic of identity as the measure of a person's true Jewishness.

Lehrer's investigation of partial Jews at the margins also illustrates how the meaning of the word *Jew* itself does not come to us predefined; it exists in dialogue, in the dynamic exchange between people. She examines identities that in contemporary Poland are encompassed not by the "conventional" and "seemingly unitary" identity categories of "Pole" and "Jew" but though a spoken and unspoken dialogue between the preconceived expectations of Jewish tourists about what should constitute the essential self of "Jewish-identified" individuals and the very different priorities of local Poles who oversee the business of Holocaust tourism. She cites the work of Charles Taylor, who argues that we always define our identity "in dialogue with, sometimes in struggle against, the identities our significant others want to recognize in us." According to Taylor, "even when we outgrow some of the latter—our parents, for instance—and they disappear from our lives, the conversation with them continues within us as long as we live."[8]

In this way Lehrer puts into relief the usefulness of the concepts of identity of cultural theorists Mikhail Bakhtin and Valentin Voloshinov. Bakhtin and Voloshinov maintained that the logic of identity is heteroglossic—resonating with many voices, vibrating with social struggles at every level.[9] In their view, concrete meanings of words are ephemeral, existing only in the specific context of being voiced, and even then the meaning is dialogic, not unitary, as it exists in the space between interlocutors and depends on the experiences and intentions of each participant in an interaction. In the abstract, words drag behind them a web of all their previous contextualized usages, each resonating with the specifics of a social interaction, so that "countless ideological threads running through all areas of social intercourse register effect in the word."[10] This web of meanings is constantly molded as words are used anew, as speakers strive to mold their meanings to serve their own intentions. Nevertheless, constructing alternatives is not an easy path, and people who challenge inherited categories are up against the weight of enforced definitions that reinforce the notion of identity as categorical.

Jonathan Freedman's essay on conversos and Crypto-Jews in the American Southwest illustrates similar clashes over partial and incomplete notions of Jewish identity among individuals living on the boundaries of identity. He too emphasizes heteroglossic performativity as "people seize on objects and signs in the world around them to create narratives about themselves and, in so doing, transvalue those objects and remake their signification." This leads to parallel paradoxes in language and identity: on the one hand, we understand and recognize words and identities as if their meanings were unambiguous, and, on the other, those meanings are ever-changing and hard to pin down. In grasping an understanding of languages and identities as heteroglossic, we must accept a certain degree of ambiguity and indefiniteness. As Freedman writes, Crypto-Jewish identity is "by definition fundamentally unverifiable, hence epistemologically unstable," as "the signs that are taken as evidence of Crypto-Jewish identity are susceptible to multiple cultural explanations, since by their very nature, they had to be illegible to a hostile community and/or the village priest." It is not just that marginal identities are best understood as heteroglossic; rather, in marginal identities it is often easier to see the processes through which identity is constituted. Freedman argues that the phenomenon of Jews in the American Southwest demands to be understood apart, that their identity is "neither 'Jewish' nor non-Jewish but somewhere in between, . . . call[ing] attention to the fluid and shifting boundaries that have defined and continue to define [both]."

Perhaps, as Freedman's investigations of identity constructions among "conversos" in the American Southwest suggest, individuals and groups will keep on defining themselves according to their own needs and desires in spite of the existing definitions and boundaries. He calls attention to the pervasiveness of thoroughly "impure," syncretizing experiences of Jews in general and concludes that in many respects "we are all Crypto-Jews."[11] What this means is that it is not just the Jewish Latino's (or the Pole's) but everyone's identity that appears as layered, contingent, constructed, and improvisational.

Essays by Calvin Goldscheider and Lila Corwin Berman capture important aspects of the process of improvising new identities under the pressure of shifting historical circumstances. Berman shows that in the face of new social realities in post–World War II America, intermarriage—long considered a threatening source of Jewish "impurity" —had to be accommodated if the survival of a distinctive ethnic identity was to persist. Goldscheider's study of recent Russian and Middle Eastern immigrants' adaptation in the United States and Canada reveals that their Jewishness is best understood not in ideological or even "spiritual" terms but as the result of social interaction and that immigrants' ability to forge or sustain a "Jewish" identity varies according to historical background, patterns of settlement, maintenance of transnational kinship and economic networks, linguistic affiliations, and the kinds of education their children receive.

The improvisational and "impure" aspects of identity are also featured in Naomi Sokoloff's analysis of recent work by Israeli writers. As her essay shows, literature has been a particularly powerful place for staging debates about "natural" and "imagined" notions of Jewish identity. Her discussion of the work of contemporary Jewish and Arab writers in Israel analyzes characters whose complex histories and contemporary lives call into question rigid categories and inherited definitions of who and what is "Jewish." The stories she examines not only depict individuals whose lived identities defy normative boundaries, but they also show an undecidability. At the same time, the stories reveal that an inclination to latch onto clear boundaries continues to be strong even after those boundaries are undermined or put into doubt. She argues that it is one of the strengths of literature that it may offer all these possibilities simultaneously. Dense, multi-layered expression "may attempt to say what could not be said other-wise and what cannot be summarized or paraphrased without losing some of its richness."

As in the stories Sokoloff examines, the essays in this volume reveal that despite the claims of those who argue for more improvisational and subjective notions of identity, assertions of who and what is "Jewish" have been a product of what Sokoloff calls "reductive stereo-types" that shut down complex characterization. Although she shows that such stereotypes work in tandem with approaches that foster mul-tivalent, open-ended depictions of motive and expressions of char-acter, what nonetheless prevails is a persistent inclination to think in terms of clear boundaries that demarcate group belonging.

The issues raised in this volume have particular relevance to Jewish identity debates; however, the insights they offer can also illuminate related struggles over language, meaning, and group definition in other contexts. My own work on language and nationality shows that the debates that arise over the question of who and what is Jewish have a parallel in the life experiences of other groups. Reading these essays on the contested nature of Jewish identity reminded me very much of the tensions between fixed and fluid conceptions of identity, plus the persistent human inclination to revert to boundaries, that I found in my fieldwork among non-Jewish Ukrainians.

In the Soviet Union a major attempt to move beyond national/ethnic/racial identities flourished in the early 1920s, when the project of constructing Sovietness invited a rejection of all oppressive standards, in art as well as in daily life. The idea was that people would eventually transcend ethnos as an identity category and that there would emerge a new Soviet person. The creation of a single world socialist economic base was expected to be accompanied by the emergence of a single world language in the superstructure, while national languages would die out.[12] The envisioned product of the changes in material, linguistic, and cultural practices was to be "Homo sovieticus." It took a new kind of human to transcend ethnicity. However, this idea was soon abandoned. As the Soviet system quickly became more and more politically authoritarian, it was much easier to rely back on the prestigious cachet of Russian language and great Russian literature and on familiar systems of categorizing people in order to control them.[13]

The construction of the Soviet person proceeded on some fronts, as living conditions (architecture, allocation of space, available furnishings, etc.) forced changes in lifestyles and attitudes.[14] However, the disruption of many of the traditional cultural and linguistic hierarchies that were in place in the Russian Empire, while originally seen as integral to the socialist revolution, disrupted centralized Russian control of the new regime. Thus Stalin chose to harness the inertia of Russian imperial habitus, appropriating the cultural values and the unconscious predispositions to build the prestige of the new Soviet regime. Russian became the dominant language, drawing on its history as the language of power in the Russian Empire. Similarly, high arts like ballet and opera continued to be revered as pinnacles of cultural achievement, to be counted with the technological achievements of the Union of Soviet Socialist Republics (USSR).

Ethnic identity, generally referred to as "nationality" in Soviet terminology (in Russian, *natsional'nost'*), eventually became more rigorously and firmly institutionalized than ever before in the USSR. It was reinforced in official practices such as documents, censuses, and cultural performances.[15] The fifth entry in every person's passport stated his or her nationality—Russian, Georgian, Kazakh, Jewish, Ukrainian, Gypsy, and so on. This reification of identity was most problematic when there was clearly unequal treatment of people of different identities, particularly with Russians being the "first among equals"—an oxymoron that points right back to a key paradox: how can people be categorically different but equal? And if categorical inequality is institutionalized, how can that be just? Can we achieve a fairer more just world, in which a Holocaust could not happen, by moving beyond categorical identities and changing the logic that underwrites our identities?

A shift away from categorical identities, however, removes clear frameworks that have reinforced minority identities in the face of the homogenizing forces of the market and mass culture. The removal of the fifth entry—nationality—from the passports of independent Ukraine was lauded by some as leading to a more inclusive society based on citizenship, while others bemoaned the loss of institutional affirmation of Ukrainianness. Even though Ukraine has gained political independence, the continued dominance of the Russian language in the media and in prestigious spheres of discourse, along with the high commercial value and expanding use of English, has impeded the resuscitation of the Ukrainian language.[16] Ironically, the European Charter for Regional or Minority Languages, signed by the state in 1996 and ratified by the Ukrainian Parliament in 1999, seemed most effective in supporting Russian, which many people saw as the former colonizer's language (tantamount to protecting the English language in India).[17] The presence of laws and other discursive practices that enshrined categories such as "Ukrainian" and "Russian," as well as the habitus that naturalized ethnic/national units, made it difficult to develop an alternative discourse. In efforts to build a democratic, independent nation-state while resurrecting Ukrainianness and overcoming the heavily Russified legacy of the Soviet regime, Ukrainian citizens are facing the paradox of embracing pluralism even while following the dominant national model of European state building. This paradox is similar to that faced by American Jews who, as Berman discusses in her essay, strove to remake "communal boundaries" without compromising the freedoms promised in a "putatively liberal, pluralistic society."

Nevertheless, in Ukraine, pluralism has been compromised by the legacy of linguistic certainties. For example, the people who speak surzhyk, the so-called impure mixtures of Ukrainian and Russian, have been widely maligned as dangerous to the integrity of cultural values. The pejoration of surzhyk substitutes for more direct discrimination against its speakers, much as the discourses about the negative value of African American English and other nonstandard Englishes often stand in for ethnic discrimination.[18]

Indeed, "natural" and predetermined notions of identity persist in spite of counterclaims and social practices that aim to challenge those boundaries. Are syncretism and hybridity inevitable in this global world, and would we all be better off to embrace them? Or is this fragmentation and individuation of identity a loss of something valuable? Can a distinct identity—Jewish or otherwise—survive if ethnic leaders and parents cannot convince their children that a categorical difference exists between their own group and others? Can identities embodied in complex ways retain their uniqueness and integrity in the face of the pressures of the homogenizing forces of neoliberalism's ideology of inclusiveness?

Whether it is a simple label or a more complex narrative explanation, words lie at the crux of definitions of who we are. Sometimes words seem inadequate to grasp complex identities, as in the oxymoronic phrasing "good bad Jews," which, as Shulamit S. Magnus points out in her essay, simultaneously propagates essentialism by continuing to apply the label "Jew" to converts away from Judaism, while disrupting its unity with conflicting qualifiers. If lived experiences often take place in the oscillation between categorical and fluid identities, human beings still crave words that establish categories to anchor them in cultural distinctiveness and to help maintain collective boundaries. At the same time, the world cries out for a more heteroglossic view of language and identity, one that helps, in the words of Brian Porter, whom Lehrer quotes, "blur the lines between 'us' and 'you,' to recognize that in many ways 'you' are also 'us.'"[19]

Notes

1. The issue of variations in meanings and connotations between translations of the "same" term in different languages is an important dimension of understanding identity, whether Jew/Juif/Jude or others. In this essay I explore the parallels between language and identity on another level, but the multilingual/multicultural discourses of particular identities are certainly worth exploring further.

2. On language ideology, see Kathryn A. Woolard and Bambi B. Schieffelin, "Language Ideology," *Annual Review of Anthropology* 23 (1994): 55–82; and Paul Kroskrity, ed., *Regimes of Language: Ideologies, Polities, and Identities* (Santa Fe, N.M.: School of American Research Press, 2000).

3. Melvin J. Tumin, "The Idea of 'Race' Dies Hard," *Commentary* 8 (July 1949): 81, quoted in Glenn, in this volume.

4. The concept of habitus, in particular as relating to language, was developed by Pierre Bourdieu in *Language and Symbolic Power*, ed. John B. Thompson, trans. Gino Raymond and Matthew Adamson (Cambridge, Mass.: Harvard University Press, 1991).

5. Ibid.

6. Benedict Anderson, *Imagined Communities: Reflections on the Origin and Spread of Nationalism* (London: Verso, 1991).

7. Fredrik Barth, *Ethnic Groups and Boundaries: The Social Organization of Culture Difference* (Oslo: Universitetsforlaget, 1969).

8. Charles Taylor, *The Ethics of Authenticity* (Cambridge, Mass.: Harvard University Press, 1991), 33.

9. Mikhail Bakhtin, "Discourse in the Novel," in *The Dialogic Imagination: Four Essays*, ed. Michael Holquist, trans. Caryl Emerson and Michael Holquist (Austin: University of Texas Press, 1981), 259–422; the essay was originally published as *Voprosy literatury i estetiki* (Moscow: Khudozhestvennaya literatura, 1975). Valentin Voloshinov, *Marxism and the Philosophy of Language*, trans. Ladislav Matejka and I. R. Titunik (Cambridge, Mass.: Harvard University Press, 1973); originally published as *Marksizm i filosofiya yazyka* (Leningrad: Priboy, 1929).

10. Voloshinov, *Marxism and the Philosophy of Language*, 19.

11. Jonathan Freedman, "Conversos, Marranos, and Crypto-Latinos: Jewish and Hispanic Crossings in the American Southwest and the Boundaries of Ethnic Identity" (paper presented at the "Boundaries of Jewish Identity" conference, University of Washington, Seattle, May 13–14, 2007).

12. Elliot R. Goodman, "World State and World Language," in *Readings in the Sociology of Language*, ed. Joshua A. Fishman (The Hague: Mouton, 1968), 729; reprinted from Goodman, *The Soviet Design for a World State* (New York: Columbia University Press, 1960).

13. David L. Hoffmann, *Stalinist Values: The Cultural Norms of Soviet Modernity (1917–1941)* (Ithaca, N.Y.: Cornell University Press, 2003); Michael Smith, *Language and Power in the Creation of the USSR, 1917–1953* (New York: Mouton de Gruyter, 1998).

14. In Victor Buchli, ed., *The Material Culture Reader* (New York: Berg, 2002), see two essays by Buchli, "Architecture and the Domestic Sphere," 207–14, and "Khrushchev, Modernism, and the Fight against *Petit-bourgeois* Consciousness in the Soviet Home," 215–36.

15. Francine Hirsch, "The Soviet Union as a Work-in-Progress: Ethnographers and the Category 'Nationality' in the 1926, 1937, and 1939 Censuses," *Slavic Review* 56, no. 2 (1997): 251–78; Yuri Slezkine, "The USSR as a Communal Apartment, or How a Socialist State Promoted Ethnic Particularism," *Slavic Review* 53, no. 2 (1994): 414–52; Katherine Verdery, *What Was Socialism, and What Comes Next?* (Princeton, N.J.: Princeton University Press, 1996), 83–87.

16. For an examination of the sociolinguistic situation in Ukraine and the historical conditions that led to it, see Laada Bilaniuk, *Contested Tongues: Language Politics and Cultural Correction in Ukraine* (Ithaca, N.Y.: Cornell University Press, 2005).

17. Laada Bilaniuk and Svitlana Melnyk, "A Tense and Shifting Balance: Bilingualism and Education in Ukraine," *International Journal of Bilingual Education and Bilingualism* 11, nos. 3–4 (2008): 350.

18. Rosina Lippi-Green, *English with an Accent: Language, Ideology, and Discrimination in the United States* (New York: Routledge, 1997).

19. Brian Porter, "Explaining Jedwabne: The Perils of Understanding," *Polish Review* 47, no. 1 (2002): 26, quoted in Lehrer, in this volume.

Bibliography

Alcalá, Kathleen. *Spirits of the Ordinary: A Tale of Casas Grandes*. San Francisco: Chronicle Books, 1997.

Aleichem, Sholom. *The Bloody Hoax*. Translated by Aliza Shevrin. Bloomington: Indiana University Press, 1991.

Allport, Gordon W. *The Nature of Prejudice*. Boston: Beacon Press, 1954.

Allport, Gordon W., and Bernard M. Kramer. "Some Roots of Prejudice." *Journal of Psychology* 22 (July 1946): 9–39.

Alter, Robert. *The Pleasures of Reading in an Ideological Age*. New York: Simon and Schuster, 1989.

Altfelix, Thomas. "The 'Post-Holocaust Jew' and the Instrumentalization of Philosemitism." *Patterns of Prejudice* 34, no. 2 (2000): 41–56.

Amossy, Ruth, and Anne Herschberg Pierrot. *Stéréotypes et clichés: Langue, discours, société* [Stereotypes and Clichés: Language, Speech, Society]. Paris: Nathan, 1997.

Anderson, Benedict. *Imagined Communities: Reflections on the Origin and Spread of Nationalism*. London: Verso, 1991.

Apel, Dora. *Memory Effects: The Holocaust and Acts of Secondary Witnessing*. New Brunswick, N.J.: Rutgers University Press, 2002.

Appelfeld, Aharon. *Bekomat hakark'a* [On the Ground Floor]. Tel Aviv: Daga, 1968.

———. *Beyond Despair*. Translated by Jeffrey M. Green. New York: Fromm International, 1994.

———. *A Table for One: Under the Light of Jerusalem*. Translated by Aloma Halter. New Milford, Conn.: Toby Press, 2006. Originally published as *'Od hayom gadol* (Jerusalem: Keter and Ben Zvi, 2001).

———. *Tzili: The Story of a Life*. Translated by Dalya Bilu. New York: Dutton, 1983. Originally published as *Hakutonet vehapasim* (Tel Aviv: Hakibbutz Hameuhad, 1983).

Aronsohn, Richard B., and Richard A. Epstein. *The Miracle of Cosmetic Plastic Surgery*. Los Angeles: Sherbourne Press, 1970.

Baer, Yitzhak. *A History of the Jews in Christian Spain*. Vol. 2, *From the Fourteenth Century to the Expulsion*. Translated by Louis Schoffman. Philadelphia: Jewish Publication Society of America, 1971.

Bakhtin, Mikhail. "Discourse in the Novel." In *The Dialogic Imagination: Four Essays*, edited by Michael Holquist, translated by Caryl Emerson and Michael Holquist, 259–422. Austin: University of Texas Press, 1981. Originally published as *Voprosy literatury i estetiki* (Moscow: Khudozhestvennaya literatura, 1975).

Barfoot, C. C., ed. *Beyond Pug's Tour: National and Ethnic Stereotyping in Theory and Literary Practice.* Amsterdam: Rodopi, 1997.

Barkan, Elazar. *The Retreat of Scientific Racism: Changing Concepts in Britain and the United States between the World Wars.* New York: Cambridge University Press, 1992.

Barth, Fredrik. *Ethnic Groups and Boundaries: The Social Organization of Culture Difference.* Oslo: Universitetsforlaget, 1969.

Barzilai, Gad. *Communities and Law: Politics and Cultures of Legal Identities.* Ann Arbor: University of Michigan Press, 2003.

———. *Wars, Internal Conflicts, and Political Order: A Jewish Democracy in the Middle East.* Albany: State University of New York Press, 1996.

Barzilai-Nahon, Karine, and Gad Barzilai. "Cultured Technology: The Internet and Religious Fundamentalism." *Information Society* 21, no. 1 (2005): 25–40.

Bauman, Zygmunt. Review of *A Social Analysis of Postwar Polish Jewry*, by Irena Hurwic-Nowakowska. *Polin: A Journal of Polish-Jewish Studies* 3 (1989): 438–42.

Ben-Amos, Dan, and Jerome R. Mintz, eds. and trans. *In Praise of the Baal Shem Tov (Shivhei ha-Besht): The Earliest Collection of Legends about the Founder of Hasidism.* Bloomington: Indiana University Press, 1970.

Ben-Eliezer, Uri. *The Making of Israeli Militarism.* Bloomington: Indiana University Press, 1998.

Ben-Rafael, Eliezer. *Jewish Identities: Fifty Intellectuals Answer Ben Gurion.* Leiden: Brill, 2002.

Ben-Ur, Aviva. "Funny, You Don't Look Jewish! 'Passing' and the Elasticity of Ethnic Identity among Levantine Sephardic Immigrants in Early Twentieth Century America." *Kolor* (Brussels), no. 2 (November 2002): 9–18.

Berman, Lila Corwin. *Speaking of Jews: Rabbis, Intellectuals, and the Creation of an American Public Identity.* Berkeley: University of California Press, 2009.

Biberman, Matthew. *Masculinity, Anti-Semitism, and Early Modern English Literature: From the Satanic to the Effeminate Jew.* London: Ashgate, 2004.

Bilaniuk, Laada. *Contested Tongues: Language Politics and Cultural Correction in Ukraine.* Ithaca, N.Y.: Cornell University Press, 2005.

Bilaniuk, Laada, and Svitlana Melnyk. "A Tense and Shifting Balance: Bilingualism and Education in Ukraine." *International Journal of Bilingual Education and Bilingualism* 11, nos. 3–4 (2008): 340–72.

Błoński, Jan. "The Poor Poles Look at the Ghetto." In *My Brother's Keeper? Recent Polish Debates on the Holocaust*, edited by Antony Polonsky, 34–52. London: Routledge, 1990. First published in *Tygodnik Powszechny*, January 11, 1987.

Bonfil, Robert. *Jewish Life in Renaissance Italy.* Berkeley: University of California Press, 1991.

Borkowicz, Jacek, Israel Gutman, and William Brand, eds. *Thou Shalt Not Kill: Poles on Jedwabne.* Warsaw: Więź, 2001.

Bourdieu, Pierre. *Language and Symbolic Power.* Edited by John B. Thompson, translated by Gino Raymond and Matthew Adamson. Cambridge, Mass.: Harvard University Press, 1991.

Boyarin, Daniel. "Interrogate My Love." In *Wrestling with Zion: Progressive Jewish-American Responses to the Israeli-Palestinian Conflict,* edited by Tony Kushner and Alisa Solomon, 198–204. New York: Grove Press, 2003.

Bramen, Carrie Tirado. "Speaking in Typeface: Characterizing Stereotypes in Gayl Jones's *Mosquito.*" *Modern Fiction Studies* 49, no. 1 (2003): 124–54.

Brodkin, Karen. *How Jews Became White Folks and What That Says about Race in America.* New Brunswick, N.J.: Rutgers University Press, 1998.

Brym, Robert, William Shaffir, and Morton Weinfeld, eds. *The Jews in Canada.* Toronto: Oxford University Press, 1993.

Buchli, Victor. "Architecture and the Domestic Sphere." In *The Material Culture Reader,* edited by Victor Buchli, 207–14. New York: Berg, 2002.

———. "Khrushchev, Modernism, and the Fight against *Petit-bourgeois* Consciousness in the Soviet Home." In *The Material Culture Reader,* edited by Victor Buchli, 215–36. New York: Berg, 2002.

Burstein, Paul. "Jewish Educational and Economic Success in the United States: A Search for Explanations." *Sociological Perspectives* 50, no. 20 (2007): 209–28.

Butler, Judith. "Imitation and Gender Insubordination." In *The Second Wave: A Reader in Feminist Theory,* edited by Linda Nicholson, 300–315. New York: Routledge, 1997.

Carlebach, Elisheva. *Divided Souls: Converts from Judaism in Germany, 1500–1750.* New Haven, Conn.: Yale University Press, 2001.

———. *Divided Souls: The Convert Critique and the Culture of Ashkenaz, 1750–1800.* Leo Baeck Memorial Lecture 46. New York: Leo Baeck Institute, 2003.

Carroll, Michael. "The Debate over a Crypto-Jewish Presence in New Mexico: The Role of Ethnographic Allegory and Orientalism." *Sociology of Religion* 63 (2002): 1–19.

Carter, Launor F. "The Identification of 'Racial' Membership." *Journal of Abnormal and Social Psychology* 43, no. 3 (1948): 279–86.

Chazan, Robert, ed. *Church, State, and Jew in the Middle Ages.* West Orange, N.J.: Behrman House, 1980.

Cheyette, Bryan, ed. *Between "Race" and Culture: Representations of "the Jew" in English and American Literature.* Stanford, Calif.: Stanford University Press, 1996.

———. *Constructions of 'the Jew' in English Literature and Society: Racial Representations, 1875–1945.* Cambridge: Cambridge University Press, 1993.

Chiswick, Carmel. *The Economics of American Judaism.* New York: Taylor and Francis, 2008.

Cinnirella, Marco. "Ethnic and National Stereotypes: A Social Identity Perspective." In *Beyond Pug's Tour: National and Ethnic Stereotyping in Theory and Literary Practice,* edited by C. C. Barfoot, 37–52. Amsterdam: Rodopi, 1997.

Coates, Paul. "Walls and Frontiers: Polish Cinema's Portrayal of Polish-Jewish Relations." *Polin: Studies in Polish Jewry* 10 (1997): 221–46.

Cohen, Asher. *Israeli Assimilation: Changes in the Definition of the Jewish Collective's Identity and Its Boundaries.* Jerusalem: Institute of the World Jewish Congress, 2002.

Cohen, Jeremy. *The Friars and the Jews: The Evolution of Medieval Anti-Judaism.* Ithaca, N.Y.: Cornell University Press, 1982.

———. "The Mentality of the Medieval Jewish Apostate: Peter Alfonsi, Hermann of Cologne, and Pablo Christiani." In Endelman, *Jewish Apostasy*, 20–47.

Cohen, Rina. "The New Immigrants: A Comparative Profile." In *From Immigration to Integration: The Canadian Jewish Experience; A Millennium Edition*, edited by Ruth Klein and Frank Dimant, 213–27. Toronto: B'nai Brith and Malcolm Lester, 2001.

Cohen, Shaye J. D. *The Beginnings of Jewishness: Boundaries, Varieties, Uncertainties.* Berkeley: University of California Press, 1999.

Cohn, Werner. "The Name Changers." *Jewish Digest* 30 (September 1984): 16–22.

Connerton, Paul. *How Societies Remember.* Cambridge: Cambridge University Press, 1989.

Cover, Robert. *Narrative, Violence, and the Law: The Essays of Robert Cover*, edited by Martha Minow, Michael Ryan, and Austin Sarat, 13–49. Ann Arbor: University of Michigan Press, 1992.

———. "Nomos and Narrative." In Cover, *Narrative, Violence, and the Law*, 95–172.

———. "The Origins of Judicial Activism in the Protection of Minorities." In Cover, *Narrative, Violence, and the Law*, 13–49.

———. "Violence and the Word." In Cover, *Narrative, Violence, and the Law*, 203–38.

Davison, Carol Margaret. *Anti-Semitism and British Gothic Literature.* London: Palgrave Macmillan, 2004.

Dawidowicz, Lucy S. *The Golden Tradition: Jewish Life and Thought in Eastern Europe.* New York: Holt, Rinehart and Winston, 1967.

Degler, Carl. *In Search of Human Nature: The Decline and Revival of Darwinism in American Social Thought.* New York: Oxford University Press, 1992.

Dollinger, Marc. *Quest for Inclusion: Jews and Liberalism in Modern America.* Princeton, N.J.: Princeton University Press, 2000.

Dominguez, Virginia. *People as Subject, People as Object: Selfhood and Peoplehood in Contemporary Israel.* Madison: University of Wisconsin Press, 1989.

Dowty, Alan. *The Jewish State: A Century Later.* Berkeley: University of California Press, 1998.

Dreisinger, Baz. "Spot the Jew." In *The Modern Jewish Girl's Guide to Guilt*, edited by Ruth Andrew Ellison, 173–75. New York: Dutton, 2005.

Efron, David. *Gesture and Environment: A Tentative Study of Some of the Spatio-temporal and "Linguistic" Aspects of the Gestural Behavior of Eastern Jews and Southern Italians in New York City, Living under Similar as Well as Different Environmental Conditions.* New York: King's Crown Press, 1941.

Efron, John. *Defenders of the Race: Jewish Doctors and Race Science in Fin-de-Siècle Europe.* New Haven, Conn.: Yale University Press, 1994.

Eilberg-Schwartz, Howard, ed. *People of the Body: Jews and Judaism from an Embodied Perspective.* Albany: State University of New York Press, 1992.

Elliott, Carl, and Paul Brodwin. "Identity and Genetic Ancestry Tracing." *British Medical Journal* 325 (2002): 1469–71. Reprinted in *BMJ USA* 3 (April 2003): 225–27.

Elliott, Donald N., and Bernard H. Wittenberg. "Accuracy of Identification of Jewish and Non-Jewish Photographs." *Journal of Abnormal and Social Psychology* 51, no. 2 (1955): 339–41.

Embacher, Helga. "Belated Reparations? Philosemitism in the Second Generation." Paper presented at the Fourth European Social Science History Conference, The Hague, February 27–March 2, 2002.

Encyclopaedia Judaica. 16 vols. Jerusalem: Keter, 1971–72.

Endelman, Todd. "Anglo-Jewish Scientists and the Science of Race." *Jewish Social Studies* 11, no. 1 (2004): 52–92.

———. "Conversion as a Response to Antisemitism." In *Living with Antisemitism: Modern Jewish Responses,* edited by Jehuda Reinharz, 59–83. Hanover, N.H.: University Press of New England, 1987.

———, ed. *Jewish Apostasy in the Modern World.* New York: Holmes and Meier, 1987.

———. *Radical Assimilation in English Jewish History: 1656–1945.* Bloomington: Indiana University Press, 1990.

———. "The Social and Political Context of Conversion in Germany and England, 1870–1914." In Endelman, *Jewish Apostasy,* 83–107.

Epstein, Joseph. "Funny, but I Do Look Jewish: The Photos of Frédéric Brenner's 'Diaspora.'" *Weekly Standard* 9, no. 14 (2003). http://www.weeklystandard.com (accessed June 17, 2005).

Feldman, W. M. *The Jewish Child: Its History, Folklore, Biology, and Sociology.* London: Baillière, Tindall, and Cox, 1917.

Felman, Shoshanna. "The Return of the Voice: Claude Lanzmann's *Shoah.*" In *Testimony: Crises of Witnessing in Literature, Psychoanalysis, and History,* edited by Shoshanna Felman and Dori Laub, 204–83. New York: Routledge, 1992.

Ferry, Barbara, and Debbie Nathan. "Mistaken Identity? The Case of New Mexico's 'Hidden Jews.'" *Atlantic Monthly,* December 2000, 6–11.

Fishberg, Maurice. *The Jews: A Study in Race and Environment.* New York: Charles Scribner's Sons, 1911.

Frank, Gelya. "Melville J. Herskovits on the African and Jewish Diasporas: Race, Culture, and Modern Anthropology." *Identities* 8, no. 2 (2001): 173–209.

Freedman, Jonathan. *Klezmer America: Jewishness, Ethnicity, Modernity.* New York: Columbia University Press, 2008.

Frenkel-Brunswik, Else. "Summary of Interview Results." In *The Authoritarian*

Personality, by Theodor W. Adorno, Else Frenkel-Brunswik, Daniel J. Levinson, and R. Nevitt Sanford, 281–86. New York: Harper, 1950.

Friedman, Menachem. *Ha-Hevrah ha-haredit: Mekorot, megamot ve-tahalikhim* [Haredi Society: Sources, Trends, and Processes]. Jerusalem: Jerusalem Institute for Policy Studies, 1991.

Fuller, B. P., M. J. Ellis Kahn, P. A. Barr, L. Biesecker, E. Crowley, J. Garber, M. K. Mansoura, P. Murphy, J. Murray, J. Phillips, K. Rothenberg, M. Rothstein, J. Stopfer, G. Swergold, B. Weber, F. S. Collins, and K. L. Hudson. "Privacy in Genetics Research." *Science* 285, no. 5432 (1999): 1359–61.

Fund, Joseph. *Pirud o hishtatfut: Agudat Yiśra'el mul ha-Tsiyonut u-Medinat Yiśra'el* [Separation or Participation: Agudat Israel Confronting Zionism and the State of Israel]. Jerusalem: Magnes, 1999.

Gassenschmidt, Christoph. "Khvol'son, Daniil Avraamovich." In *YIVO Encyclopedia*, 1:890.

Gebert, Konstanty. "Divided by a Common Book." In *The Best of Midrasz 1997*, 21. New York: American Jewish Committee, 2008.

———. "Jewish Identities in Poland: New, Old, Imaginary." In *Jewish Identities in the New Europe*, edited by Jonathan Webber, 161–67. London: Littman Library of Jewish Civilization, 1994.

Gerber, Jane S. *The Jews of Spain: A History of the Sephardic Experience*. New York: Free Press, 1992.

Gillis, John R., ed. *Commemorations: The Politics of National Identity*. Princeton, N.J.: Princeton University Press, 1994.

Gilman, Sander L. *Difference and Pathology: Stereotypes of Sexuality, Race, and Madness*. Ithaca, N.Y.: Cornell University Press, 1985.

———. *Jewish Self-Hatred: Anti-Semitism and the Hidden Language of the Jews*. Baltimore: Johns Hopkins University Press, 1986.

———. *The Jew's Body*. New York: Routledge, 1991.

———. *Making the Body Beautiful: A Cultural History of Aesthetic Surgery*. Princeton, N.J.: Princeton University Press, 1999.

———. *Smart Jews: The Construction of the Image of Jewish Superior Intelligence*. Lincoln: University of Nebraska Press, 1996.

Ginzburg, Shaul. *Meshumodim in tsarishn rusland: Farshungen un zichroynes vegn yidishn lebn in amolikn rusland* [Apostates in Tsarist Russia: Researches and Memoirs of Jewish Life in Russia of Former Times]. Vol. 2 of *Historishe verk* [Historical Work]. New York: Tsiko Bikher Farlag, 1946.

Glazer, Nathan. *American Judaism*. Chicago: University of Chicago Press, 1957.

Glenn, Susan A. *Daughters of the Shtetl: Life and Labor in the Immigrant Generation*. Ithaca, N.Y.: Cornell University Press, 1990.

———. "In the Blood? Consent, Descent, and the Ironies of Jewish Identity." *Jewish Social Studies* 8, nos. 2–3 (2002): 139–52.

———. "The Vogue of Jewish Self-Hatred in Post–World War II America." *Jewish Social Studies* 12, no. 3 (2006): 95–136.

Glick, Leonard B. "Types Distinct from Our Own: Franz Boas on Jewish Identity and Assimilation." *American Anthropologist* 84, no. 3 (1982): 545–65.

Goffman, Erving. *Stigma: Notes on the Management of Spoiled Identity*. New York: Simon and Schuster, 1986. Originally published in 1962 by Prentice-Hall.

Goitein, S. D. *A Mediterranean Society*. 3 vols. Berkeley: University of California Press, 1967.

Goldenweiser, Alexander. "The Jewish Face." *Reflex*, October 1927, 10.

Goldscheider, Calvin. "Are American Jews Vanishing, Again?" *Contexts* 2, no. 1 (2003): 18–24.

———. *Israel's Changing Society: Population, Ethnicity, and Development*. 2nd rev. ed. Boulder, Colo.: Westview Press, 2002.

———. *Jewish Continuity and Change: Emerging Patterns in America*. Bloomington: Indiana University Press, 1986.

———. *Studying the Jewish Future*. Seattle: University of Washington Press, 2004.

Goldscheider, Frances, and Calvin Goldscheider. *Leaving Home before Marriage: Ethnicity, Families, and Generational Relations*. Madison: University of Wisconsin Press, 1993.

Goldstein, Eric. *The Price of Whiteness: Jews, Race, and American Identity*. Princeton, N.J.: Princeton University Press, 2006.

Goldstein, Sidney, and Calvin Goldscheider. *Jewish Americans: Three Generations in a Jewish Community*. Englewood Cliffs, N.J.: Prentice-Hall, 1968.

Goldstein, Sidney, and Alice Goldstein. *Jews on the Move: Implications for Jewish Identity*. Albany: State University of New York Press, 1996.

Goodman, Elliot R. "World State and World Language." In *Readings in the Sociology of Language*, edited by Joshua A. Fishman, 715–36. The Hague: Mouton, 1972. Originally published in Elliot R. Goodman, *The Soviet Design for a World State* (New York: Columbia Press, 1960), 264–84.

Gordon, Milton. *Assimilation in American Life: The Role of Race, Religion, and National Origins*. New York: Oxford University Press, 1964.

Gross, Jan. *Neighbors: The Destruction of the Jewish Community in Jedwabne, Poland*. Princeton, N.J.: Princeton University Press, 2001.

Grossman, Avraham. *Pious and Rebellious: Jewish Women in Medieval Europe*. Waltham, Mass.: Brandeis University Press, 2004.

Gruzenberg, O. O. *Yesterday: Memoirs of a Russian-Jewish Lawyer*. Edited by Don C. Rawson. Berkeley: University of California Press, 1981.

Grynberg, Henryk. "Poles Inherited Some of the Jewish Tragedy." In *The Best of Midrasz 1997*, 37–38. New York: American Jewish Committee, 2008.

Habell-Pallan, Michelle. *Loca Motion: The Travels of Chicana and Latina Popular Culture*. New York: New York University Press, 2005.

Haiken, Elizabeth. *Venus Envy: A History of Cosmetic Surgery*. Baltimore: Johns Hopkins University Press, 1997.

Halberstam, Judith. *Skin Shows: Gothic Horror and the Technology of Monsters*. Durham, N.C.: Duke University Press, 1995.

Halkin, Hillel. *Across the Sabbath River: In Search of a Lost Tribe of Israel*. New York: Houghton Mifflin, 2002.

Harrison, Bernard. "Talking Like a Jew: Reflections on Identity and the Holocaust." *Judaism* 45, no. 4 (1996): 3–28.

Harshav, Benjamin. *Explorations in Poetics.* Stanford, Calif.: Stanford University Press, 2007.

Hart, Mitchell B. "Racial Science, Social Science, and the Politics of Assimilation." In *Science, Race, and Ethnicity: Readings from Isis and Osiris*, edited by John P. Jackson, 99–128. Chicago: University of Chicago Press, 2002.

———. *Social Science and the Politics of Modern Jewish Identity.* Stanford, Calif.: Stanford University Press, 2000.

Hartman, Harriet, and Moshe Hartman. *Gender and American Jews: Patterns in Work, Education, and Family in Contemporary Life.* Waltham, Mass.: Brandeis University Press, 2009.

Hartman, Moshe, and Harriet Hartman. *Gender Equality and American Jews.* Albany: State University of New York Press, 1996.

Heinze, Andrew. *Jews and the American Soul: Human Nature in the Twentieth Century.* Princeton, N.J: Princeton University Press, 2004.

Herskovits, Melville J. "Franz Boas as Physical Anthropologist." In *Franz Boas, 1858–1942*, edited by A. L. Kroeber et al. *American Anthropologist*, n.s., 45, no. 3 (1943): 43–49.

———. "Who Are the Jews?" In *The Jews: Their History, Culture, and Religion*, edited by Louis Finkelstein, 1151–71. New York: Harper and Brothers, 1949.

Hertz, Deborah. *How Jews Became Germans: The History of Conversion and Assimilation in Berlin.* New Haven, Conn.: Yale University Press, 2007.

———. *Jewish High Society in Old Regime Berlin.* New Haven, Conn.: Yale University Press, 1988.

Herz, Cary. *New Mexico's Crypto-Jews: Image and Memory.* Albuquerque: University of New Mexico Press, 2008.

Hirsch, Francine. "The Soviet Union as a Work-in-Progress: Ethnographers and the Category 'Nationality' in the 1926, 1937, and 1939 Censuses." *Slavic Review* 56, no. 2 (1997): 251–78.

Hobson, Laura Z. *Gentleman's Agreement.* New York: Simon and Schuster, 1946. Reprint, New York: Dell, 1962.

Hoffmann, David L. *Stalinist Values: The Cultural Norms of Soviet Modernity (1917–1941).* Ithaca, N.Y.: Cornell University Press, 2003.

Hofnung, Menachem. *Democracy, Law, and National Security.* London: Aldershot, 1996.

Holtzman, Avner. "Zitron, Shemu'el Leib." In *YIVO Encyclopedia*, 2:2133–34.

Honigmann, Peter. *Die Austritte aus der Jüdischen Gemeinde Berlin, 1873–1941* [Departures from the Jewish Community of Berlin, 1873–1941]. Frankfurt am Main: Peter Lang, 1988.

hooks, bell. *Black Looks: Race and Representation.* Boston: South End Press, 1992.

Hordes, Stanley. *To the End of the Earth: A History of the Crypto-Jews of New Mexico.* New York: Columbia University Press, 2005.

Horowitz, Brian. *Jewish Philanthropy and Enlightenment in Late-Tsarist Russia.* Seattle: University of Washington Press, 2009.

Horowitz, Elliott. "Too Jewish? And Other Jewish Questions: A Review Essay." *Modern Judaism* 19, no. 2 (1999): 195–206.

Hsia, R. Po-Chia. *The Myth of Ritual Murder: Jews and Magic in Reformation Germany.* New Haven, Conn.: Yale University Press, 1988.

Hulbert, Ann. *Raising America: Experts, Parents, and a Century of Advice.* New York: Knopf, 2003.

Igo, Sarah. *The Averaged American: Surveys, Citizens, and the Making of a Mass Public.* Cambridge, Mass.: Harvard University Press, 2007.

Jackson, John L., Jr. "The Soles of Black Folk: These Reeboks Were Made for Runnin' (from the White Man)." In *Race Consciousness: African-American Studies in the Next Century*, edited by Judith Jackson Fossett and Jeffrey A. Tucker, 177–90. New York: New York University Press, 1996.

Jackson, John P., ed. *Science, Race, and Ethnicity: Readings from Isis and Osiris.* Chicago: University of Chicago Press, 2002.

Jacobs, Janet Liebman. *Hidden Heritage: The Legacy of the Crypto-Jews.* Berkeley: University of California Press, 2002.

Jacobs, Joseph. *Studies in Jewish Statistics.* London: D. Nutt, 1891.

Jacobson, Matthew Frye. *Whiteness of a Different Color: European Immigrants and the Alchemy of Race.* Cambridge, Mass.: Harvard University Press, 1998.

Jervis, Lisa. "My Jewish Nose." In *Adiós, Barbie: Young Women Write about Body Image and Identity*, edited by Ophira Edut, 62–67. Seattle: Seal Press, 1998.

Kahn, Susan Martha. *Reproducing Jews: A Cultural Account of Assisted Conception in Israel.* Durham, N.C.: Duke University Press, 2000.

Kashua, Sayed. "Cinderella." Translated by Vivian Eden. *Words without Borders: The Online Magazine for International Literature*, December 2006. http://www.wordswithoutborders.org/article.php?lab=Cinderella (accessed May 17, 2009).

———. "Herzl ne'elam behatsot" [Herzl Disappears at Midnight]. *Ha'aretz*, October 3, 2005.

Katz, Jacob. *Exclusiveness and Tolerance: Studies in Jewish-Gentile Relations in Medieval and Modern Times.* New York: Schocken, 1962.

———. "Though He Sinned, He Remains an Israelite." *Tarbiz* 27 (1958): 203–17.

Keren, Michael, and Gad Barzilai. *Hishtalvut kevutsot "periferyah" ba-hevrah uva-politikah be-'idan shalom* [Inclusion of "Peripheral" Groups in Law and Society in Times of Peace]. Jerusalem: Israel Democracy Institute, 1998.

Keret, Etgar. *Tsinorot* [Pipelines]. Tel Aviv: Am Oved, 1992.

Kessel, Barbara. *Suddenly Jewish: Jews Raised as Gentiles Discover Their Jewish Roots.* Hanover, N.H.: University Press of New England, 2000.

King, Karen Ann Russell. "Surviving Modernity: Jewishness, Fieldwork, and the Roots of American Anthropology in the Twentieth Century." Ph.D. diss., University of Texas at Austin, 2000.

Kirshenblatt-Gimblett, Barbara. "The Corporeal Turn." *Jewish Quarterly Review* 95, no. 3 (2005): 447–61.

Kisch, Guido. *Judentaufen: Eine historisch-biographisch-psychologisch-soziologische*

Studie besonders für Berlin und Königsberg [Jewish Converts: A Historical-Biographical-Psychological-Sociological Study, Particularly for Berlin and Konigsberg]. Berlin: Colloquium Verlag, 1973.

Klebenov, Tilia. "*Chai* There: Subtle Ways Jews Tell Other Jews They're Jewish." *Jewish Magazine* 29 (February 2000). http://www.jewishmag.com/29mag/chai/chai.htm (accessed June 17, 2005).

Kleeblatt, Norman. "'Passing' into Multiculturalism." In *Too Jewish? Challenging Traditional Identities*, edited by Norman Kleeblatt, 3–38. New York: Jewish Museum; New Brunswick, N.J.: Rutgers University Press, 1996.

Klein, Judith Weinstein. *Jewish Identity and Self-Esteem: Healing Wounds through Ethnotherapy*. New York: Institute on Pluralism and Group Identity, American Jewish Committee, 1980.

Kroskrity, Paul, ed. *Regimes of Language: Ideologies, Polities, and Identities*. Santa Fe, N.M.: School of American Research Press, 2000.

Kugelmass, J. Alvin. "Name-Changing—and What It Gets You: Twenty-five Who Did It." *Commentary* 14 (August 1952): 145–50.

Kugelmass, Jack. "Bloody Memories: Encountering the Past in Contemporary Poland." *Cultural Anthropology* 10, no. 3 (1995): 279–301.

Kunin, Seth D. "Juggling Identities among the Crypto-Jews of the American Southwest." *Religion* 31 (2001): 41–61.

———. *Juggling Identities: Identity and Authenticity among the Crypto-Jews*. New York: Columbia University Press, 2009.

Kupper, Ruta. "Kol yisrael aravim zeh le-zeh" [All Israelis Are Responsible for One Another]. *Ha'aretz*, November 13, 2007.

Kurin, Richard. *Reflections of a Culture Broker: A View from the Smithsonian*. Washington, D.C.: Smithsonian Institution Press, 1997.

LaCapra, Dominick. *Writing History, Writing Trauma*. Baltimore: Johns Hopkins University Press, 2001.

Lederhendler, Eli. *The Road to Modern Jewish Politics: Political Tradition and Political Reconstruction in the Jewish Community of Tsarist Russia*. New York: Oxford University Press, 1989.

Leerssen, Joep. "The Downward Pull of Cultural Essentialism." In *Image into Identity: Constructing and Assigning Identity in a Culture of Modernity*, edited by Michael Wintle, 31–52. Amsterdam: Rodopi, 2006.

———. "The Rhetoric of National Character: A Programmatic Survey." *Poetics Today* 21, no. 2 (2000): 267–92.

———. "Types, Tropes, and the Poetics of Conventionality." *Poetics Today* 22, no. 3 (2001): 691–96.

Lehrer, Erica. "The Only Jewish Bookshop in Poland." *Pakn Treger*, no. 36 (Summer 2001). http://www.yiddishbookcenter.org/story.php?n=101.

Lehrer, Leibush. "The Dynamic Role of Jewish Symbols in the Psychology of the Jewish Child in America." *YIVO Annual of Jewish Social Science* 6 (1951): 37–72.

———. "Jewish Belongingness of Jewish Youth." *YIVO Annual of Jewish Social Science* 9 (1954): 137–65.

Levenson, Alan T. *Between Philosemitism and Antisemitism: Defenses of Jews and Judaism in Germany, 1871–1932.* Lincoln: University of Nebraska Press, 2007.

Levinson, Nathan Peter. *"Ketzer" und Abtrünnige im Judentum: Historische Porträts* [Cutting off from Jewish Society: Historical Portraits]. Hannover: Lutherisches Verlagshaus, 2001.

Levy, Yagil. *Israel's Materialist Militarism.* New York: Macmillan, 2007.

Liebman, Charles S. *Li-heyot be-yahad: Yahase datiyim-hiloniyim ba-hevrah ha-Yiśre'elit* [To Live Together: Secular-Religious Relations in Israeli Society]. Jerusalem: Keter, 1990.

Liebman, Charles S., and Elihu Katz. *The Jewishness of Israelis: Responses to the Guttman Report.* Albany: State University of New York Press, 1997.

Lindzey, Gardner, and Saul Rogolsky. "Prejudice and Identification of Minority Group Membership." *Journal of Abnormal and Social Psychology* 45, no. 1 (1950): 37–53.

Lippi-Green, Rosina. *English with an Accent: Language, Ideology, and Discrimination in the United States.* New York: Routledge, 1997.

Litvak, Olga. "The Literary Response to Conscription: Individuality and Authority in the Russian-Jewish Enlightenment." Ph.D. diss., Columbia University, 1999.

Lock, Margaret. "Breast Cancer: Reading the Omens." *Anthropology Today* 14, no. 4 (1998): 7–16.

López, Albert. "My Crypto-Jewish Self." *Kulanu.* http://www.kulanu.org (accessed January 21, 2008).

Lourie, Anton. "The Jew as Psychological Type." *American Imago* 6 (June 1949): 119–55.

Lowenstein, Steven M. *The Berlin Jewish Community: Enlightenment, Family, and Crisis, 1770–1830.* New York: Oxford University Press, 1994.

Macgregor, Frances M. Cooke. *Facial Deformities and Plastic Surgery: A Psychosocial Study.* Springfield, Ill.: Charles C. Thomas, 1953.

Maciejko, Pawel. "Frankism." In *YIVO Encyclopedia,* 1:540–44.

Magnus, Shulamit S. "Kol Ishah: Women and Pauline Wengeroff's Writing of an Age." *Nashim: A Journal of Jewish Women's Studies and Gender Issues* 7 (2004): 28–64.

———. "Pauline Wengeroff and the Voice of Jewish Modernity." In *Gender and Judaism: The Transformation of Tradition,* edited by T. M. Rudavsky, 181–90. New York: New York University Press, 1995.

Mahler, Raphael. *Hasidism and the Jewish Enlightenment: Their Confrontation in Galicia and Poland in the First Half of the Nineteenth Century.* Philadelphia: Jewish Publication Society of America, 1985.

Malešević, Siniša. *The Sociology of Ethnicity.* New York: Sage, 2004.

Marcus, Jacob Rader. *The Jew in the Medieval World: A Source Book.* Rev. ed. Cincinnati: Hebrew Union College Press, 1999.

Marks, Jonathan. "Ashley Montagu, 1905–1999." *Evolutionary Anthropology* 9 (2000): 111–12.

Medem, Vladimir. *The Life and Soul of a Legendary Jewish Socialist: The Memoirs of Vladimir Medem.* Translated by Samuel A. Portnoy. New York: Ktav, 1979.

Melammed, Renée Levine. *Heretics or Daughters of Israel? The Crypto-Jewish Women of Castile.* New York: Oxford University Press, 1999.

Mendes-Flohr, Paul. *German Jews: A Dual Identity.* New Haven, Conn.: Yale University Press, 1999.

Miller, Nancy K. "Hadassah Arms." In *People of the Book: Thirty Jewish Scholars Reflect on Their Jewish Identity,* edited by Jeffrey Rubin-Dorsky and Shelley Fisher Fishkin, 154–56. Madison: University of Wisconsin Press, 1996.

Milosz, Czeslaw. "Ars Poetica?" In *The Collected Poems: 1931–1987,* translated by Czeslaw Milosz and Lillian Vallee, 101. New York: Ecco Press, 1988.

Mintz, Alan. *Ḥurban: Responses to Catastrophe in Hebrew Literature.* New York: Columbia University Press, 1984.

Mintz, Steven. *Huck's Raft: A History of American Childhood.* Cambridge, Mass.: Harvard University Press, 2004.

Montagu, M. F. Ashley. "Race Theory in the Light of Modern Science." In *The Jewish People: Past and Present,* 1:1–9. New York: Jewish Encyclopedic Handbooks, Central Yiddish Culture Organization, 1946.

Moskowitz, Eva. *In Therapy We Trust: America's Obsession with Self-Fulfillment.* Baltimore: Johns Hopkins University Press, 2001.

Moss, Kenneth B. "Ahi'asaf." In *YIVO Encyclopedia,* 1:22.

Mosse, George. *Toward the Final Solution: A History of European Racism.* New York: Howard Fertig, 1975.

Most, Andrea. "Re-imagining the Jew's Body: From Self-Loathing to 'Grepts.'" In *You Should See Yourself: Jewish Identity in Postmodern American Culture,* edited by Vincent Brook, 37–68. New Brunswick, N.J.: Rutgers University Press, 2006.

Nathan, Debbie. "Cross Ways: Hispanics Search for the Origins of Their Unique Faith That Fuses Jewish Tradition with the Celebration of Christ." *Houston Press,* January 17, 2002.

Nathans, Benjamin. *Beyond the Pale: The Jewish Encounter with Late Imperial Russia.* Berkeley: University of California Press, 2002.

Nebel, Almut, Dvora Filon, Bernd Brinkmann, Partha P. Majumder, Marina Faerman, and Ariella Oppenheim. "The Y Chromosome Pool of Jews as Part of the Genetic Landscape of the Middle East." *American Journal of Human Genetics* 69, no. 5 (2001): 1095–1112.

Netanyahu, Benzion. *The Origins of the Inquisition in Fifteenth-Century Spain.* New York: Random House, 1995.

Neulander, Judith S. "Crypto-Jews of the Southwest: An Imagined Community." *Jewish Folklore and Ethnology Review* 16 (1994): 64–68.

———. "Folk Taxonomy, Prejudice, and the Human Genome: Using Disease as a Jewish Ethnic Marker." *Patterns of Prejudice* 40 (2006): 381–98.

———. "The New Mexican Crypto-Jewish Canon: Choosing to be 'Chosen' in Millennial Tradition." *Jewish Folklore and Ethnology Review* 18 (1994): 19–58.

————. Review of *To the End of the Earth: A History of the Crypto-Jews of New Mexico*, by Stanley Hordes. *Shofar: An Interdisciplinary Review of Jewish Studies* 25 (2007): 179–81.

Norton, Mary Beth. *Founding Mothers and Fathers: Gendered Power and the Forming of American Society.* New York: Knopf, 1996.

Novak, William, and Moshe Waldocks, eds. *The Big Book of Jewish Humor.* New York: HarperCollins, 1981.

Noy, Dov. *Jewish Folk Songs in Russia.* Ramat Gan, Israel: Bar Ilan Press, 1991.

Oberman, Heiko A. *The Roots of Anti-Semitism in the Age of Renaissance and Reformation.* Translated by James I. Porter. Philadelphia: Fortress Press, 1981.

Ockman, Carol. "'Too Jewish? Challenging Traditional Identities': Jewish Museum." *ArtForum* 35, no. 1 (1996): 106–7.

Ornan, Uzi. "Anachnu Ha'Knaanim" [We Are the Canaanites]. *Svivot* 33 (December 1994). http://www.snunit.k12.il/heb_journals/svivot/33061.html (accessed May 6, 2009).

Peled, Yoav. "Ethnic Democracy and the Legal Construction of Citizenship: Arab Citizens of the Jewish State." *American Political Science Review* 86 (1992): 432–43.

Peled, Yoav, and Gershon Shafir. *Being Israeli: The Dynamics of Multiple Citizenship.* Cambridge: Cambridge University Press, 2002.

Peleg, Yaron. *Israeli Culture between the Two Intifadas: A Brief Romance.* Austin: University of Texas Press, 2008.

Petrovsky-Shtern, Yohanan. "'The Guardians of Faith': Jewish Traditional Societies in the Russian Army; The Case of the Thirty-fifth Briansk Regiment." In *The Military and Society in Russia, 1450–1917*, edited by Eric Lohr and Marshall Poe, 413–34. Leiden: Brill, 2002.

Piper, Adrian. "Passing for White, Passing for Black." *Transitions* 58 (1992): 4–32.

Plotnicov, Leon, and Myrna Silverman. "Jewish Ethnic Signalling: Social Bonding in Contemporary American Society." *Ethnology* 17, no. 4 (1978): 407–22.

Polonsky, Antony, and Joanna B. Michlic, eds. *The Neighbors Respond: The Controversy over the Jedwabne Massacre in Poland.* Princeton, N.J.: Princeton University Press, 2003.

Porter, Brian. "Explaining Jedwabne: The Perils of Understanding." *Polish Review* 47, no. 1 (2002): 23–26.

Raskin, Richard. *Life Is Like a Glass of Tea: Studies of Classic Jewish Jokes.* Philadelphia: Jewish Publication Society, 1992.

Reinharz, Jehuda. *Fatherland or Promised Land: The Dilemma of the German Jew, 1893–1914.* Ann Arbor: University of Michigan Press, 1980.

Richardson, Laurel. "Looking Jewish." *Qualitative Inquiry* 9, no. 5 (2003): 815–21.

Rimmon-Kenan, Shlomith. *Narrative Fiction: Contemporary Poetics.* London: Methuen, 1983.

Robertson, Ritchie. *Heine.* New York: Grove Press, 1988.

Romano, Renee. *Race Mixing: Black-White Marriage in Postwar America.* Cambridge, Mass.: Harvard University Press, 2003.

Rose, Anne C. *Beloved Strangers: Interfaith Families in Nineteenth-Century America.* Cambridge, Mass.: Harvard University Press, 2001.

Rosenberg, Bernard, and Gilbert Shapiro. "Marginality and Jewish Humor." *Midstream* 4, no. 2 (1958): 70–80.

Rosenblit, Marsha L. *The Jews of Vienna, 1867–1914: Assimilation and Identity.* Albany: State University of New York Press, 1983.

Ross, Dorothy. *The Origins of American Social Science.* New York: Cambridge University Press, 1991.

Ross, Theodore. "Shalom on the Range: In Search of the American Crypto-Jew." *Harper's* 319 (December 2009): 76–84.

Rumbaut, Rubén, and Alejandro Portes. *Ethnicities: Children of Immigrants in America.* Berkeley: University of California Press, 2001.

Saldívar, José. *Border Matters: Remapping American Cultural Studies.* Berkeley: University of California Press, 1997.

Saussure, Ferdinand de. *Course in General Linguistics.* Translated by Wade Baskin. New York: McGraw-Hill, 1959. Originally published as *Cours de linguistique générale* (Paris: Payot, 1916).

Schlör, Joachim. "From Remnants to Realities: Is There Something beyond 'Jewish Disneyland' in Eastern Europe?" *Journal of Modern Jewish Studies* 2, no. 2 (2003): 148–58.

Schnur, Susan. "As an Adopted Child, All I Wanted Was Real Jewish Hair." *Lilith* 20, no. 1 (1995): 15.

Scholem, Gershom. "Jacob Frank." In *Encyclopaedia Judaica,* 7:55–72.

Scholes, France. "Troublous Times in New Mexico, 1659–1670." *New Mexico Historical Review* 12 (1937): 380–452.

Schorsch, Ismar. *Jewish Reactions to German Anti-Semitism, 1870–1914.* New York: Columbia University Press, 1972.

Schwartz, Yigal. *Aharon Appelfeld: From Individual Lament to Tribal Eternity.* Waltham, Mass.: Brandeis University Press, 2001.

Scodel, Alvin, and Harvey Austrin. "The Perception of Jewish Photographs by Non-Jews and Jews." *Journal of Abnormal and Social Psychology* 54, no. 2 (1957): 278–80.

Seidman, Naomi. "Fag-Hags and Bu-Jews: Toward a (Jewish) Politics of Vicarious Identity." In *Insider/Outsider: American Jews and Multiculturalism,* edited by David Biale, Michael Galchinsky, and Susannah Heschel, 254–68. Berkeley: University of California Press, 1998.

Shahar, Charles, and Howard Magonet. *Immigration and Language.* Pt. 5 of *2001 Census Analysis: The Jewish Community of Montreal.* Toronto: United Israel Appeal Federations Canada, May 2005.

Shaked, Gershon. "Appelfeld and His Times: Transformations of Ahashveros, the Eternal Wandering Jew." *Hebrew Studies* 36 (1995): 87–100.

——. *Sifrut az, kan, ve'akhshav* [Literature Then, Here, and Now]. Tel Aviv: Zmora-Bitan, 1993.

Shavit, Yaacov. *Me 'Ivri 'ad Kena'ani* [From Hebrew to Canaanite]. Tel Aviv: Domino, 1987.

Silk, Mark. *Spiritual Politics: Religion and America since World War II*. New York: Simon and Schuster, 1988.

Sion, Brigitte. "Where Have All the Sephardim Gone?" European Sephardic Institute. http://www.sefarad.org/publication/lm/036/6.html (accessed January 21, 2008).

Skorecki, Karl, Sara Selig, Shraga Blazer, Robert Bradman, Neil Bradman, P. J. Warburton, Monica Ismajlowicz, and Michael F. Hammer. "Y Chromosomes of Jewish Priests." *Nature* 385 (January 2, 1997): 32.

Slezkine, Yuri. "The USSR as a Communal Apartment, or How a Socialist State Promoted Ethnic Particularism." *Slavic Review* 53, no. 2 (1994): 414–52.

Slutsky, Yehuda. *Ha-itonut ha-yehudit rusit ba-me'ah ha-t'sha esreh* [The Jewish Russian Press in the Nineteenth Century]. Jerusalem: Mosad Bialik, 1970.

———. "Saul Ginsburg." In *Encyclopaedia Judaica*, 7:582–83.

———. "Zitron, Samuel Leib." In *Encyclopaedia Judaica*, 16:1186.

Smith, Michael. *Language and Power in the Creation of the USSR, 1917–1953*. New York: Mouton de Gruyter, 1998.

Sokoloff, Naomi B. "Aharon Appelfeld." In *The Dictionary of Literary Biography*. Vol. 299, *Holocaust Novelists*, edited by Efraim Sicher, 17–30. Detroit: Gale Research, 2004.

———. "Life/Writing: Appelfeld's Autobiographical Work and the Modern Jewish Canon." In *Arguing the Modern Jewish Canon: Essays on Literature and Culture in Honor of Ruth R. Wisse*, edited by Justin Cammy, Dara Horn, Alyssa Quint, and Rachael Rubinstein, 371–85. Cambridge: Center for Jewish Studies, Harvard University, 2008.

Sollors, Werner, ed. *Theories of Ethnicity: A Classic Reader*. New York: New York University Press, 1996.

Spiel, Hilde. *Fanny von Arnstein: A Daughter of the Enlightenment, 1758–1818*. Translated by Christine Shuttleworth. New York: Berg, 1991.

Stanislawski, Michael. *For Whom Do I Toil? Judah Leib Gordon and the Crisis of Russian Jewry*. New York: Oxford University Press, 1988.

———. "Jewish Apostasy in Russia: A Tentative Typology." In Endelman, *Jewish Apostasy*, 189–205.

———. *Tsar Nicholas I and the Jews*. Philadelphia: Jewish Publication Society, 1983.

Stearns, Peter. *Anxious Parents: A History of Modern Childrearing in America*. New York: New York University Press, 2003.

Steinlauf, Michael. *Bondage to the Dead: Poland and the Memory of the Holocaust*. Syracuse, N.Y.: Syracuse University Press, 1997.

Stocking, George W. *Race, Culture, and Evolution: Essays in the History of Anthropology*. Chicago: University of Chicago Press, 1982.

Sutton, Wesley K., Alec Knight, Peter A. Underhill, Judith S. Neulander, Todd R. Disotell, and Joanna L. Mountain. "Toward Resolution of the Debate regarding Purported Crypto-Jews in a Spanish-American Population:

Evidence from the Y Chromosome." *Annals of Human Biology* 33, no. 1 (2006): 100–111.

Taylor, Charles. *The Ethics of Authenticity.* Cambridge, Mass.: Harvard University Press, 1991.

Tec, Nechama. *In the Lion's Den: The Life of Oswald Rufeisen.* New York: Oxford University Press, 1990.

Teter, Magda. "Conversion." In *YIVO Encyclopedia,* 1:348–51.

Thomas, Mark G., Michael E. Weale, Abigail L. Jones, Martin Richards, Alice Smith, Nicola Redhead, Antonio Torroni, Rosaria Scozzari, Fiona Gratrix, Ayele Tarekegn, James F. Wilson, Cristian Capelli, Neil Bradman, and David B. Goldstein. "Founding Mothers of Jewish Communities: Geographically Separated Jewish Groups Were Independently Founded by Very Few Female Ancestors." *American Journal of Human Genetics* 70, no. 6 (2002): 1411–20.

Tobias, Henry. *A History of the Jews in New Mexico.* Albuquerque: University of New Mexico Press, 1990.

Toch, Hans H., Albert I. Rabin, and Donald M. Wilkins. "Factors Entering into Ethnic Identifications: An Experimental Study." *Sociometry* 25 (September 1962): 297–312.

Tokarska-Bakir, Joanna. "Poland as the Sick Man of Europe? Jedwabne, 'Post-memory,' and Historians." *Eurozine,* May 30, 2003. http://www.eurozine.com/article/2003-05-30-tokarska-en.html (accessed April 4, 2009).

Tumin, Melvin J. "The Idea of 'Race' Dies Hard." *Commentary* 8 (July 1949): 80–85.

Turner, Victor. *From Ritual to Theatre: The Human Seriousness of Play.* New York: PAJ Publications, 1982.

Vaisman, Daria. "My Life as a Shiksa Jew." *Jewish Student Press Service,* June 9, 2005. http://www.shmoozenet.com/jsps/stories/0998Daria.shtml (accessed June 17, 2005).

Velasco, Juan. "Automitografías: The Border Paradigm and Chicana/o Auto-biography." *Biography* 27, no. 2 (2004): 313–38.

Verdery, Katherine. *What Was Socialism, and What Comes Next?* Princeton, N.J.: Princeton University Press, 1996.

Volkov, Shulamit. "The Dynamics of Dissimilation: Ostjuden and German Jews." In *The Jewish Response to German Culture: From the Enlightenment to the Second World War,* edited by Jehuda Reinharz and Walter Schatzberg, 195–211. Hanover, N.H.: University Press of New England, 1985.

Voloshinov, Valentin. *Marxism and the Philosophy of Language.* Translated by Ladislav Matejka and I. R. Titunik. Cambridge, Mass.: Harvard University Press, 1973. Originally published as *Marksizm i filosofiya yazyka* (Leningrad: Priboy, 1929).

Wade, Nicholas. "Gene Test Shows Spain's Jewish and Muslim Mix." *New York Times,* December 8, 2008.

Weinfeld, Morton. *Like Everyone Else . . . but Different:The Paradoxical Success of Canadian Jews.* Toronto: McClelland and Stewart, 2001.

Wengeroff, Pauline. *Memoiren einer Grossmutter: Bilder aus der Kulturgeschichte der Juden Russlands im 19. Jahrhundert* [Memoirs of a Grandmother: Scenes from the Cultural History of the Jews of Russia in the Nineteenth Century]. 2 vols. Berlin: Poppelauer, 1908–10.

———. *Memoirs of a Grandmother: Scenes from the Cultural History of the Jews of Russia in the Nineteenth Century.* 2 vols. Translated, with introduction, notes, and commentary, by Shulamit S. Magnus. Stanford, Calif.: Stanford University Press, in press.

Whitfield, Stephen. *The Culture of the Cold War.* Baltimore: Johns Hopkins University Press, 1991.

Wilder, Esther. "Socioeconomic Attainment and Expressions of Jewish Identification: 1970 and 1990." *Journal for the Scientific Study of Religion* 35, no. 2 (1996): 109–27.

Woolard, Kathryn A., and Bambi B. Schieffelin. "Language Ideology." *Annual Review of Anthropology* 23 (1994): 55–82.

Yerushalmi, Yosef Hayim. *Freud's Moses: Judaism Terminable and Interminable.* New Haven, Conn.: Yale University Press, 1991.

TheYIVO Encyclopedia of Jews in Eastern Europe. Edited by Gershon David Hundert. 2 vols. New Haven, Conn.: Yale University Press, 2008.

Zipperstein, Steven J. *Elusive Prophet:Ahad Ha'am and the Origins of Zionism.* Berkeley: University of California Press, 1993.

———. "Heresy, Apostasy, and the Transformation of Joseph Rabinovich." In Endelman, *Jewish Apostasy,* 206–31.

———. *The Jews of Odessa:A Cultural History, 1794–1881.* Stanford, Calif.: Stanford University Press, 1985.

Zitron, Shmuel Leib. *Avek fun folk, tipn un silueten funm noyenten ovor* [Gone from the People, Types and Silhouettes from the Recent Past]. 4 vols. Warsaw: Ahiasaf, 1920.

———. *Me'ahorei hapargod: Mumarim, bogdim, mitkhahshim* [From behind the Screen: Converts, Traitors, Deniers]. Vilna: n.p., 1925.

Zubrzycki, Geneviève. *The Crosses of Auschwitz: Nationalism and Religion in Post-Communist Poland.* Chicago: University of Chicago Press, 2006.

Zurawik, David. *The Jews of Prime Time.* Hanover, N.H.: University Press of New England / Brandeis University Press, 2003.

Contributors

GAD BARZILAI is Professor of Political Science, Law, and International Studies in the Jackson School of International Studies and the Law, Societies, and Justice Program at the University of Washington. He is the Lucia S. and Herbert L. Pruzan Professor of Jewish Studies and serves as the chair of the Jewish Studies Program at the University of Washington. He is a former Professor of Political Science and Law at Tel Aviv University. He is the author of numerous articles, several edited volumes and monographs, and four books, including *Communities and Law: Politics and Cultures of Legal Identities* (University of Michigan Press, 2003), which won the Yonathan Shapiro Prize for the best book in Israel Studies awarded by the Association of Israel Studies.

LILA CORWIN BERMAN is Associate Professor of History at Temple University. She holds the Murray Friedman Chair in American Jewish History and directs the Feinstein Center for American Jewish History. She is the author of *Speaking of Jews: Rabbis, Intellectuals, and the Creation of an American Public Identity* (University of California Press, 2009) as well as several articles, including "Jews and the Ambivalence of Middle Classness" (*American Jewish History*, 2008).

LAADA BILANIUK is Associate Professor of Anthropology at the University of Washington. Her book *Contested Tongues: Language Politics and Cultural Correction in Ukraine* (Cornell University Press, 2005), won the Best Book in Slavic Linguistics award of the American Association of Teachers of Slavic and East European Languages. In it she examines purism and Ukrainian-Russian language mixing to understand the process by which modern societies seek to confer or deny social legitimacy to others based on language ideology. She is currently researching the cultural politics of music and popular culture in Ukraine.

JONATHAN FREEDMAN is Professor of English and American Studies at the University of Michigan. He is the author of *The Temple of Culture: Assimilation and Anti-Semitism in Literary Anglo-America* (Oxford University Press, 2000) and *Klezmer America: Jewishness, Ethnicity, Modernity* (Columbia University Press, 2008). He has also edited (with Sara Blair) a volume of essays called *Jewish in America* (University of Michigan Press).

SUSAN A. GLENN is the Howard and Frances Keller Endowed Professor in History and a member of the Jewish Studies Program faculty at the University of Washington. She is the author of *Daughters of the Shtetl: Life and Labor in the Immigrant Generation* (Cornell University Press, 1990), which won the American Historical Association's Joan Kelly Memorial Prize, and *Female Spectacle: The Theatrical Roots of Modern Feminism* (Harvard University Press, 2000). Her recent articles include "In the Blood? Consent, Descent, and the Ironies of Jewish Identity" (*Jewish Social Studies*, 2002) and "The Vogue of Jewish Self-Hatred in Post–World War II America" (*Jewish Social Studies*, 2006). She serves on the Academic Council of the American Jewish Historical Society.

CALVIN GOLDSCHEIDER is Samuel Ungerleider Jr. Professor Emeritus of Judaic Studies and Professor Emeritus of Sociology at Brown University. His recent books include *Israel's Changing Society: Population, Ethnicity and Development* (Westview Press, 2002); *Cultures in Conflict: The Arab-Israeli Conflict* (Greenwood Press, 2002); *Studying the Jewish Future* (University of Washington Press, 2004); and *Immigration, Gender, and Family Transitions to Adulthood in Sweden* (University Press of America, 2006).

SUSAN MARTHA KAHN is Associate Director of the Center for Middle Eastern Studies at Harvard University and Lecturer in the Department of Near Eastern Languages and Literatures. Her book *Reproducing Jews: A Cultural Account of Assisted Conception in Israel* (Duke University Press, 2000) won the National Jewish Book Award and the Eileen Basker Memorial Prize, given by the Society for Medical Anthropology in recognition of outstanding research on gender and health.

ERICA LEHRER is Assistant Professor in the Department of History and the Department of Sociology and Anthropology at Concordia University in Montreal, where she also holds the Canada Research Chair in Post-Conflict Memory, Ethnography, and Museology. She is the author of "Repopulating Jewish Poland—in Wood" (*Polin: Studies in Polish Jewry*, 2003) and "Jewish? Heritage? In Poland? A Brief Manifesto and an Ethnographic-Design Intervention into Jewish Tourism in Poland" (*Bridges: A Jewish Feminist Journal*, 2007). She also translated from Polish to English the book *Difficult Questions in Polish-Jewish Dialogue*, edited by Maciej Kozlowski, Andrzej Folwarczny, and Michal Bilewicz, (Jacek Santorski, Agencja Wydawnicza, 2006). She is completing a book manuscript titled "Remaking Memory: How Jews and Poles Are Salvaging Jewish Heritage in Poland," based on ethnographic fieldwork in Poland, Israel, and the United States.

SHULAMIT S. MAGNUS is Associate Professor of Jewish Studies and History at Oberlin College. She is the author of *Jewish Emancipation in a German City: Cologne, 1798–1871* (Stanford University Press, 1997) and articles on Jewish women's history and ritual. The first volume of her critical edition of the memoirs of Pauline Wengeroff (1833–1916), *Memoiren einer Grossmutter*, is forthcoming from Stanford University Press in 2010; the second volume is in process.

NAOMI B. SOKOLOFF is Professor of Near Eastern Languages and Civilization, Professor of Comparative Literature, and the past Samuel and Althea Stroum Endowed Chair in Jewish Studies at the University of Washington. She has published widely on modern Hebrew literature, she is the author of *Imagining the Child in Modern Jewish Fiction* (Johns Hopkins University Press, 1992), and she has coedited several collections of essays. Her recent publications include "Life/Writing: Aharon Appelfeld's Autobiographical Work and the Modern Jewish Canon," in *Arguing the Modern Jewish Canon*, ed. Justin Cammy et al. (Center for Jewish Studies, Harvard University Press, 2008).

Index

Aaron, priestly line of descent from, 14

Abrams, William, 103

Adorno, Theodor W., 76

Age of Wonders, The (Appelfeld), 50

Agudath Yisrael, 29

Ahiasaf house, 137, 138–39

Akeda, 51

Alcalá, Kathleen, 192

Aleichem, Sholom, 159n45, 160n58

Aleksandrov, [P. A.], 148–49

Allport, Gordon W., 75–76

All Whom I Have Loved (Appelfeld), 50

Alter, Robert, 63n21

Altneuland (Herzl), 60

American Jewish Committee, 18, 100

American Jewish experience: community and identity, 110–25, 128–31; Crypto-Jews in Southwest, 188–202; intermarriage, 91–109, 116, 117, 119–20, 126–27; narratives of, 189; visual stereotypes and Jewish identity, 64–90

American Jewish Joint Distribution Committee, 15

American Jewish Year Book, 102–3

American Journal of Human Genetics, Diasporic communities study in, 14

"American" look, 72, 73, 75, 87n31

ancestry, genetic tracing of. *See* population genetics

Anderson, Benedict, 206

Anti-Defamation League, 83

anti-race science, 67–72, 74–75, 85n9, 86n21, 86n26, 87n31

antisemitism: and anti-race science, 67–72, 74–75, 85n9, 86n21, 86n26, 87n31; and blood libel trials, 144–45, 148–49, 159n45; Christian,

133–34, 183n13; experience of, as theme of Hobson's *Gentleman's Agreement*, 72–74; Goldenweiser's "Jewish Face," 69; Kupernik on anti-Jewish writing, 147; Nazi, 13, 68, 69–71, 74, 173, 183n13; and the other, 180; Polish, 165, 174–75, 180, 183n13, 185n26; racial determination and awareness experiments and, 71–72, 75–76, 87–88n45; Russian writers and, 150; social reality of, in Appelfeld's "Transformation," 43–53, 60–61; and threat of "secret Jew," 78–79

anusim (Heb., "forced ones"): rabbinate on, 194–95; Society for the Study of Crypto-Jews and Anusim, 191–92; vs. *conversos*, 191

apostates, Jewish, in tsarist Russia, 132–60

Appelfeld, Aharon, 50, 52; "Transformation," 43–53, 60–61

Arab Palestinians in Israel: and Hebrew-language study, 63n25; Kashua as voice for, 45–46, 58, 60–61; in Kashua's "Herzl Disappears at Midnight," 43–46, 53–61; military service and, 37; non-Jewish citizenship and, 34; on restricting Jewish identity, 34, 35; right of return and, 29, 34, 35, 41n10; on territorial citizenship, 34, 35

Arab Work (sitcom, Kashua), 60

"Arkadi Haliwa Takes the Number Five" (Keret), 53–54

Arnsteiner, Joseph von, 135

Ashkenazi Jews: in American Southwest, 192; genetic ties to Middle Eastern

Library of Congress Cataloging-in-Publication Data
Boundaries of Jewish identity /
edited by Susan A. Glenn and Naomi B. Sokoloff.
p. cm.
"A Samuel and Althea Stroum Book."
Includes bibliographical references and index.
ISBN 978-0-295-99054-5 (hardback : alk. paper)
ISBN 978-0-295-99055-2 (pbk. : alk. paper)
1. Jews—Identity.
2. Jews—United States—Identity.
3. Jews—Israel—Identity.
4. Jews—Europe—Identity.
I. Glenn, Susan A. (Susan Anita)
II. Sokoloff, Naomi B.
DS143.B76
2010305.892'4—dc22
2010033490

LaVergne, TN USA
15 October 2010
200859LV00001B/172/P